Barrett and his Book Elicit Rave Reviews

"If you keep going on the p   ping a
real service to your country."   tant
Secretary of the Treasury and

CW00606755

"Counterculture Kevin's jo   nis badly-
needed Muslim perspective…
– Morgan Reynolds, former director, Criminal Justice Center, National
Center for Policy Analysis

"Barrett has plenty of important things to say. This is a voice people
need to hear in this hour." – William Hare, author, Amazon top reviewer.

"A reluctant activist, Keith Barrett reminds us that the journey to truth
is unpredictable, shape-shifting, and never-ending." – Professor Tamar
Frankiel, University of Riverside.

"With disarming candor, Kevin Barrett takes us on a fascinating
journey in his struggle for 9/11 truth. A terrific read!" Jim Fetzer,
Distinguished McKnight Professor Emeritus, University of Minnesota

"You're terrific! Masha'Allah. I just love to see American grit don a
kefi and give 'em what for! May God watch over you, aid you, and
protect you and yours." – A. K. Dewdney, Professor Emeritus, U.of
Western Ontario, *Scientific American* mathematics columnist, 1984-1993.

"Some of us who seek a real investigation of what happened on 9/11
approach the whole question in a gingerly and "gentlemanly" way.
We think the obvious cover-up makes it clear that the administration has
much to cover up, but we state radical theories in moderate tones.
Accordingly, we are rather dull to read. Kevin Barrett tells the appalling
truth as he sees it in ways more appropriate to its shocking nature. That
includes a lot of humor. He is never dull. The truth he tells includes the
truth of his own story, the real beliefs of the Muslim community to
which he belongs, and the implications of the growing evidence that
9/11 was a false flag operation. If the real investigation we seek ever
transpires, this will owe much to him… I am deeply moved and
impressed by his leadership… I know it will take his kind of activism to
make anything happen." – John B. Cobb, Jr., Professor of Theology,
Emeritus, Claremont School of Theology

"Kevin Barrett is a man of honor and integrity. His spirituality shows
in his tireless efforts to put the truth out there, regardless of
consequence. This book speaks truth that people need to realize and
quickly." – Meria Heller, Talk Radio Host, www.meria.net

while Reactionaries Rage...

"The problem is, at the University of Wisconsin, they have no standards. This guy would have been gone at Boston University, my alma mater, in a heartbeat. The chancellor there, John Silber – this guy would be in the Charles River floating down toward the harbor." – Bill O'Reilly, Fox News TV Toxic Talk Show host

"You're a very angry man. You're a conspiracy nut." – Sean Hannity, Fox News TV Verbal Thuggery Unit

"How come a public institution will accord any kind of job other than cleaning the bathrooms to a person who says these things?" – Edward Luttwak, neocon author, *Coup d'Etat: A Practical Handbook.*

"This guy didn't rip off Charlie Sheen. Charlie Sheen probably ripped off him." – Jessica McBride, WTMJ Radio, Milwaukee

"Blurbs" we'd like to see

"Kevin Barrett is the Michael Moore of 9/11 truth." – Michael Moore

"Michael Moore is Kevin Barrett for 9/11 wimps." – Kevin Barrett

"Barrett takes no prisoners. Heads off to Kevin Barrett!" – al-Zarqawi

"We're not sure we're gonna be able to contain these wildfire conspiracy theories. We've seen such a terrible loss of credibility. Maybe the best thing to do is pull this book." – "Lucky Larry" Silverstein, CEO, Faulty Towers USA.

"Hervorragende Schlagfertigkeit!" – *Der Spiegel*

"If you thought Osama was a hardcore anti-imperialist Muslim, get a load of Kevin Barrett." – William Blum, author of *Killing Hope.*

"If you thought William Blum was a hardcore anti-imperialist American, get a load of Kevin Barrett. If I were forced to spend the rest of my life on dialysis in a cave in Afghanistan and could only bring one book, I would choose *Truth Jihad.*" – Osama Bin Laden [tape delivered to al-Jazeera, authenticated by CIA]

"If I were stuck in an undisclosed location for an undisclosed length of time, this is the book I would *not* want to bring with me." – Dick Cheney

"Stick THIS in your undisclosed location, Cheney." – Kevin Barrett

"If 'telling it like it is' can get you into paradise, Barrett will be sipping ethereal wine and snuggling virgins with me any day now." – Howard Cosell

Amazon Top Reviewer Wm. Hare Compares Barrett to Mencken, Rabelais

Kevin Barrett takes the reader on a fascinating personal journey, culminating in a total commitment to the organization he founded, the Muslim-Jewish-Christian Alliance for 9/11 Truth. His breezy prose and succinct social commentary remind one of H. L. Mencken. America's legendary pundit would have cheered Barrett's puncturing of establishment myths in his search for the truth behind the 9/11 atrocities.

Barrett's gift for verse and sidesplitting satire in *Truth Jihad* also recall Rabelais, the ribald genius of France; Barrett has taught and studied in Paris, too. He makes admirable use of humor, realizing that without it, life would be too somber to bear in Bush America, under the Damocles sword of a neocon armageddon.

As a practicing Muslim, Barrett is well placed to analyze the current epidemic of Islamophobia. One of the most valuable insights in *Truth Jihad* is his clever scrutiny of the geopolitics of neocon propaganda, which smears Muslims with the terrorist label, as a ploy to despoil their land of its fabulous oil wealth.

Author Eric Larsen Praises Barrett's Multifaceted *Truth Jihad*

Kevin Barrett has emerged as one of the most dedicated, eloquent, humane, humorous, and influential figures in the 9/11 Truth movement. *Truth Jihad* is an event of significance, both for the Truth movement itself and for the present state of publishing. It is a book not only true, but, unlike any other work on the subject, it's a powerful and most intensely appealing combination of the humane, the authentic, the personal, the universal, the impassioned, the reasoned, the thoughtful, the irreverent, the reverent, the serious, the satiric, and—hardly infrequently—one of the funniest things you're ever likely to read.

It's also the story of his own life as student, as writer, married man, convert to Islam, father, and emergent public figure who hilariously and powerfully advances the cause of 9/11 Truth.

As you read *Truth Jihad*, you will be stirred by its earnest yet funny, intellectual yet comradely, theoretical yet also perfectly blunt telling of the plain and obvious truth about 9/11, and by its homage to life, nation, people, family, children—and, above all, to a future that's intact, whole, honest, and true.

May such a future come to be. Somehow.

Buy the book. Read the book. Treasure it. If, as with *A Nation Gone Blind*, you find *Truth Jihad* going unreviewed in the "mainstream" papers — well, given the way things are now in our unwell and endangered nation, you can take such an ignoring of it as a credit to the book for being in fact a huge, moving, humane, and passionate voice for the truth—exactly the sort of thing that does not get reviews in these dark and compromised days.

Truth

The best jihad is a word of truth flung in the face of a tyrant.

– The Prophet Muhammad

Big Lie

They followed the very correct principle, that in the greatness of a lie there is always a certain potency of believability, because the broad masses of people are sooner corrupted in their inmost hearts than they are consciously or intentionally bad; and thus in the primitive simplicity of their nature, they more easily fall victims to the big lie than the small one, since they themselves sometimes tell little fibs, but would be too ashamed to tell great lies. Such falsehoods do not even occur to them, so they can not believe others capable of the colossal impudence of these most scandalous distortions. Even when faced with the facts in such a case, they will still linger in doubt and waver and continue to suppose there must be some truth to it. This is known all too well by the boldest cliques of liars in this world, who thus put it despicably to use.

– Adolf Hitler, *Mein Kampf*

Jihad

The Zaheer brothers in the San Francisco Bay Area released their first hip-hop album entitled "Jihad," Arabic word for struggle. Jihad stands for the greatest struggle within oneself. To seek knowledge, justice and balance within oneself – this is jihad. – A. S. Ghazali, Pakistanlink.com.

"We used to go by 'Jihad'… But after Sept. 11, it was misinterpreted to mean holy war, and that's not the message we bring at all," Ameer Zaheer told the San Jose Mercury News.

A millenium earlier, it was reported by the sage Al-Ghazali (d. 1111), that the true meaning of *Jihad* is the search, striving or effort to gain knowledge.

So let our Truth Jihad begin.

Courage

"Courage is the Desire to Seek the Truth, Whatever It May Be; Patriotism is the Courage to Speak the Truth, In the Face of Tyranny."

– J-P. Leonard

Truth Jihad

My Epic Struggle

against the

9/11 Big Lie

by Kevin Barrett, PhD.

PROGRESSIVE PRESS

Progressive

2007

Truth Jihad

My Epic Struggle

against the

9/11 Big Lie

Published by Progressive Press,
PO Box 126, Joshua Tree, Calif. 92252,
www.ProgressivePress.com

ISBN: 0-930852-99-0 ISBN-13: 978-0-930852-99-3
Library of Congress CIP Data applied for
Length: 83,000 words
Printed in the USA. First Printing: March/April 2007

"FALSE FLAG FACTS and PHYSICS" filler items, editing,
and layout by John-Paul Leonard/ Progressive Press.
Cover design graphics by J-P.L. and Sandra Taylor –
The Graphic Page, on a concept from K. Barrett.
Tile pattern from Jameh Mosque, Yazd, Iran, courtesy of
www.gardenvisit.com photo gallery, retouched and translated
thanks to Prof. Hussein Mollanazar, Tehran, Iran (see p. 50).
News ticker headlines by *The Onion* and CNN.

Distribution: Amazon, Baker & Taylor, Disticor Canada,
Ingram, Gazelle UK, independent bookstores and
the 9/11 Truth Movement

Topics: 9/11, conversion to Islam, autobiography,
dissent, humor, false-flag terror, bigotry, witch
hunting, censorship and media bias, academic
freedom, return to American ideals

Dedication

To all of my 9/11 truth friends and colleagues—
you know who you are—
without whom this book could not have been written.

And to Fatna, Hakim and Karim.
Having a truth jihadi for a husband and father isn't easy,
but I hope you'll have a better world for it.

TABLE OF CONTENTS

Publisher's note

Millions of people now know the main arguments for the thesis "9/11 was an inside job," starting from the controlled demolition of the World Trade Center buildings No. 1, 2 and 7. Even a champion of orthodoxy like *Time Magazine* was obliged to note that the "9/11 Truth Movement" is no longer "a fringe phenomenon. It is a mainstream reality."*

Kevin Barrett takes this now-familiar thesis as a springboard to new territory in *Truth Jihad*. Like Jack Kerouac in *On the Road*, Barrett has written a gospel for a new generation of post-9/11 skeptics. This ebullient book strikes a confident keynote for this sudden coming of age. It is a tonic draft of courage for millions of disenfranchised 9/11 truthers – and for the uneasy majority who sense that America, once a beacon of ideals for humanity, is no longer on the right track.

As author and activist, Barrett stands as a giant, uncowed figure in the best American tradition of Thoreau, Whitman, and Clemens. His *Truth Jihad* is half autobiography, half polemic, and half humor. Serious themes of academic freedom, freedom of thought, religious faith, and rigorous reason vs. mass-media propaganda and "dumbing-down" all mingle with a celebration of life by a generous spirit and sharp wit.

Truth Jihad is the first "9/11 Truth" book that is not *primarily* tasked with proving 9/11 was an inside job to our fellow humanity, who remain blindly trapped inside the mainstream media bubble. For millions of us the facts are already painfully clear now – as is the frustration of trying to convey the harsh truth to those who aren't ready for it. *Truth Jihad* is a sharing of that experience, and an affirmation of life and literature after 9/11 – a lively celebration of art, freedom, truth and protest.

~~~~~

*On Sept. 3, 2006, *Time Magazine* published a lead article, "Why the 9/11 Conspiracies Won't Go Away," conceding, "The population of world No. 2 [9/11 conspiracy theorists] is larger than you might think. A Scripps-Howard poll of 1,010 adults last month found that 36% of Americans consider it "very likely" or "somewhat likely" that government officials either allowed the attacks to be carried out or carried out the attacks themselves. Thirty-six percent adds up to a lot of people. This is not a fringe phenomenon. It is a mainstream political reality."

Authors' Preface

This book's cover, and its title, may scare some readers. They may assume that my *Truth Jihad* is a bloody holy war, fought by someone who thinks he is in full possession of the truth—a violent, ignorant fanatic who wants to impose his own version of truth on everyone else.

As you read this book, I think you will discover that this is not the case. But you should not start with any misconceptions. So please keep this in mind: *I do not, cannot know the whole truth about what happened on September 11th, 2001.* What I do know is that the official version, *The 9/11 Commission Report*, is, as David Griffin has written, "a 571-page lie."[1]

This book is not about the Big Lie of the *9/11 Commission Report* or the hundreds of little lies it contains. That task was already accomplished, within months of the *Report*'s issuance, in *The 9/11 Commission Report: Omissions and Distortions* by David Ray Griffin.[2] Seminal works for those who want to take a serious look at the evidence about what may or may not have happened on September 11th, 2001 are the following:

The New Pearl Harbor by David Ray Griffin[3]
The War on Freedom by Nafeez Ahmed[4]
9/11 Synthetic Terror: Made in USA by Webster Griffin Tarpley[5]
9/11 Mysteries (DVD) by Avatar Productions

Please refer to these works, and to the other books and websites listed in the bibliography, for evidentiary discussions. For now, let me offer an extremely brief summary of a very few of the great many reasons to consider the *9/11 Commission Report* a lie, a whitewash, an undisguised, blatant, shameless cover-up.

The *9/11 Commission Report* is a catalogue of sins of omission and commission. It ignores virtually all of the abundant evidence that contradicts its pre-ordained conspiracy theory: 19 hijackers carried out the attacks, led by a dialysis patient in a cave in Afghanistan without the help or foreknowledge of any government or intelligence agency. It ignores reliable reports from the BBC and other sources that many of the alleged 19 hijackers are still alive.[6] It ignores overwhelming evidence that many of these "19 hijackers" were/are not Muslims at all, much less extremists, but boozing, whoring, pork-chop-eating secular types who appear to have been intelligence agents playing a role assigned to them, who trained at Maxwell Air Force Base Officer's School in Alabama, and who today continue to live and work in Morocco, Tunisia, and Saudi

Arabia.[7] It ignores the fact that none of these alleged hijackers' names, nor any other Arab names, were on any of the flight manifests.[8] It ignores the fact that Bin Laden repeatedly denied involvement in 9/11 during the fall of 2001 and even deplored the attacks as un-Islamic—and that the "Fatty Bin Laden" "confession tape" of December, 2001 features a "Bin Laden" who does not look very much like Bin Laden,[9] and that leading experts think some or all of the post-2001 "Bin Laden tapes" are fake.[10] The FBI itself confirms that Bin Laden is "not wanted for 9/11" because there is "no hard evidence" against him.[11]

The Commission ignores the fact that the head of Pakistan's ISI, a close ally of the CIA, wired $100,000 to Atta shortly before the 9/11 attacks, and then was called to Washington D.C. where he spent the week leading up to the attacks conferring with various top US officials.[12] It ignores the obvious controlled demolition of a massive skyscraper that was never hit by a plane—the ultimate 9/11 smoking gun, World Trade Center Bldg. 7—and the apparent confession of the over-insured landlord-of-six-weeks, Netanyahu-buddy Larry Silverstein, that Building 7 was "pulled," i.e. demolished with explosives.[13] It ignores virtually all of the evidence that the Twin Towers were likewise demolished.[14] It lies and states that the interior core of the Towers consisted of "hollow elevator shafts" rather than 47 massive core columns holding up the building—columns that would have been left sticking hundreds of feet out of the rubble had there actually been an absurdly improbable "pancake collapse" of the kind imagined by the Commission.[15] It ignores most of the dozens of burning questions that have been raised about the many improbabilities surrounding the alleged hijacking of Flight 77 and its supposed crash into the Pentagon.[16] It ignores eyewitness testimony and other evidence suggesting that the "let's roll" story of Flight 93's demise is a lie.[17] It ignores Treasury Secretary Norman Mineta's sworn testimony to the Commission placing Dick Cheney in command in the White House bunker shortly after 9:15, and issuing an apparent "don't protect our nation's capital" stand-down order at around 9:30; the Commission lies by saying that Cheney did not even get to the White House bunker until after 10:00—contradicting not only Mineta's testimony, but also statements by terror czar Richard Clarke.[18]

On those rare occasions when the Commission does acknowledge the existence of evidence contradicting its thesis, it distorts that evidence outrageously. Thus we learn that George Bush kept reading about pet goats to schoolchildren during an alleged massive aerial surprise attack, rather than assuming his Commander in Chief's role, because he did not want to frighten the children. This is a sickeningly puerile and patronizing "explanation," even for a *Report* written at a seventh-grade reading level. It ignores the fact that the Secret Service should have whisked the President off to safety, and made sure he was carrying out his Constitutional role as Commander-in-Chief of a nation under surprise attack, at the barest hint of any such attack. (Had this all been merely a case of outrageous criminal incompetence, we would have heard of demotions, firings, and prosecutions; but as far as we know no Secret Service agents—nor any FAA, NORAD, FBI, or CIA agents—have been fired, prosecuted, or even reprimanded; some have been promoted.)

The Commission's obfuscation and lies cannot hide the fact of a strong prima facie case of high treason against all US officials complicit in the unconstitutional, apparently pre-planned transfer of Commander-in-Chief powers from the President to the Vice President, who has absolutely no Constitutional authority to assume such a role. The Commission's decision to allow the President and Vice President to avoid testifying separately under oath, but instead to meet informally with the Commission *together*, without allowing Commissioners to record the proceedings or even take notes, makes every member of the 9/11 Commission complicit in this prima facie act of high treason. (Those who know guilty demeanor when they see it should watch Bush's post-9/11-Commission-meeting Rose Garden Press Conference, available as a separate file on Michael Moore's *Fahrenheit 9/11* DVD.)

Likewise, the Commission wildly distorts the three radically incompatible, increasingly ludicrous accounts offered by the military to explain why not one of the allegedly hijacked airliners was even intercepted, much less shot down. (Interception is standard procedure for any off-course plane—there had been 67 cases earlier in 2001—and it usually takes less than 20 minutes.) That the military was lying—not just spinning the truth, not just embellishing, but lying outrageously—was so obvious that Senator Mark Dayton (D-MN) almost broke down crying on the Senate podium as he tried to come to terms with it immediately after the *Report* was released. Shortly after Dayton's earth-shaking but almost unreported Senate speech blasting the NORAD lies, "terrorist threats" forced the Senator to evacuate his entire staff from his Washington D.C. office, return to Minnesota, and announce his impending retirement.

The *Commission Report*, as Dayton said, glosses over the military's lies, accepting the third and most ridiculous of NORAD's stories as the gospel truth, without asking for the faintest shred of evidence to support it. Now, in July 2006, we have learned that at least some Commissioners say they wanted to report the blatantly lying military officials for possible perjury prosecutions.[19] So why didn't they? Why did the *9/11 Commission Report* pretend to swallow the military's lies unquestioned? What kind of a *Report* is this?

Short answer: The *9/11 Commission Report* is a farce. It is an insult to the thousands who died that day, to their surviving family members, and to the tens of thousands who have died in the Cheney regime's criminal wars of aggression that could never have happened without the 9/11 "New Pearl Harbor."

Four of the bravest 9/11 widows are the so-called Jersey girls—Patty Casazza, Monica Gabrielle, Mindy Kleinberg, and Lorie Van Auken of the Family Steering Committee for the 9/11 Independent Commission. These four heroines fought for an investigation of 9/11 during the 440 days of Cheney-regime stonewalling that preceded the establishment of the absurdly under-funded and under-mandated Commission. (Compare that 440-day wall of silence to what happened after previous disasters like Pearl Harbor, JFK, and the Space Shuttle crash, when investigations were launched almost immediately.)

Here is what 9/11 widows Patty Casazza, Monica Gabrielle, Mindy Kleinberg, and Lorie Van Auken have to say about the Commission's cover-up of perjury by NORAD officials:

> Recent stories in the Washington Post, the New York Times, as well as the release of the transcripts of the NORAD tapes in Vanity Fair, clearly show that the 9/11 Commission failed in its duties.
>
> According to current reports, the Commission knew that it had been deceived by NORAD. In May 2003, representatives of NORAD testified, in full regalia, before the 9/11 Commission equipped with an easel and visual aids to highlight NORAD's timeline for the day of 9/11. In June 2004, NORAD testified again, changing its previous testimony. The new timeline blamed the lack of military response on late notification by the FAA.
>
> The Commissioners never determined or explained why there was a discrepancy between the two sets of testimonies. Governor Kean is quoted in the Washington Post article as saying "we, to this day don't know why NORAD told us what they told us, it was just so far from the truth ... It's one of those loose ends that never got tied."[20]

Blatant, undisguised perjury by top US military officials is a "loose end"? Well, yes, I suppose it is. So are the eleven alleged hijackers who are known to be still alive. So is the abundance of molten steel produced by all three major WTC building collapses—ironclad physical evidence proving beyond a reasonable doubt that all three buildings were demolished with explosives.[21]

It is time to admit that the entire *9/11 Commission Report* is one gigantic "loose end" that has completely unraveled the fabric of Constitutional governance in this country. Are you willing to live with a 571-page lie as the official record of the most important historic event of the 21st century? Are you willing to live with a 571-page lie that has served as the basis for two criminal wars of aggression, and many massive catastrophic rollbacks in Constitutional civil liberties, that were all ordered and implemented as policy—not just as contingency plans—*before* the event that allegedly made them necessary?[22]

If your answer is yes, I submit that you are insane. Then again, maybe you think I am the one who's insane. I do get occasional emails informing me that I am insane, to which I reply: Anyone crazy enough to email a crazy person to tell him he's crazy...is crazy!

If you are willing to live with that Big Lie known as the *9/11 Commission Report*, then one of us must be crazy.

Before you jump to conclusions about which one of us that is, please take the time to inform yourself. Read the books recommended above, and check out some of the other sources, including video and auditory evidence, listed in the appendix. Take a look at my account of how I got to where I am today, and read some of my book reviews and polemical and satirical pieces that are included in this volume. While you may conclude that I have led an unusual, eventful and not always respectable life, and that some of my experiences have been stranger than fiction, I doubt that you will finish this book thinking that I am a lunatic, or that my opinions on 9/11 are entirely baseless.

Then again, maybe you will. It's your call.

Kevin Barrett

Lone Rock, Wisconsin

August 20th, 2006

Part 1: The Making of a Truth Jihadi

By the pen and what they write with it,
You are not, by God's favor given you, a madman.
–Qur'an 68: 1-2

Introduction: Nichols' Offer I Couldn't Refuse: Friday, June 30ᵗʰ, 2006

Bismillah ar-rahman ar-rahim: In the name of God, the Compassionate, the Caring:

It was just a few days after Steve Nass had made me famous. Nass, a Bushite Wisconsin state assemblyman, had called a press conference and demanded I be fired from my job as a University of Wisconsin lecturer. Why? Because I had dared to speak my mind about 9/11 on a talk radio show.

Suddenly deluged with media interview requests, my cell phone and landline both ringing off the hook, I ducked out of the house for a few minutes and made a quick run to the post office. There—whether coincidentally, sychronistically, or by the will of Allah—I encountered John Nichols, editor of Madison's left-leaning daily newspaper, the *Capital Times*.

Nichols is one of the very few mainstream journalists who really *is* a journalist. Unlike the legion of hacks in corporate-media employ, Nichols is sharp, witty, eyes-wide-open and in full possession of his ethics. He literally wrote the book on Cheney—*Dick, the Man Who Is President*—and he published two of my 9/11 truth op-eds when no other American newspaper would have dared.

I greeted him with something like "You're the only journalist in town who isn't trying to reach me. Or did the NSA tip you off that I was heading for the post office?" It did seem odd, or at least ironic. Here I was fleeing a pack of slavering journalists who wouldn't give my phone a rest, and who should I run into but John Nichols, the only journalist in America I would have gone out of my way to talk to. He was sitting cross-legged on the concrete sidewalk, his back against the glass panel beside the post office door, chatting nonchalantly on his cell phone, looking like a curly-blond bespectacled undersized smiling-Buddha laying in wait to ambush me.

I sat down beside him and we chatted for most of the hour that remained before my Wisconsin Public Radio interview with Ben Merens. He asked how I was holding up under media assault, and expressed amusement at the incomprehension of some of his journalistic colleagues, like the one who called him up and asked "How can you publish this crazy Barrett guy?" John's reply: "Because he's asking good questions."

I asked why no journalists would take on 9/11. Anybody who could get to Morocco or Saudi Arabia could probably get an interview with one of the eleven alleged suicide hijackers who were known to be still alive. Wouldn't this be bigger than Watergate? Nichols allowed that it would, but didn't think it would be possible to set off a 9/11 Watergate as things currently stood. "Journalism is dead," he said. What passed for journalism, he explained, was mostly just infotainment controlled by a few corporations with a de facto monopoly and a common anti-democratic agenda.

I asked Nichols what he made of the fact that Cheney, not Bush, had been the acting Commander-in-Chief during the 9/11 attacks—a treasonous violation of the Constitution that must have been pre-arranged by high officials with foreknowledge of the attacks. Nichols admitted that after reading Paul Thompson's *Complete 9/11 Timeline*, he had realized that Cheney's account of his actions and whereabouts on 9/11 was obviously a lie.

So why wouldn't individuals at least stand up and speak their minds? Why was I the only one who would say in public what so many people thought? Nichols agreed that 9/11 skepticism was rife among the intelligentsia. "Get a few drinks in people and they'll say these things in hushed tones."

So why not say them sober, in broad daylight and with full-throated voice?

"People know that once they speak out on this issue they'll be typecast for life," Nichols said. "Nobody will ever again be able to see them whole, as a complex person with many facets and interests. They'll wear a permanent label reading 'conspiracy theorist.' Most people can't handle that."

Nichols went on to say that now that I, Kevin Barrett, was a famous conspiracy theorist, people might be interested in learning about me as a person, in order to understand why I was willing to say in public what others hardly dared whisper in private. He said that his publishers might be interested in a book about what it was like to be such a hardcore dissident in post-9/11 America. A lot of people felt like dissidents, he allowed, but a Muslim arguing in public that 9/11 was an inside job was a special case. That level of dissidence arouses public curiosity. I should write a book, Nichols said, and call it *American Dissident.*

This is that book—sort of. Here you have some of my best screeds, diatribes, letters, parodies, book reviews and miscellaneous writings on 9/11, framed with my own account of how I became America's most famous Muslim 9/11 "conspiracy theorist." It was my writings, many of them first published at http://mujca.com, that set me on the road to 9/11-revisionist fame. They attracted an enthusiastic following, making me a well-known 9/11 skeptic and MUJCA a leading 9/11 website, long before right-wing radio host Jessica McBride and Wisconsin State Assemblyman Steve Nass launched their witch-hunt. In fact, it was the popularity and over-the-top outrageousness of my writings that caught the attention of Nass and Jessica McBride in the first place. As McBride put it with admiring incredulity during our interview, "This Barrett guy isn't just another conspiracy theorist ripping off Charlie Sheen. He's one of the leading conspiracy theorists in the country. Charlie Sheen probably ripped off *him!*"

McBride was especially outraged by my parodies, such as my real letter to the Secret Service inquiring whether it was okay to speculate about the capital punishments that might await our treasonous president. On the other hand, she thought my satirical letter to Governor Doyle was "pretty funny"—and she was even more amused that the governor himself didn't get it, immediately calling a press conference to announce that I had sent him a crazy letter, "some kind of diatribe" that underlined my apparent unfitness to teach.[23] It was my satirical and polemical writings, with their paradoxically light-hearted dark humor, that won me a following, amusing even the likes of McBride, and triggered the barrage of publicity. This book collects the best of these writings, along with my account of the personal struggle I experienced while producing them.

My *Truth Jihad* has a two-part structure corresponding to the two senses of the term *jihad*. That much-maligned word simply means "struggle" and, in its classic religious sense, links two distinct concepts. First, there is the "greater jihad"— the struggle to be a good person, to annihilate one's petty egotistical side and become a cipher for the will of God. Second, there is the "lesser jihad"—the political or military struggle to defend the community from its enemies.

This book is both a lesser jihad and a greater jihad. The polemical writings are a form of lesser jihad. They represent my best attempt to defend my communities—the American community as well as the Muslim community—from the same enemy: The top US officials who, as the preponderance of evidence indicates, must have orchestrated the 9/11 attacks and falsely blamed them on Muslims, in order to trigger a "new American century" of aggressive war against Muslim-majority countries, while destroying the American tradition of Constitutional governance by erecting a fascist dictatorship capable of waging this new hundred-years-war. By telling the truth about 9/11, I am waging nonviolent lesser jihad, in hopes that the pen may prove mightier than the sword.

The autobiographical side of this book represents a greater jihad whose aim is another kind of truth, the truth of the soul. Telling the truth about one's personal life is always a struggle, and few autobiographical writers rise to the occasion. Of those who do, even fewer happen to be Muslims. There may be a handful of great Muslim autobiographical writers— I would include Ibn al-'Arabi and Mohammed Assad in this category— but there are few if any who write *as Muslims* while producing anything resembling the modern Western tell-it-all-style autobiography. The West's tradition of autobiography grows out of the confessional style of St. Augustine, while its characteristic modern mode of intellectual autobiography hails from the essays of Montaigne. The notion that confessing one's sins in a garrulously personal manner can yield authenticity underlies this Western tradition. Muslims usually prefer to drape a gauzy veil of oblique and tactful reticence over the intimate personal details of their lives, while avoiding an excessively personal mode of discourse.

Modesty is a major Muslim virtue, and saying "I" is inherently immodest. Hence this book, an autobiographical account by a Western-educated Muslim truth jihadi, is a paradoxical, quixotic project. If I sometimes rend the veil too forcefully, or not forcefully enough, I hope the reader, and Allah, will forgive me. More importantly, I hope the reader will forgive me for following the counsel of the *malamatiyya*, or Blame Seekers, the greatest speak-truth-to-power tradition ever, by insisting that my ultimate allegiance is not to the reader, nor to a leader, nor even to any community—whether American or Muslim—but to God and God alone.

Ground Zero: September 11th, 2001

On Tuesday morning, September 11th, 2001, I was on my way to a Folklore discussion section when I first heard the rumors about planes hitting the World Trade Center. As a Teaching Assistant, my job was to lead a discussion about folklore, not current events, so I kept the discussion on-topic. On the way out of the classroom the halls were buzzing: "*Two* planes crashed into the World Trade Center, and both towers just collapsed!"

My first thought: Somebody's going to make a lot of money off this. The military budget's going to double. And then from somewhere deep inside my cranium, a grumpy, paranoid little voice, piped up: They'll blame the Muslims and go to war. Then I thought: No, the wacko Zio-extremists like Steve Emerson will try to blame the Muslims, just like after Oklahoma City. But it will turn out to be homegrown terrorists again. Truth will out.

The grumpy little voice, it turned out, was on to something. Within hours of the attacks, television personalities were saying "this has all the earmarks of al-Qaida," and brandishing the names of nineteen alleged Arab hijackers, all of whom presumably had the telltale marks on their ears. One of the earmarked hijackers had somehow lost his passport as the plane crashed into the building— maybe he pulled it out of his pocket and flung it skyward at just the right moment—and the magic passport, leading a life as charmed as Kennedy's magic bullet, had floated to the pavement unharmed, to be discovered and turned over to the authorities as evidence. Mohammed Atta's equally charmed suitcase, chalk-full of such "evidence" as a parody of an Islamist's will—what better place to keep your will than a suitcase on board a plane you're going to fly into a building!—miraculously missed its connection at Boston's Logan Airport, so it could be discovered and brandished to the world as proof that the deed was done by Muslim extremists.

Why Atta would book a flight from Maine to Boston with a tight connection, rather than just fly out of Boston, was another interesting question. And how did he manage to leave rental cars at both the Maine and Boston airports? There certainly was an over-abundance of "evidence" implicating these guys!

It looked like a done deal—too done of a deal, if you asked me.

That Thursday in class, I told the students what I knew about al-Qaida, which meant "the base," meaning the CIA database of Arab mujahideen recruited to fight on behalf of US interests in Afghanistan and across the southern flank of the Russian empire. The students were interested, but didn't seem to want to contemplate the possibility that al-Qaida was still a CIA front. In fact, a wave of television-fueled hysteria had washed over the nation, and nobody wanted to see the event for what it was—a crime, not an act of war. If we had been told the truth that this monstrous attack was a crime, the crime would have been investigated, and the perpetrators sought out and punished. Instead, the television talking heads, egged on by the Bush administration, endlessly repeated that this was another Pearl Harbor, an act of war. There was no point in trying to find out who had attacked us. We already knew who did it. It was THEM – Muslims, Arabs, foreign fanatics, darker-skinned people who live outside our borders. The appropriate response was to slaughter a whole lot of dark-skinned people with bombs and tanks and artillery. That would show THEM. The precise identities of whoever had planned and carried out the monstrous crimes of 9/11 was of absolutely no importance. Killing foreigners was the only thing that mattered now.

I was appalled by the psychotic zeitgeist, by the legions of lunatics waving flags while cheering the Bush junta's destruction of the very liberties those flags symbolized. It seemed the whole nation had gone insane. But despite the ever-increasing number of holes in the official story, I remained skeptically agnostic about the question of what had really happened on September 11th, 2001. It would take me two years to realize that it had been an obvious inside job, that the evidence proving this was overwhelming, and that the perpetrators were hiding in plain sight, in "undisclosed locations" at the highest levels of the U.S. government.

Once I understood this—it hit me in early December, 2003—my life changed drastically. For a few weeks I agonized about what to do. Should I continue as before, occasionally forwarding e-mails with alternative analyses of events to selected friends and colleagues? Or should I commit myself to a career of activism?

I quickly chose to not only involve myself in the 9/11 truth movement, but to commit to it. The old saw has it, "In a ham-and-eggs breakfast, the chicken is involved, but the pig is committed." That may sound like an odd metaphor for a Muslim to use, but so be it. Commitment is like marriage as opposed to dating (another odd metaphor for a Muslim!) It involves a giving over of one's being, a sort of self-sacrifice predicated on acceptance of mortality. Once one understands that at least some top US officials, who sit in front of consoles with red buttons that could kill billions of people, are willing to slaughter almost 3,000 of their own people in pursuit of more and more power, one realizes that organizing effective resistance is a potentially dangerous undertaking. One can either involve oneself—hesitantly, nervously, fearfully—or one can commit oneself. True commitment requires relinquishing fear of death, and achieving peace and contentment in the face of one's potential murder, torture, persecution, what-have-you—even in the face of the possibility that one's family could suffer, perhaps atrociously, for one's actions.

I had been involved in activist causes before, but never committed. I had demonstrated against the Vietnam War while still a kid. I had marched against apartheid. I had spent most of a year campaigning for a nuclear weapons freeze. I had demonstrated against Gulf War One, helping shut down San Francisco for a day to protest that awful crime against the people of Iraq. I had written letters defending the Palestinians. I had campaigned for two presidential candidates capable of thinking an original thought, Gary Hart and Jerry Brown. (I didn't agree with them on everything, just as I do not agree with Russ Feingold today on many issues, but I respected Hart's and Brown's grey matter just as today I respect Feingold's quixotic defense of the Constitution.)

When I realized that 9/11 had almost certainly been an inside job, and that clear, obvious, overwhelming, in-your-face evidence made this obvious to anyone willing to take an honest look at the matter, I knew that this issue was not like other issues. I had been attracted to the nuclear weapons freeze because it was so obviously more important than other issues. After all, if the nuclear stockpiles are not eliminated, they will eventually be used, and then all other issues will be moot.

Likewise with 9/11. All of the horrible US policies that are destroying the world—criminal wars of aggression, the destruction of liberty at home and abroad, ever-increasing economic inequality and injustice, the inculcation of mass stupidity and utter annihilation of critical thinking among most of the US population, the "legalization" of torture and first use of nuclear weapons, the waste of precious resources on military spending, and the consequent destruction of the earth's biosphere— grow directly out of the 9/11 Reichstag Fire, just as the evils of Nazism grew out of the original Reichstag Fire. Without the Reichstag Fire, Hitler would have been unable to abolish constitutional governance and launch his criminal wars of aggression that ultimately claimed 50 million lives. Likewise, without the 9/11 neo con job, few of the present planet-destroying US policies would have been possible.

If the German people had figured out that Hitler was behind the Reichstag Fire, they might have risen up in rebellion—even though nobody died in that blaze. If the American people understood that top officials of their own government had orchestrated the destruction of the World Trade Center and the murder of thousands of Americans in pursuit of a criminal agenda, they would certainly rise up in rebellion, and turn their nation's policies 180 degrees away from that criminal agenda. They would cut the military budget to a tiny fraction of what it had been before the 9/11 Reichstag Fire. They would withdraw not just from the imperial wars 9/11 had incited, but from empire itself, reclaiming the great American anti-imperialist tradition of 1776. They would arrest the super-rich criminals who were complicit in 9/11, and institute the mother of all trust-busting eras to shatter the monopolies, especially the media monopolies, into thousands of tiny, locally-owned pieces, and redistribute the criminals' wealth to the people. They would put their money into roads, schools, housing, and other life-supporting activities, instead of death-dealing ones. They would concentrate their energies on developing technologies to cope with the coming economic-energy-environmental crisis, and build railroads and alternative power stations rather than new kinds of bunker-busting nuclear weapons. They would embrace international co-operation and demilitarize first outer space, and then, gradually, the planet itself, leaving locally-based militias, and maybe a couple of nuclear subs per nation for insurance against invasion, as the only form of military power. And they would reclaim their freedom of speech and expression and dismantle the police state that has been riding America's back like an evil spirit since the National Security State replaced constitutional democracy back in 1947.

It was not just a matter of life or death, I realized. It was far more important than that. At the deepest soul level, I decided that I had no interest in living in a world without 9/11 truth, nor in leaving such a world to my children. I felt I would gladly sacrifice everything I had, everything I knew—even the lives of everyone I knew, the universe itself, the cosmos, EVERYTHING—in an all-out battle to see that the perpetrators of 9/11 did not get away with their crimes. This would be my truth jihad.

David Griffin, the Christian philosopher-theologian and 9/11 activist whose work has so influenced me, has been asked whether he fears for his life. David's reply: "If they take me out, my books will shoot to the top of the New York Times bestseller list. And if they don't, I'll get to write my *Summa Theologica* in peace. It's a win-win situation."

The Traveler

As a child I was a traveler. The older I get, the more I would rather stay home and read.

I once wrote a pseudo-country song about my traveling origins for one of my two punk bands. It started like this:

I was born in a gas station rest-room
Out beside Ol' Highway 23
Underneath the paint-chipped dispenser of prophylactics
The ladies' room was occupied ya see
Or maybe they just couldn't [off-key] FIND THE KEY!

Actually I was born in Madison General Hospital in Madison, Wisconsin, on February 9th, 1959, at some ungodly hour in the morning. But I did get dragged around the highways and byways of U.S. America a lot while still young and impressionable.

My dad, Pete Barrett, was a pretty amazing character. The son of a high school math teacher who later excelled as football coach, then principal, Pete built a boat with the help of his uncle while in his early teens, won scholarships to Cornell and the Webb Institute of Naval Architecture, and later earned a law degree and a Ph.D. in finance. He also taught engineering at two universities even though he never quite completed his engineering Ph.D. because he refused to learn German. He was also a successful businessman. More than anyone else, he was responsible for growing North Sails from the one-loft operation it was when he got there to the worldwide chain it is today. A world-class racing sailor, he competed in three Olympics and won a silver medal in Tokyo in 1964 and a gold medal in Acapulco in 1968. The silver medal would have been a gold except that he brushed against a mark he was rounding, sailed the rest of the race in first place, but refused to cross the finish line even though nobody had seen his infraction. His failure to finish that race cost him the gold medal. That kind of ruthlessly self-sacrificing honesty in sailboat racing is almost unheard of; normally nobody likes to admit to an infraction. Giving up a gold medal for a foul unperceived by others has probably never happened before, nor will it ever happen again. The story became a legend in sailing circles. The lesson I have drawn from this story is simple but profound: Better to sacrifice everything you desire than live with a lie.

My mom was no slouch herself—and still isn't. (She hasn't quite caught on to 9/11 truth yet, but she's getting there.) She met my dad on a mountain-climbing trip, and continued to climb, ski and sail beside him throughout his life. She handled our very complex family logistics and raised her three children while my dad was competing in academia, sailing, and business. She even crewed for my dad in Olympic-class sailboat racing, though they never quite reached the Olympics together. As her children left grade school she completed her CPA and served as accountant for North Sails, later establishing her own practice.

When I was born, my dad was 24, my mom was 19, and both were young, hungry, and restless. We moved seven times before I reached sixth grade, and took countless cross-country station-wagon trips, most of them to the many sailboat regattas my dad loved competing in. We moved so often, and traveled so much, that I felt like my real home was in the back of the family station wagon, clutching a book and intermittently watching a sailboat trailing along behind the car.

Though I never liked school, I loved reading, which became both a home-away-from-home and another way of traveling. I learned to read at age three, and by age six, when I skipped first grade, I was reading at a sixth grade level. As a kid I had lousy literary taste—I liked crappy mass-produced 20th-century adventure serials like the Hardy Boys and the Oz books over good 19th-century stuff like Twain, Stevenson, and Dickens. (I did not yet realize that I was growing up in a culture that was being relentlessly dumbed-down.) One thing I will say for my taste, though, was that I loved Edgar Allen Poe—and still do. Though I originally learned French to read Rimbaud, one of the highlights of my *francophonie* was discovering Baudelaire's translations of Poe, which are at least as good as the originals.

Reading, for me, became mixed up with traveling. I remember books based on where I was when I read them. For example, I read a mediocre juvenile book called *Henry Reed's Journey* as we drove across the California and Arizona deserts to Lake Mead, where the Colorado River is temporarily denied its wanderlust by the Hoover Dam. I also remember reading an anti-dam screed called *Big Dam Foolishness* on that same trip, and being impressed by the arguments it mounted against Egypt's Aswan Dam even as I gazed at America's Aswan, Hoover Dam. At that time I must have been in fourth or fifth grade.

The same pattern continued as I grew up and read better books. I recall Hesse's *Steppenwolf* as the book I re-read at age 19 while driving through the Mojave Desert and then turning north along the California-

Nevada border toward King's Canyon National Park and Yosemite. I remember first encountering Philip K. Dick, America's greatest postwar author, on a boat in the Virgin Islands at age fourteen or fifteen—which would have been 1973 or 1974. I encountered Colin Wilson's work in an old stone farmhouse near Plymouth in the south of England en route to hitchhiking around Cornwall and Wales at age seventeen. And I will never forget reading *The New Testament* cover to cover, in French, while taking trains to view the many landmark churches and cathedrals in the Paris region in 1988. Though I knew I would never be a Christian, that experience made Jesus one of my spiritual teachers, and revealed to me the beauty of Christianity.

As a reading traveler and traveling reader, I was perpetually in search of meaning, a destination that was always around the next bend. This gave my life a certain unsettled and unsettling quality. My parents never quite understood what my traveling and reading were about. They read Agatha Christie novels as a diversion from their lives' hypercompetitive grind. And they usually traveled either to compete in a sailboat race—the clear-cut goal being "get there and win"—or on business. Even when on vacation, they worked with furious single-minded determination at having a good time, often by engaging in expensive, logistically complex tasks that entailed a fair amount of physical discomfort. They backpacked with the best backpacking equipment, climbed mountains with ropes and pitons, skied with up-to-date ski equipment, sailed sailboats with Harken blocks and North sails, and generally did everything possible to single-handedly keep the recreational accessories industry afloat.

Impressed by the success of "new journalists" Hunter S. Thompson and Tom Wolfe, I majored in journalism at the University of Wisconsin-Madison and managed to graduate in 1981 with a B average and a bad hangover, my literary-artistic ambitions still basically intact. After messing around with a full-time gig as a proofreader, some freelance writing, and lots of freelance editing, with writing poetry and fiction and singing in punk bands as my real occupation, I wound up in San Francisco studying literature and the teaching of composition. It looked like a straight-forward way for a bookish guy to make a living, should I ever decide to stop living rent-free in a motor home on the streets.

While living in San Francisco from 1981 through 1994—except for a couple years each in Seattle and Paris, and a few junkets to Mexico and Central America—I wrote two novels that I never tried to publish. The first was a pretentious, partially-pornographic potboiler called *Humbert,*

Lolita and the Marquis de Sad, which, as its name indicates, involved a love triangle and a fair amount of kinky sex. It would have been perfect for Maurice Girodias, the Frenchman who published banned-in-the-USA works by Henry Miller, J.P. Donleavy, Lawrence Durrell, Pauline Réage, Jean Genet, Frank Harris, William S. Burroughs, Raymond Queneau, George Bataille, and Gregory Corso. Unfortunately, the USA stopped banning pretentious, mildly naughty books in the 1960s, so there was no longer a market for this type of work. That was precisely why I chose to write such a book—it parodied the tawdry stuff Girodias's authors produced mainly for money but occasionally to literary effect. In fact, it was a sort of love song to that type of book. I have always been attracted to authors like these, and like Philip K. Dick and Fyodor Dostoevsky, who write desperately, at high speed, mainly for money, yet who somehow produce "tawdry" literary masterpieces. The fact that I was privately writing such a book, at a relaxed pace, with absolutely no interest in ever publishing it, was what, in my young mind, gave the whole project literary value. Some of *Humbert* was inspired by sexual escapades with a lovely eighteen-year-old stripper-poet who broke off her affair with Corso—by then an ancient relic—to go out with me. Her graphic account of our affair has been published, but I will not tell you where to look for it.

If *Humbert* was never, ever meant for publication, the same cannot be said of *The Electric Elk*. That novel, a permanent work-in-progress, recounts the exploits of a hero named Edsel Edison, who is condemned to the meaningless drudgery of a door-to-door sales job. The product he sells is called the Edison Edfone, a walkman-like, or should I say ipod-like contraption that is worn atop the head like a pair of antlers, broadcasting custom-tuned EMF frequencies as well as muzak and greatly enhancing the wearer's efficiency in both the workplace and recreational arenas. The Edison Edfone comes in an array of models, ranging from the cheap, none-too-effective Workingman's Edfone—the kind Edsel wears, since he cannot afford a better model—all the way up to the Executive Edfone, which costs a king's ransom or even a CEO's salary. Edsel is permanently out of sorts about carrying the same name as the inventor of the device, and what's worse, his own Edfone is constantly breaking down and blasting him with psychotic-rage EMF bursts and maddening muzak at precisely the most inopportune moments. Unfortunately, or perhaps fortunately for Edsel's continued employment prospects, living without Edfones permanently affixed to one's head has become impossible in the toxic, ultra-high-stress world of the near future. For one thing, they have basically become the equivalent of today's cell phones and internet interfaces, and no other communications devices exist. For another, they soothe the user's brainwaves like an interactive tranquilizer, making it possible to bear the horrors of the techno-dystopia they represent.

The title *The Electric Elk* refers to the Irish Elk, a beast that reportedly grew larger antlers every generation due to male head-bashing competition for females, until finally the poor animals could no longer lift their heads off the ground and quietly went extinct. My techno-adaptation of this concept is fairly self-explanatory.

I never really finished *The Electric Elk*, nor did I ever have any plans to do so. Unlike *Humbert*, however, it was never a purely private writing project, so there is no compelling reason why it could not be submitted for publication. One day, insha'allah, when 9/11 truth prevails, I may travel back to the future and finish it.

~~~~

Excerpt from Barrett's Wikipedia biography: Early Life

In the early 1990s, Kevin Barrett received master's degrees in both English literature and French from San Francisco State University and married a Moroccan-born Muslim woman. He converted to Islam in 1992.

Barrett returned to the University of Wisconsin-Madison in 1995. The U.S. State Department gave him a Fulbright Scholarship in 1999 to study a year in Morocco. He received a Ph.D. in African languages and literature with a minor in folklore from the University of Wisconsin-Madison in 2004, focusing his dissertation on the topic of Moroccan legend. Barrett has taught English, French, Arabic, American Civilization, Humanities, African Literature, Folklore, and Islam at colleges and universities in the San Francisco Bay area, Paris, and Madison, Wisconsin.

~~~~~

FALSE FLAG FACTS

How could anyone take the risk to leave such obvious smoking guns? Because that is just what people will think – and the media will cover it up. False flag tactics work amazingly well, even when exposed: no one is punished, and the gains are not undone. As long as it is little known, the simple principle of reverse action is an enormous source of power for the elites over mankind – like fire in Greek legend, when Prometheus defied the gods and brought its forbidden secret to empower the people.

My *Jahiliyya*:[24] "Adulthood" pre-1993 Reversion to Islam

I was never the world's likeliest candidate for Islamic saintliness, much less martyrdom. Some of my friends and all of my enemies used to describe me as a boozer and a womanizer.

I didn't see it that way. Sure, I liked women—some of them, anyway. What was wrong with that? A few of them I really, *really* liked, which led to four affairs that could be called long-term relationships. I had no interest in marriage, though. As the saying goes, why buy a cow when you can get the milk for free. Were it not for Islam, I am sure that I never would have gotten married. Islam, to my mind, more or less makes marriage mandatory; while the culture I lived in before Islam, my "jahiliyya" or pre-Islamic ignorance, made it seem utterly pointless. The Prophet Muhammad, peace upon him, is reported to have said, "Marriage is half of your religion," and the Qur'an makes it absolutely clear that sex outside of marriage is a serious breach. Without those injunctions, or something like them, why would anyone get married?

And while I am confessing my sins, I might as well point out that I always liked wine and beer. Throughout the 1980s and into the early 1990s I used to swill countless pints of Guinness at the Plough and Stars pub on Clement Street in San Francisco. When I first discovered the place you could get a pint of first-rate Guinness—first-rate by American standards at least—for 50 cents during the 5:00 to 7:00 happy hour. (By the 1990s it had gone up to a buck a pint, but nobody I knew was complaining.) Though I still remember the gay Irishman who used to play "In the 'Derry Air" over and over on the jukebox, the place was pretty straight as San Francisco bars went. Like the ironically-named Dicks, the only straight bar in the Castro, the Plough and Stars was a workingman's pub that wasn't necessarily the best place to meet women, but still a great place to hang out. The Plough and Stars was owned by an IRA sympathizer, and I learned much later that the crew of Irish house painters I used to drink with were actually IRA fugitives.

In addition to cheap Guinness and revolutionary Irish rhetoric, I also enjoyed cheap wine and poetry. My favorite way to meet women was to attend poetry readings and invite them back to my place for a glass of wine. What most guys didn't understand, I learned from experience, is that the average male, especially the materially-successful or otherwise attractive one, is looking for a relatively dumb woman. Their egos can't handle brilliant, spirited, articulate ladies. There were plenty of intelligent, creative, beautiful women going begging for male companionship at those poetry readings! And most of the male poetry-fanciers were ugly, nerdish, or egomaniacal—usually all three at once. Not much competition there. Being fairly bright, reasonably good looking, and not all that much of an asshole, I pretty much had it made.

I used to invite women—sometimes singly, sometimes in groups—to my own private wine-tasting parties. How did I manage that while living in a motor home on the streets at an income way below the poverty line? Easy. I acquired my variegated vintages at a bargain-basement joint called the Canned Food Warehouse off Folsom Street in the Mission District. It offered $10 to $20 bottles of wine for one or two bucks a bottle. The catch was that some of the bottles had gone bad. I would buy several bottles of every vintage and host a wine-tasting party in my motor home. The idea was to taste each bottle, throw out the bad ones, and swill from the good ones. The next day, the bad ones, as well as the unfinished good ones if there were too many of them, would be returned to the Canned Foods Warehouse for a full refund. Though usually too hung-over to communicate effectively, I still somehow managed to get those refunds for more than a decade. When the Warehouse finally ended its automatic refund policy I was probably the reason.

My taste for cheap-but-decent wine continued for a year or two after my conversion to Islam. Habits are hard to shake, and excuses are always easy to come by. My excuse was that I didn't know much about the religious rules, but I knew from observation that some Muslims drank while others didn't. So I decided to be one of those who drank. Twisting the Qur'an on a procrustean bed, I interpreted the English translations of the various verses about wine in such a way as to allow for some ambiguity.

The first sign that God found my interpretation less than satisfactory came early on in my first Ramadan fast. I broke the fast according to the sunna, with a date and a bit of milk, then prayed the evening prayer... and finally sat down to a delicious dinner that I chased with a full bottle of red wine.

The next day I woke up feeling like a sick infidel dog. And that afternoon, while standing beside the Islam bookshelf in the Berkeley Public Library, I experienced the first and worst of the migraines that have plagued me intermittently ever since. My whole visual field was gradually enveloped in flashing zig-zagging lightning bolts decorated with neon rattlesnake patterns. Blinded, I felt my way out of the library and into the optometrist's shop around the corner. The optometrist quickly diagnosed me: I was suffering from typical pre-migraine auras. Get ready for the worst headache of your life, he told me.

Sure enough, it hit me like a Night Train freight train. I was out of commission for two days. I wrote it off as a message from Allah: "Keep it to half a bottle during Ramadan."

~~~~~

Excerpt from Barrett's Wikipedia biography: Controversy

Barrett first drew attention to his views by writing letters to the editor of the Madison Capital Times and Wisconsin State Journal, in which he claimed that Muslims had nothing to do with the attacks: "As a Ph.D. Islamologist and Arabist I really hate to say this, but I'll say it anyway: 9/11 had nothing to do with Islam. The war on terror is as phony as the latest Osama bin Laden tape." Barrett has also asserted that other purported terrorist attacks, including the July 7, 2005, London bombing, and the March 11, 2004, Madrid bombing, were the actions of a "special wing of, probably, U.S. or western military intelligence," and not Islamic terrorists.

Following a June 28, 2006 talk radio segment on WTMJ, Barrett's views came to the attention of Wisconsin Governor Jim Doyle, U.S. Representative Mark Green, and State Representative Stephen L. Nass. After conducting a 10-day review of Barrett's past teaching and plans for the class, UW-Madison Provost Patrick Farrell determined that Barrett was fit to teach.

On July 11, 2006, Barrett appeared on the television show "The O'Reilly Factor", and the show's host, Bill O'Reilly, said about Barrett, "This guy would have been gone at Boston University, my alma mater, in a heartbeat… in the Charles River floating down, you know, toward the harbor." In response, Barrett filed a complaint with the FCC.

Barrett has edited "9/11 and American Empire" (vol. 2) from Interlink Books, published in Dec. 2006.

In Fall 2006 Kevin Barrett began hosting a talk show twice a week on the GCN Live Network called The Dynamic Duo, and weekly on the RBN Network with a show called Truth Jihad.

CNN's Anderson Cooper broadcast a fairly sympathetic story on Barrett on Nov. 22, 2006, which became the most popular video of the week on YouTube.

~~~~~

The Prophet Muhammad "raised woman from the status of a chattel to complete legal equality with man… for the first time in human history made universal brotherhood a fact and principle of common law."
– Mohammad Marmaduke Pickthall, *The Meaning of the Glorious Qur'an.*

Sex and the Hermeneutics of Suspicion

I have always loved sex, ever since my first four-year-old fantasies of rubbing up against the teenage babysitter. Now, as a parent, I think it is a very good thing that my wife and I have never hired teenage babysitters, because I'd probably have the exact same fantasies. Some of us, in some ways, never really grow up. Or maybe we do. Maybe growing up is realizing that you never grow up, recognizing your limitations, and staying away from temptation. Muslims seem a lot more mature about this than non-Muslim Americans. Muslims have a saying that "if a man and a woman are in a room together, there is always a third person present—the shaytan!" They recognize the power and ubiquity of the sexual drive that God gave us, and manage it through a social code designed to stop problems before they begin. Many non-Muslim Americans seem to be in denial about their sexuality—they don't like to admit that sex is a lot more powerful than they are. So they often get themselves into situations where the sex drive can take over, leading to problems like teenage pregnancies, rampant venereal disease, date rape, broken marriages, and so on.

It isn't that Islam is puritanical. There is plenty of room for licit sexuality in classical Islam. Oversexed men are allowed more than one wife, on condition that they work hard enough and productively enough to completely support their wives and children—and that they treat all their wives equally, and satisfy them all sexually. If you think about these conditions, you can probably understand why very few Muslim men through the ages have had more than one wife. Theoretically, the possibility of polygamy should channel the extra energy of oversexed men in productive directions, forcing them to work harder earning an honest living so they can support their larger family.

Compare that to what often happens to oversexed, ambitious men and their wives in today's USA. To take one classic example—an extreme one, I admit—an ambitious, presumably oversexed and under-brained Republican politician here in Wisconsin, the author of a law called The Defense of Marriage Act, was recently caught cheating on his wife—and with a married woman, no less! In an Islamic culture, this guy would have to quit the Republican Party and get a real job. (Islam forbids making a living through criminal enterprises.) Then he would work overtime, negotiate with his wife about the possibility of taking another wife into the household, and either get more nooky from his first wife, or negotiate permission to take a second bride. The one thing he would NOT be allowed to do is sneak out and cheat, undermining two marriages in the process.

Women, in Islam, are guaranteed complete financial support and sexual satisfaction from their husbands, who are absolutely *not* allowed to cheat. The classic *hudud* punishment of stoning to death for adultery was rarely enforced, in part because it required three witnesses to the actual genital penetration to obtain a conviction. Like other *hudud* punishments, this one was designed to dissuade socially destructive behavior without having to be enforced much, if at all. Just the image of being stoned to death is enough to underline how serious a transgression adultery is, and to dissuade most people from engaging in it, just as the image of losing a limb is enough to greatly discourage or even eliminate theft. (Please note that these rules are gender-neutral, and that allegedly Muslim cultures that focus on punishing female misbehavior while ignoring or condoning male misbehavior are un-Islamic.)

Islamic law courts from past ages reveal many lawsuits brought by wives demanding full sexual satisfaction from their husbands. That sounds pretty progressive and feminist, no? Remember, just a hundred years ago, the best medical minds in the West were discussing the hotly-debated scientific question, "Are women capable of feeling sexual pleasure?" The standard answer at the time was "no."

Not so progressive-and-feminist-sounding is the Islamic rule that unlike husbands, wives are *always* allowed only one sexual partner at a time. (Remember, this is also the case for the vast majority of Muslim men; polygamy is for a tiny minority.) Given the possibility of legitimate polygamy, is the ban on polyandry sexist? or only a way to ensure that children know who their parents are. Men are understandably reluctant to support children they don't know are theirs. If children are born to women who have more than one lover, the possibility that the resulting children will not be taken care of—and that male rivalry may erupt in violence—is always present.

The often-overlooked point is that in virtually all cultures known to anthropology, marriage rules are basically about harnessing extra male energy and making it available to women and children, so that the next generation will be taken care of. Islam's rules seem to accomplish this in an unusually harmonious way. Of course, in today's hyper-individualist society of ME-ME-ME, the individual whim is sacrosanct, while the basic needs of the group, especially its less fortunate members, are mostly forgotten. To such a society, the classical Islamic norms seem unjust, since they are all about motivating individuals to live for something greater than the self and its whims. Ultimately, in the Islamic worldview, we are here for the hard work of spiritual development, not the easy pleasure of selfish satisfactions, and society should be set up to create the harmony and the ethic of self-transcendence that encourage spiritual development, while allowing satisfaction of healthy, moderate needs and desires.

I suppose this all sounds rather bizarre to many of my readers. How did I, the child of nice lapsed Unitarian Midwestern parents, become a defender of polygamy? Perhaps it was because I saw from early on that American sex and marriage rules, inherited from Christian culture, are tainted with hypocrisy, repression and denial. (With fathers like the self-flagellating Augustine and the self-castrating Origen, it is not surprising that Christianity has a few hang-ups.) As a teenager I got a crash course in the hermeneutics of suspicion from my high school librarian, Charlotte Smith. She taught me suspicion of science by recommending Velikovsky —a quack, I later learned, but an interesting one. She ingrained me with metaphysical suspicion by placing in my eager hands books by the likes of Kurt Vonnegut, Herman Hesse, and Philip K. Dick. And she fueled my suspicions about the way sexuality is expressed and repressed by giving me access to the forbidden books of the Pewaukee High School library, including Erica Jong's *Fear of Flying* and Philip Roth's *Portnoy's Complaint.* More importantly, she directed me to the works of Sigmund Freud. I read *The Interpretation of Dreams* at age sixteen, and quickly learned to interpret my own dreams and delve into my own unconscious. (What I found in my dreams was even more bizarre than what Freud had suggested—they seemed to include precognitive material, as John Donne explains in *An Appointment with Time.*)

While still a teenager, I came to the conclusion that polite society simply could not deal with sex and death. I discovered Jim Morrison's charisma-laced poetry in the cutout bin of the local record store, and bought all The Doors albums for 69 cents each. That was in 1973. By 1984, when those records were stolen from my motor home, they were worth considerably more than that.

In 1975 I learned about the one death America *really* could not deal with: the murder of JFK. Mark Lane, Lee Harvey Oswald's lawyer and the author of the seminal JFK assassination book *Rush to Judgment,* came to a local community college to lecture. I watched Lane show the Zapruder film, which—as everyone but Gerald Posner knows—shows the president being murdered by a head-shot from the right front, his brains blown out of his skull backwards and to the left. Lane then showed a slide of *Life* magazine's reprint of the head-snap frames. Unbelievably, the frames were printed in reverse order, giving the false impression that President's head was being blown forward, not backward—which is what would have happened had Oswald actually shot JFK from behind as the Warren Commission claimed.

After doing some reading, I grew convinced that a massive, obvious, in-your-face cover-up had followed the death of JFK and protected the real murderers. Polite society, of course, did not want to deal with this, any more than it wanted to admit that we are sexual beings and that little boys and their dads fantasize about the babysitter. Some things we simply do not talk about! But then, some of us do. The subculture of people who talk frankly about sex has grown enormously since my high school days, as has the subculture of people who talk frankly about the JFK assassination. And today, the subculture of people who talk frankly about 9/11 has moved out of the internet and into the mainstream. Chalk up a victory for truth, and give partial credit to Sigmund Freud and the hermeneutics of suspicion.

~~~~~

FALSE FLAG FACTS

We were very pleased that *Publishers Weekly* chose to review this book (as you may have guessed from the cover), even though they damned it with faint praise. After a nod to his bellettristic flourish, the spin was that the author supplied no proofs that 9/11 was an inside job – because he didn't have any: "he doesn't back conclusions with hard facts, directing readers to other books and Web sites to learn the "truth"… he's preaching to the converted."

The real problem is Kevin's facts are *too* hard for them (see p. 9-10). All the videos mentioned here can be viewed free online on google, youtube or trutube. But if your argument is not liked, they dispute or ignore any facts you bring. History is awash with more false-flag exploits by the Anglo-American empire than anyone, yet they won't see it. Each time I post these hard-to-face facts on Wikipedia, they are quickly torn down. I started Youpedia.net as a haven for refugees from such Wiki'd mob censorship.

Why would the weak provoke the strong to make war and wipe them out? No country is completely crazy. It stands to reason: this Empire grew by provoking wars when it saw a strategic advantage – always with a figleaf of false pretexts to mollify moral sentiment.

It's widely acknowledged Bush lied and a million died in Iraq. His Daddy ditto, and now come more lies and war drums on Iran. Why is the 9/11 lie so hard to see? Because it was the Big Lie of the 21st century.

Le Paris d'Amérique (November, 1988 – July 1989)

I am often asked the question: If government agents really did blow the World Trade Center to kingdom come, fly a military plane and/or missile into the Pentagon, create an illusion of suicide hijackings, and then cover the whole thing up... how in the world could they get away with it? Are the Bush Boyz really that smart? My answer, though I am usually too polite to say it, is: *No, it isn't that they're that smart—it's that you're that stupid.*

Most journalists, I am sorry to say, are complete idiots. They will believe anything you tell them no matter how outlandish, if it fits the kind of pre-fabricated "story" that will help their employers sell advertisements. And the general public, aside from those who use genuinely alternative sources, will believe just about anything the journalists tell them, no matter how preposterous.

I know all this from experience. I helped feed information that was not just false, but utterly hallucinatory—downright phantasmagoric, even—to the French mainstream media. Then I watched them lap it up and report the hallucination as reality on the nightly news and in all the mainstream papers and newsmagazines. Since French journalists are by and large at least three times as smart and four times as skeptical as their American counterparts, I shudder to think how easy it was for Rove, Wolfowitz and Co. to hoodwink the American people on 9/11.

The *Paris d'Amérique* hoax took place between late 1988 and spring 1989. I was living in a tiny $200-a-month maid's quarters near the Bastille, taking three literature seminars including one with Hélène Cixous, teaching a course on *La Civilisation Américaine* and trying to convince the students it wasn't an oxymoron, conducting a research project on the French critical reception of Philip K. Dick, and playing starting center for the *Université Paris VIII* basketball team—which will give you an idea just how short, and how bad, French college basketball players were.

One day some friends came to visit from Prague. I invited them to a café near the Bastille, a rock n' roll themed joint with pictures of Elvis on the walls. While we were sipping *bière américaine* and chatting, a group of four twenty-something ragamuffins at a nearby table caught my eye. They looked to be in their late teens, with long unkempt hair and torn T-shirts and blue jeans giving them a resemblance to the early Ramones.

They beckoned me over to their table and excitedly showed me a newsmagazine, *Le Nouvel Observateur*—the French equivalent of *Newsweek*. They opened it and showed me an article about themselves, complete with large color photos. The guys were apparently in a rock band. They were pictured playing electric guitars and drums. One of the pictures showed them posing with a guy who looked a bit like me. The story explained that the French rock group *Les Casse-Pieds*, "the Pain-in-the-Necks," used to play for spare change in the Paris metro—until they were discovered by an Australian-born Hollywood director named Christopher Maudson and cast in his soon-to-be-released major motion picture.

The band-members explained that they had hoaxed the French media. There was no such film, nor was there any such director as "Christopher Maudson." They had made the whole thing up, and the media had bought it. They had found an Australian traveler in the youth hostel who was willing to give interviews as "Christopher Maudson." Unfortunately he had recently returned to Australia. But since I looked a bit like him... would I mind posing as a famous nonexistent Hollywood director?

I replied with the French equivalent of "uh, yeah, well, sure, maybe" and gave them my phone number. Several days later my phone rang. I had an interview with *L'Express*, the *Time* magazine of France, in a couple of hours. Could I meet the band at the Bastille metro stop in half an hour? I agreed, not quite understanding what I was getting myself into.

The *Casse-Pieds* met me at the station. Together we boarded a train toward the southwest suburbs. The band—Daniel, Phillipe, and Jo—played in the aisles of the train while the singer Manu shouted in my ear a vain attempt to impart information about who I was and what kind of movie I had made.

I believe my soon-to-be friend Manu was Manu Chao, who would later become almost as famous in "reality" as the *Casse-Pieds* were then famous in the imagination of the French media. Yet when I look at photos of the now-famous Manu Chao, he looks almost as different from the Manu I remember as the "Fatty Bin Laden" of the infamous December, 2001 "confession video" looks from Osama. The Manu I fondly recall, like the real Bin Laden, was *skinny*. And kind of hyper and nervous. The famous Manu I now see in photos seems to have a reasonably well-muscled, mesomorphic build, and his face looks nowhere near as bony as the one in my fading memory. Maybe Manu Chao was taking speed back in 1988, or just not getting enough to eat. I've googled the *Casse-Pieds* and found that Manu Chao was indeed one of them at the time, so I guess now that he's famous he just looks a lot better-fed and more mature. Hope I run into him again some day—the guy is a trip and a half.

And speaking of a trip and a half, I will never forget my expedition to the interview where I became a famous French impostor. Our metro destination was a huge, warehouse-style building in the *banlieue*. Inside was a gigantic music industry exposition, with stages for live bands and dozens of booths for record labels, radio stations, bands, publicists, newspapers, magazines, and other music-biz excrescences. Upon entry, I was quickly surrounded by media people dying to get a word or a photo op with the "famous Hollywood director." The journalist from *L'Express* quickly shepherded me away to a private area, posed me for photographs on a Harley, and sat me down for an interview. It seemed like a big fantasy, and all I had to do was play along. I answered her questions as best I could, given the premise that I was a celebrated film director, sometimes pretending my French wasn't quite up to understanding the precise nature of her inquiry. At one point I amazed and impressed even myself by telling her that I was good friends with Francis Ford Coppola. The worst moment came when she asked me about the title of my soon-to-be-released film. I had forgotten; or maybe Manu had never told me. I mumbled a bit, and finally said that I was not at liberty to discuss that issue due to a dispute with the producers.

When I left that warehouse exposition I was in a state of existential shock. Had I really just given an interview to France's leading newsmagazine? Had I really convinced them that I was a famous Hollywood director? Whose fantasy was this, anyway?

Two weeks later—in early December, 1988—we were the cover story of the *Express de Paris* supplement. The article was lavishly illustrated with photos of the band in various poses, alongside photos of me next to those of Tom Waits and Willy DeVille, the two alleged stars of my imaginary movie. The article described how I had discovered the *Casse-Pieds* and immediately known that they would be the next big thing in America. I had taken them to a mansion in the French countryside and given them a screen test. Then I had flown them to Hollywood, where they partied with famous movie stars and rock musicians. The shooting had taken a month or so. Now it was in the can. The film *Le Paris d'Amérique* was due out in June.

All of this was news to me. I hardly recognized anything from our interview, though the article did mention my close friendship with Francis Ford Coppola.

From there, the hoax just kept on keeping on. By the time I left France in August 1989 we had fooled both of France's leading newsmagazines, its three leading newspapers, at least two of the five television networks, and all the rock n' roll radio shows. Whenever a journalist discovered that she had been fooled, we asked for and received discreet silence so we could fool others. Some were angry at first, but most took it as the amazing, hilarious spoof that it was and got into the spirit of the thing.

The highlight, for me, was the involvement of Yves Boisset. He was a well-known director of B-grade *policier* detective flicks, which the reviewers regularly savaged. Boisset didn't like the media too much, so he happily agreed to help us with our little hoax.

One day in winter 1989 Boisset invited us into a Left Bank metro station where he was shooting a scene for his next film. He told us he'd help us make a commercial for our bogus movie. After he was done shooting his own scene, he filmed me pretending to direct Manu, Daniel, Phillipe, and Jo as they ran through the metro station and boarded a train. I twirled my right arm like a windmill and drew a finger across my throat as I yelled out directors' remarks like "Okay, roll it! Great, a little more expression, fine, excellent. Cut! Cut!" My fake Australian accent sounded ridiculous to me, but nobody else seemed to mind.

While I knew Boisset was making a commercial for our imaginary movie, I had no idea what it would look like or where, if anywhere, it would air. A month after the filming I had almost forgotten about it. Late one night I was heading back to downtown Paris after partying in the suburbs with some Greek friends. Two Greek girls and I stumbled down the stairs into the metro to catch the last train, our brains singing with hashish. As we arrived trackside I happened to glance up at *Le Tube*, the closed-circuit TV system that played nonstop in metro stations all over Paris. My synapses all short-circuited at once when I saw the image of myself on *Le Tube* "directing" the *Casse-Pieds* as they raced to catch a metro train. A stentorian narrator expressed amazement at the skill of Hollywood studio technicians who were able to create such an amazingly lifelike replica of the Paris Metro at their studio in Hollywood.

I looked around me at the real metro. I looked up at *Le Tube*. The three-minute ad for *Le Paris d'Amerique* was playing on an endless loop, with its video simulacrum of the real metro acting as a simulacrum of a fake metro in Hollywood that was acting as a simulacrum of the real metro in Paris. The tape loop went on and on. The last train never came. Suddenly the real metro around me looked like a simulacrum. The girls whose arms had just been linked with mine looked like mannequins. Through a torn veil I thought I saw a glimpse of Reality that was so Real it made all of this look cheap, tawdry, utterly fake, a bad imitation of an imitation of an imitation.

The *Paris d'Amérique* hoax aroused my metaphysical curiosity: What was real, what was fake, and how could we tell the difference? It also taught me a valuable lesson: The media does not report reality. Instead, it creates a wish-fulfillment fantasy for its audience. French people have a deep-seated wish that a French pop music group could do what the Beatles, the Rolling Stones, the Who, the Sex Pistols, and other British groups have done: Make it big in America. Feed them the story that fulfills their wishes and they'll buy it hook, line and sinker. And once they've bitten, they'll never let go. Journalists just won't admit they've been fooled. They'd rather keep the hoax going by keeping mum, even if they have to fool themselves and ignore the evidence of their own senses, rather than fess up and admit they've been duped.

Back in America, land of the naïve, the good-hearted, and the hopelessly gullible, selling a fake terrorist attack would be a snap. If four dreamy French ragamuffins could hoax the hardboiled cynics and skeptics of their media, imagine what Karl Rove and a team of CIA covert operations professionals could do in the USA. If a huge, horrific attack on America were to take place, Americans would have an overwhelming, deep-seated wish that it be a foreign attack, not an inside job. A foreign attack would offer righteousness, moral clarity, and an easy answer to the question of what to do: Just obey your leaders, celebrate your patriotism, repeat "united we stand" over and over. An inside job would be… unthinkable. Once the media had bitten on the "foreign attack" wish-fulfillment fantasy it would never let go, no matter how much evidence later came to light.

~~~~~
### FALSE FLAG FACTS

The 9/11 Big Lie is a Very Big Lie: 9/11 was a multi-faceted operation, and the myriad loose ends that give away the lie can make it hard to decide where to start. One looks for smoking guns that should be clear to anyone. Global Outlook magazine lists 26 anomalies, 911truth.org has its Top 40 talking points, and David Griffin counts 115 holes in the "571-page lie," the 9/11 "Omission Report" (enough smoking guns for all the firing squads we need! See p. 85) On these pages we'll mention some tell-tale holes in the Big Lie, from history to physical evidence, from motive to modus operandi.

# Dr. Weirde (January 1992 – August 1995)

Since childhood I have always known that deeper layers of reality hide beneath the surface of appearances. In esoteric Islamic thought, the surface appearance is called *thahir*, while the deep reality is known as *batin*.

For example: America's surface appearance is a vast wasteland of shopping malls and glittering neon arabesques along a road to nowhere and endless night. Beneath the depressingly monotonous façade, however, lurks a myriad of reality-places, each with its own unique historical imprint and spiritual signature.

San Francisco has more of these places than any American city I know, which is one reason I spent thirteen years there. I used to bicycle around San Francisco wondering: Which City Hall window did the homophobic lunatic Dan White slip through en route to murdering gay-rights icon Harvey Milk and abrasively liberal mayor George Moscone? Which of the houses flanking Golden Gate Park on Fulton Street was the Jefferson Airplane mansion? Where, somewhere just off Haight Street, was the Grateful Dead's house? Where did Norton I, the bum who declared himself Emperor of the United States and Protector of Mexico, live? Where was Patty Hearst's hideout? Where did Jim Jones set up his People's Temple? Where did the beatnik poets hang out? And where did Charles Manson live with his Family?

One foggy night I was wandering through the Mission District with a 105 degree fever looking for a supermarket with aspirin and cold orange juice. From around a corner twenty feet in front of me a tall, bespectacled figure in a mad hatter top-hat wrapped in a long black cloak appeared and turned his baleful gaze upon me. He was wearing mirror sunglasses that seemed to emit light, not just reflect it. Dazed, I lurched against a wall and stared at the apparition. On the black top hat glowed the luminous white letter W.

The figure disappeared into the night and I returned home with my orange juice. Gradually the fever went away. But for weeks afterward, every time I looked in a mirror, I thought I caught a glimpse of Dr. Weirde—or so I named him—lurking somewhere in the background.

From such humble beginnings *Dr. Weirde's Weirde Tours: A Guide to Mysterious San Francisco* (Last Gasp, 1994) was born. It was the first and best weird tour guide. Many are its flattering imitations—guides to the bizarre and outré sights of various American cities, states, and regions.

Writing under the pen name Dr. Weirde, I tried to peel away the layers of time and accident to get at the lovably twisted soul of Baghdad-by-the-Bay. My book got good reviews from André Codrescu among others, and sold out two print runs in its first year. It even became an assigned textbook for the course on San Francisco at San Francisco State University.

Dressed in a long black cloak, mad hatter top-hat and mirror sunglasses, I gave talks and slideshows to promote the book at Bay Area libraries and bookstores. I also made occasional radio and TV appearances, and got comfortable with being a public figure. (Little did I know that I was preparing myself for the future, when Steve Nass would make me a famous conspiracy theorist.)

The project had taken shape in my mind before I reverted to Islam, and I finished it during my first two years as a Muslim. I didn't see any contradiction between being a Muslim and being my naturally weirde self, and I still don't. But now that I have grown into a more serious Muslim skin, I am no longer interested in making a career of that sort of weirdeness, some of which borders on debauchery.

At one level, *A Guide to Mysterious San Francisco* was a lark, an entertainment, a commercial enterprise whose major purpose was amusement. But beneath the surface, the whole project was a heartfelt love song to the weird and wonderful city I had made my own. And if anyone doubts that it was a labor of love, please note that I did all of the design, photography, typesetting, layout, and publicity myself—and that producing a book with literally thousands of illustrations on a PC in 1994 was a project that only a lover or a madman would attempt.

If you would like to read samples of this book, just google Weirde – don't forget the e on the end, which distinguishes me from all the other weird people who have passed through San Francisco.

~~~~~

FALSE FLAG FACTS: FROM THE IRA TO IRAQ

http://groups.yahoo.com/group/WarOnFreedom/message/3269, a collection of articles posted by Irish Scholars for 9/11 Truth. In a nutshell, British SAS army bombmakers infiltrated both sides to foment religious "troubles" and give Britain an excuse to hold on to Northern Ireland. They are in Iraq now with the same tactics, setting Sunnis against Shiites, to prolong military rule while they steal the oil – and blame their own terror attacks on Iran. British terror commandos have been caught red-handed, and many "IED" bombs bear their signature technology.

The Vision (January 1993)

"Why did you convert to Islam?" That is what people ask at parties, instead of the usual "what do you do?" if they know you are an American revert.

A *what?* That's right, a revert—pronounced REE-vert. Muslims believe that every child is born good, innocent, in full submission to God. No original sin here! Sex and aggression are gifts of God—there is nothing inherently wrong with them, they just need to be regulated, like all human needs and desires, in the interest of social and spiritual harmony. This goodness and naturalness is deep human nature—what Muslims call *fitra*. So when you come to Islam, you're coming *back* to Islam. You are not converting from one religion to another, but reverting to your original deep human nature.

While I like this idea, I am not sure that I like the word. REE-vert sounds too much like PREE-vert, which is what we used to call our friends in high school, in mock redneck vernacular, when we pretended to suspect them of sexual deviation: "What are you, some kinda PREE-vert?"

To me, the word *revert* conjures up the image of a kind, polite, innocent Muslim with a flat tire walking into the Dew Drop Inn to use the phone. "What'll it be, podner?" "I'm sorry, I don't drink—I'm Muslim." The louche, dicy denizens of the bar size him up through sotted glares. "Ya-all don't look like no Muslim, boy. Y'all look lahk you should be a good ole Christian Amerikkin pay-tree-ott. What the hell's WRONG with you?"

"I'm a revert."

Hoots and hollers all around. "Duh mah ears deceive me, Joe Bob, or did he just say he's a PREEEE-vert?" The denizens howl and screech like a pack of rabid chimpanzees as they chase the poor Muslim revert out of the bar and down the street, where they are suddenly conscripted by a passing army recruiter and sent off to rape, torture and kill dark-skinned Muslims in a distant land blessed by abundant energy resources, while our hypothetical revert thanks Allah and his lucky stars that he is a white, red-blooded American Muslim... and vows to get a cell phone and stay out of *haram* juke-joints in the future.

Anyway... though I don't much like the word *revert* it does describe my experience of coming back to the primordial religion, to primordial human nature. "Trailing clouds of glory do we come," Wordsworth wrote of the luminous state of submission and oneness from which we emerge as little children. I remember moments of indescribable awe and beauty: Watching reflections play across the rear window of the family station wagon; tasting ripe raspberries in my grandparents' back yard; hearing music in the buzz of insects, and knowing that the vast fragrant field of weeds had been made for us, just as surely as if it had been well-tended cropland.

For me, this is a poetic consciousness: Words trigger these memories and associations. Proust used words as his *madeleine*, as have so many poets in so many ways. I was trained in literature, and took to the Romantics and symbolists, so the notion that amazingly apt words could evoke such ecstasy has been part of my lived experience since my early twenties.

And that's how I came to Islam at age 35. Through words. Words and a vision.

It began with harsh, astringent words, illusion-shattering words, words that corresponded to the first half of the *shahada*, the Muslim profession of faith: *There is no god...*

During the last 500 miles of my 3000-mile Amtrak journey from San Francisco to New York, I was finishing Gore Vidal's *Golgotha* and regaling my fellow partiers in the lounge car with its mockeries of religion. (Mock on, mock on, Voltaire, Vidal!) At one point I invented a comedy routine whose gist was that the Jews had invented the world's worst idea, the Christians had somehow augmented its idiocy, and the Muslims had brought it to its sublime nadir of perfect awfulness.

Hilarious, no? I thought so. So did my fellow passengers. But while I mocked Islam, a small voice inside me was saying, "You don't know what the bleep you're talking about—you don't know anything about Islam!"

Debarking in New York just after the climax of my comic monologue, I caught the L train to Brooklyn, toward the friend's couch I was looking forward to collapsing on. Exiting the subway with my traveling companion, John—the only other lunatic intellectual in my high school class, then a professional squatter and homeless-organizer in New York City—I was dragged bodily into the L café to celebrate our arrival in Brooklyn. There I sipped espresso—and beheld the Moroccan Muslim beauty who would soon become my wife.

When I learned she was Muslim, my monologue no longer seemed funny, but darkly ironic. I felt like God was nudging me hard, in the ribs, with a very big, very sharp elbow.

A few nights later I had a vision while in a hypnagogic state—that wonderful place where you're neither awake nor asleep, but lucid-dreaming somewhere in-between. I was climbing a desert mountain and arrived at the top. On the other side of the mountain, sprawling magnificently below me, was a splendid, luminous city, at the same time vaguely Middle Eastern and not of this earth. It was self-evidently a holy city, with a sacred glow emanating from within, as if it were built with stones of congealed light.

When I finally let go of the vision, I knew that the rest of my life would be a pilgrimage to that holy city. Later, a trip to the library confirmed that the two signature monuments in my dream city were the Great Mosque in Mecca and the al-Aqsa mosque in Jerusalem, whose most famous section is the Dome on the Rock.

~~~~~

Glazed tile with couplet praising the Prophet Muhammad,
Jameh Mosque, Yazd, Iran. (see p. 50).

Visionary Words

Shortly after bearing witness to this vision of a single holy city housing both the Grand Mosque and the Masjid al-Aqsa, I encountered Hakim Bey's *TAZ*, an anarchist manifesto that reads like pure poetry. Its poetics, and many of its references, pointed me in the direction of Islamic mystical poetry in the line of Rumi, Jami, Hafiz, and Ibn al-'Arabi. As I read *TAZ* and the Muslim mystics, I flashed back on the Sufi Traditionalists I had read a few years earlier for a Kabala course with Jacob Needleman.

Needleman, the editor of the Penguin *Arcana* series on mysticism, has a planetary reputation as one of the wisest spiritual heads in academia. But I had never heard of him when I walked into his Kabala classroom at San Francisco State University in early September 1989. I was looking for a class in the Teaching of Composition—which seemed like a pretty good way for a literary ne'er-do'well like me to make an honest living—and accidentally walked into the wrong room. Needleman was rambling on in his inimitable style, giving little sign of noticing me as I slunk in late. I took a seat in the back and listened to what I assumed was going to be a lecture on Composition Pedagogy. Fifteen minutes into the lecture, I suddenly realized that I had some bad news and some good news. The bad news: Whatever the subject matter was, it definitely was not English Composition. The good news: Whatever it was, it beat Composition Pedagogy all to hell.

Needleman's Kabala class left an indelible mark on me, though I would be hard-pressed to say exactly what that mark was. His rejection of the modern, industrial world, with its idolatrous faith in materialism and scientism, made sense to a guy who dug the Romantics, luddites, and anarchists. His interest in Gurdjieff struck a chord in me. But his Traditionalist religious outlook, with its hard monotheistic core, was utterly foreign to my utterly non-monotheistic background. Having been brought up a lapsed Unitarian—which is as lapsed as it gets—and going from there to Freud, Jung, existentialism, Zen, and so on, I had absolutely no idea what the word *God* was supposed to mean.

One day, right around the time of the Loma Prieta earthquake of 1989, Needleman said something about the irreducibly essential nature of monotheism. I raised my hand and objected: Just what *was* monotheism? What did *God* mean, anyway? And what was wrong with polytheism? Needleman glared at me, his large head and twinkling eyes somehow combining gravity with levity, and paraphrased Louis Armstrong on jazz: If you don't know what monotheism is, you ain't never gonna know. Something quintessentially Platonic happened. For a split second I knew that I did know. Or, rather, I remembered. Then I forgot again. A few weeks later, a lovely, cow-eyed, intensely spiritual Jewish girl in the class tried to remind me. I turned down her invitation to come over and listen to madrigals. Had I accepted that invitation, my life might have taken a rather different turn. But however different the road, it would have led to the same place.

Needleman's Sufi Traditionalists… Hakim Bey… Jami, Hafiz, Rumi and Ibn al-'Arabi… it was, in a word, *maktoub*, a Muslim word for destiny whose literal meaning is "it was written." The idea is that your destiny is written in an archetypal holy book, the Book of Destiny, expressing the ineluctable will of Allah. Apparently God had decided that I was to become a Muslim. And who was I to argue with God? I had already been through the argue-with-God thing when I had plumbed the *Book of Job* as background for *Moby Dick*, Philip K. Dick, and the youthful sorrows of my own too-oft-unsatisfied dick. *Been there, done that.* If the rabbis wanted to go on arguing with God for all eternity, trying to blame Him for what happened to Job and what happens to all of us—not just the Jews, rabbi!—that was their own damned business. After the vision, and the words, I was past the point of arguing. I said "Okay, God, you've won. Your Reality ends the dispute."

I took the shahada: "There is no god… but God! And Muhammad is the messenger of God." Those words, uttered in Arabic before two witnesses, make the speaker a Muslim.

So now I was a Muslim. But what did that imply?

Not much at first. Other than marriage, my life more or less continued as before, except with a God-intoxicated subtext.

To tell the truth, getting married changed me a lot more, or at least a lot faster, than becoming Muslim did. And when we had our first child, almost two years after marriage, it changed me a lot more, and a lot faster, than Islam *or* marriage had.

I started getting serious about taking care of my family—about living for other people, not just for myself. I cut down on alcohol but did not eliminate it. I learned the rudiments of the *salaat* prayer but did not perform it regularly. Most notably, I found myself with a sense of loving commitment to my wife and children. And *al-hamdullilah* that sense of God-intoxication never really left me.

The Word

After bathing in oceans of mystical words, splashing in streams of words, plunging in pure sweet lakes and timeless rivers, dancing in warm spring rain, I knew I had to go to the source: The Qur'an, the Word of God.

To read the Qur'an, I needed to learn Arabic. Unfortunately I am a mediocre language-learner. It had taken me many years to become fully fluent in French, and I had never really mastered Spanish. Arabic is a much harder language to learn than French and Spanish put together.

I took a mini-course in Palestinian Arabic. It was great fun—the teacher was a fiery, joyful woman who loved Levantine culture and cuisine as well as the Palestinian cause. Parties at her house were delicious affairs for the brain as well as the taste buds. But I never really got the hang of Palestinian dialect. And I could tell that even if I did, it wasn't going to open up the secrets of the Qur'an.

I tried studying formal Arabic on my own and made very little progress. I listened to Arabic tapes on my Walkman as I bicycled around Berkeley, and absorbed some of the sounds without making much overall progress. I finally realized that I would never really learn Arabic unless I forced myself to—by subjecting myself to the discipline of a Ph.D. program.

That was what everyone was telling me I should do anyway. I had been going around calling myself Dr. Weirde, author of the cult classic tour guide parody *Dr. Weirde's Weirde Tours: A Guide to Mysterious San Francisco.* "I'm not a real doctor," I always explained. "But I do have two master's degrees. Take that, Dr. Science!" My friends and academic colleagues thought I was crazy for earning two master's degrees. Why not just get a Ph.D.? Why shouldn't Dr. Weirde become a real doctor?

Egged on by eggheads, desperate to learn Arabic, and ready to take life one degree more seriously, I applied to the University of Wisconsin-Madison, where the Arabic program is housed in the Department of African Languages and Literature. An Arabic program with an African slant seemed perfect for me, since I wanted to focus on North Africa in general and Morocco in particular. I applied to U.W.-Madison— conveniently located near where several members of my family lived— and was accepted. They even offered me a generous grant that would pay for my studies and living expenses during the first year. It was an offer I couldn't refuse. I left *A Guide to Mysterious San Francisco* in the hands of Ron Turner of Last Gasp, the publisher who had sprung R. Crumb on an unsuspecting world. Then with wife, newborn baby and possessions loaded into my 1964 blue-and-white bullet-shaped Travco motor home, I hitched up my 1964 airstream trailer behind it and drove from San Francisco to Wisconsin.

Then came the hard part. I struggled with Arabic from 1995 through 1999, when I moved to Morocco on a Fulbright dissertation research grant. The year in Morocco helped push me over the hump. When I got back to the US in summer 2000 I could read Qur'an. Slowly; laboriously; imperfectly. No matter. Perfection is God's alone. The rest of us are slow learners—and admittedly, some of us are a lot slower than others.

~~~~~

About the Cover Design

Front and center a photo of Kevin riding a gaily caparisoned Moroccan pony lends a light, refreshing touch. To frame it I used an image of tilework from the Jameh mosque in Yazd, Iran (see p. 46). Its symmetry and proportions served as marvelously faithful guides in creating the front cover.

Prof. Hussein Mollanazar graciously provided meanings of the couplet, that is glazed in the centre rosette in the photo, from a classical mystical poem by the the 12th century poet Isfahani, praising the prophet Mohamed. The words:

<div dir="rtl">مطلع اشراق نور سرمدی   مهبط جبریل وحی ایزدی</div>

matla'-e eshraq-e noor-e sarmadi / ascendance of the effulgence of light eternal,
mahbat-e Jebril o wahy-ye izadi / descent of Gabriel of revelation divine.
matla' – place of arising, dawn, rising star, the ascendant, auspicious beginning.
eshraq; neoplatonic Illuminism; radiance, from the root *sharq* with the meanings to shine, sunrise, East, Orient;
matla'-eshraq, the dawn, a title of the Prophet Mohamed, or of the succession of the first twelve imams or "dawns," or of the illuminist Sufi sage Suhrawardi.
noor – light. sarmadi – eternity.
mahbat, place of descent, landing place, cradle.
mahbat-e Jebril, descent of Gabriel; a title of the Prophet Mohamed.
wahy, inspiring, revealing, suggesting or giving an idea or impression.
izadi, divine; the city of Yazd; the Yazidi mystical cult. (Sarmadi and izadi are the only old Persian words in the couplet, the other six come from Arabic).

Various meanings could be derived by meditating on this one couplet. To me, the image arose of the dawning of knowledge from the East. May God forbid the descent of destruction from the West on that cradle of humanity's inspiration! Prof. Mollanazar notes that the last line can mean "You are the place where divine revelation descends," addressed to the Prophet – or perhaps also to the illumined mystic devotee. Persian is written from right to left. The ascent stanza begins by descending and ends in an ascent on the left, whence the stanza about descent arcs upwards and meets the first on the descent – in a flow reminiscent of the two halves of the Chinese Yin-Yang symbol. Meaning, not the beginnings, but the endings of things really count? – JPL

Another Vision (1997)

But that's getting ahead of ourselves. Back in 1993, the vision of the holy city brought me to Islam. It got me reading English interpretations of the Qur'an. By 1995 I was in a Ph.D. program learning Arabic. But to tell the truth—and that's what we're here for, isn't it?—that magnificent vision, life-changing as it was, did not make me a particularly good Muslim overnight. Actually I was a pretty bad one for several years.

I cut down on alcohol but didn't eliminate it. I learned to pray—more or less. Actually I never learned the postures and recitations properly. I rarely saw the inside of a mosque. I did fast for Ramadan, but as we have seen, I was too dumb to stop drinking wine during the holy month, and got walloped with migraines as a result.

Looking back, I can see that my initial approach to Islam was influenced by the Protestant culture I had grown up in. "Read the book yourself, eschew ritual" was the hallmark of the Protestant outlook. I read and interpreted the English versions of the Qur'an on my own— a problematic enterprise, I knew, since the Arabic original was the only true Qur'an. But that didn't stop me from inventing unorthodox interpretations. I decided that for me, alcohol was not illicit, merely discouraged. I arrived at this unusual reading by ignoring the consensus view that earlier Qur'anic verses were abrogated by later ones. And when I moved from the wine heaven of California to beery Wisconsin, I conveniently decided that the ban on wine did in fact apply to me—for the Qur'an bans wine, but mentions no other form of alcohol, with the possible exception of a verse *praising* mead, an early form of honey-beer. Since beer was not explicitly banned—maybe even praised—I deemed myself free to enjoy the many brews that are a staple of Wisconsin social life.

My struggle to give up wine and beer before Allah blasted my brain to bits with migraines and shot my liver full of holes is commemorated by a collection of poems I wrote entitled *From the Brewpub of Ruin*, a takeoff on Rumi's poems written "from the tavern of ruin." Wine is a common Sufi metaphor for Divine knowledge, the intoxication one feels when the presence of God is especially close. When that sensation departs, the lover-beloved-love (for the mystic plays all three roles by turn, with God playing the others) experiences heartbreak and loss. The Tavern of Ruin is a Sufi metaphor for the heartbroken state of being intoxicated with God, yet aware of the impossibility of losing oneself utterly and permanently in Him. Some say that Omar Khayyam's *Rubaiyat* is one such Sufi allegory disguised as a paean to wine, women and song.

Aware of the impossibility of losing myself utterly and permanently in the divine fumes and glittering bubbles of that sacred ambrosia known as microbrew, I expressed my own heartbroken loss—loss of the Divine while drinking beer, loss of beer in my long-term movement toward the Divine—in the Omar Khayyam parody that opens *From the Brewpub of Ruin*. My conceit in this poem was that one should, in good Muslim fashion, avoid drinking worldly wine, so that one may sip the wine of paradise in the life to come. As for beer, however...

Drink Beer with Old Khayyam

Awake! For evening's luscious neon light
Pulses and gleams through boundless strip-mall'd night.
Hark, there's a sign! "Brewpub of Ruin" it spells.
No words were e're more welcome to my sight.
Drink beer with old Khayyam, and leave the wine
To ripen slow on paradisian vine,
For beer grows weak and stale and flat with age,
While God's grapes can endure the wrath of time.
A wallet full of credit cards and thou,
Wine's paradise can wait, beer's here and now.
And if I die before the bill arrives,
How dey gonna repossess deir suds n' chow?
"A mortgage and a paycheck sweet!" crow some,
While others slave for better things to come.
I'll take the beer in hand and waive the rest,
Sipping in rhythm to a different drum.
And those who husbanded the golden grain,
The malt, barley and hops, with labor'd pain,
Are naught but fools who strove to own the clouds,
But never got a chance to taste the rain.
Think! In this brewpub where we briefly stay,
Whose flashing neon lights spell Night and Day,
How kings and princes, presidents and popes
Drank their allotted fill, then went their way.
I came into this brewpub, *why* not knowing,
Nor *whence*, like free beer willy-nilly flowing,

And out of it, like foam from off a glass,
Scattered I fly, fate willy-nilly blowing.
Refill my pint! What good's it to repeat
How time keeps reeling off beneath our feet:
We stagger toward a sourly stinking grave,
But beer of here and now is always sweet.
Why hurry coffee-addled toward your fate,
Worrying all the while 'bout time and date?
You'll never be on time. Relax! More beer!
The jetliner of time is always late.
A barley seed of wisdom did I sow,
And with my beer-piss watered it to grow,
And this was all the Harvest that I reaped:
I came like new-tapp'd ale,
            And like a fart I go.

I blamed my fondness for beer on my Irish ethnic origins. Actually I am only a little over a quarter Irish, but that didn't stop me from claiming that a taste for Guinness was deep in my DNA. Being a born-and-bred Wisconsinite was also a convenient excuse. Fancying myself an Irish Muslim, I invented a folkloric ballad about my struggle against the evil hops and barley.

Ballad of an Irish Muslim

I was born in County Kerry with a Guinness in me hand
That thick white foam washed o'er me like the waves wash o'er the sand
One great black wave broke on me brain and washed me sins (sense) away
And I became a Muslim... on that glahrious drunken day... but now...

Refrain:
Me drinkin' days are done—hamdullilah! (praise God!)
Me drinkin' days are done—insha'allah! (if God so wills!)
Raise your glass to this Irish Muslim
Whose drinkin' days are done.

I joined the Sally Rovers and I had a glahrious time

Captured meself four English wives and a hundred concubines
Took me wives and treasure and built a palace in old Salee
From whence I turned toward Mecca... and prayed five times each
day
And I prayed: me drinkin' days are done—hamdullilah!
Me drinkin' days are done—incha'allah!
Raise your glass to this Irish Muslim
Whose drinkin' days are done.

But one dark day...
I was captured by the English, thrown in an English jail
They beat me with their paddy sticks until my heart did fail
They threw me in the River Thames and left me there for dead
But when I floated by a pub I sniffed (sniff-sniff)... and lifted up
me head
And I said: Me drinkin' days aren't done—not quite yet
Me drinkin' days aren't done—no such luck ye limeys!
Raise yer glass to this Irish Muslim... whose drinkin' days aren't
done

They offered me some Guinness and I drank up their supplies
When I told 'em I was Muslim, why they couldn't believe their eyes
The said, "What sort of Muslim is this who drinks a dozen pints?"
I said "Ye should've seen me drink before I saw the light!"
Me true drinkin' days are done (ye call this drinkin'?)
Me drinkin' days are done (ha! t'ain't drinkin', this!)
Raise yer glass to this Irish Muslim... whose drinkin' days are done
(fer all practical porposes)

Now there are two verses in the Koran concernin' alcohol
One of 'em says "don't drink too much," the other says "don't
drink atall"
One verse is fer the Irish and the other's fer the rest
And though I'm too drunk to know which is which, I'm afraid that
I can guess

Refrain:
Me drinkin' days are done—hamdullilah!
Me drinkin' days are done—insha'allah!
Raise your glass to this Irish Muslim
Whose drinkin' days... are done.

I gradually gave up even beer, and felt the better for it. Even my immature version of Islam was not without value, since it helped me become a more mature, serious, compassionate person. After conversion and marriage I gave up womanizing, and settled into a faithful monogamous relationship with my wife—the first time in my life I had even *wanted* to stick to one woman, much less actually done so. I focused hard on my work and studies, and was able to support my family, after a fashion, while making progress toward a Ph.D. My natural selfish hedonism was tempered by my relationship with God and other human beings, especially my family. Despite a couple of lapses into bad behavior and too much microbrew, I managed to live a more honorable life than I had in my pre-Muslim days.

One night, however, I had another vision that seemed to nudge me harder in the direction of Islam. Though it came in a dream, the vision stood out from its dream surroundings and made an impression I would never forget.

In the vision I saw myself in a beautiful, Islamic-styled religious building with a square courtyard. It looked like something from the Alhambra, which I had visited in 1989, four years before my conversion, and fallen in love with.

I climbed a stairway from the courtyard into the building and met a Muslim professor I knew. He was with a group of other prominent, respected Muslims, whose precise functions I did not understand. They were in a vast hallway overlooking the courtyard. They solemnly approached me and asked me to lead the *salaat* prayer. I panicked. I could not refuse their request, but I did not know how to lead the prayer. Overcoming my fear, I went ahead and led the prayer to the best of my abilities, choosing my words and gestures with instinct and intuition, making it up as I went along, but feeling divinely guided as I did so.

When I awoke from the vision, I was deeply disturbed. I felt simultaneously honored and ashamed. Honored, because I had been chosen by a group of pious, prestigious Muslims to serve as their imam; and ashamed, because I had never learned the prayers well enough to lead them correctly.

I vowed I would become a good Muslim, one worthy of leading such a group in prayer. I decided to give up alcohol. And I decided that I would learn to pray properly, and to recite Qur'an at least well enough to serve as imam if called upon to do so.[25]

Morocco

When I got to Morocco, I recognized the building with the courtyard from my dream—the place where I had led the *salaat* prayer for the first time. It was the Merinid medersa (religious college) in Salé, built in 1333 by Sultan Abou al-Hassan Ali. Behind it is the zawiyya of Sidi Abdullah bin Hassoun, the patron saint of Moroccan travelers.

I had dreamed of the place more than a year before I saw it. When I finally got there, it was empty. The guidebook had said that a caretaker would ask for ten dirhams admission. But there was no caretaker. The doors were wide open for me, but nobody was inside.

I wandered through the halls of the madersa like a ghost. The corridors were much narrower than they had appeared in my dream. The tiny cubicles where the students had lived made my old college dorm room seem huge by comparison. Still, the place had a feeling of expansiveness, as if it were hovering on the edge of infinity, ready to drift off at any moment. The courtyard, in particular, seemed vast and mysterious. The tile walls, topped by delicately carved stucco and woodwork, pulsated with arabesque rhythms. They seemed ready to melt into a shimmering, boundless mirage, a rich and complex world of visionary light-patterns that underlies and gives birth to material reality.

I spent two hours in that madersa. Its emptiness and amplitude resonated with me and gave me an overwhelming feeling of peace. That feeling—and not the contents of the twelve seventy-pound suitcases full of the worldly belongings of myself, my wife, and my two children—is what I really brought back from Morocco.

My official reason for spending a year in Morocco was a Fulbright scholarship for dissertation research. I wanted to study the use of supernatural images in Moroccan legends. I had been struck by the richness of Moroccan supernatural folklore during my previous visit in 1997, and wondered what it all meant. Having studied American supernatural legends, and written about some of them for *A Guide to Mysterious San Francisco*, I was struck by the way that Moroccan legends, as opposed to American ones, all seemed intricately tied into a strong tradition of religious symbols and values.

Oddly enough, my dissertation work on Moroccan legend provided excellent training for my later deconstruction of the myth of 9/11—a myth that has now become a legend. How is that? Let me define my

terms. A myth, in folklorist parlance, is a sacred narrative whose users—
the people who tell and listen to it and consider it sacred—strongly
believe it to be true, to the point that disbelievers may be accused of
heresy. One common, core type of myth found in most of the world's
cultures is the *myth of origins*, which explains how the current social order
came to be, and implicitly or explicitly justifies it. Typically a myth of
origins involves a bifurcation between light and dark, good and evil,
before and after, us and them. For religious Christians and Jews, *Genesis* is
a myth of origins. And for the ever-shrinking number of Americans who
are still true believers in the "war on terror," the official story of 9/11,
enshrined in the Kean-Zelikow Report, is a sacred myth. I know this
from painful personal experience, having been hounded as a heretic for
questioning it.

Though the official story of 9/11 was scripted as a sacred myth—and
Philip Zelikow, whose academic training is in the creation and
manipulation of myths, would seem a likely candidate for the role of
Royal Mythographer—it has since been drifting away from the category
of myth, and toward that of legend. Legends are like myths in that they
often recount improbable, amazing, or supernatural events. But whereas
myths are viewed as sacred and true by those who use them, legends are
defined as stories that turn on an explicit or implicit debate on belief.

You are not allowed to debate the truth of a myth. If you do, the
myth's users will be very upset. Steve Nass is an excellent example of a
primitive tribesman who goes bananas when someone questions his
sacred myth.

Legends, however, are defined *by the fact that their users are questioning
them—questioning what really happened as well as what it means.* Did Jesus
really turn water into wine? Anyone who asks this question has taken a
sacred myth and turned it in the direction of legend. Did such-and-such a
Sufi saint really turn a Christian's wine into water, and thereby revert that
Christian to Islam? When Moroccans tell stories like that, they aren't
trying to enforce an official code of belief, but are instead playing around
with sacred meanings and staging an open-ended debate about such
beliefs, and the value systems that are bound up with them.

I loved the legends I heard in Morocco. And I loved thinking about
them, wondering about their meaning, trying to understand why they
were told and retold.

What does this have to do with my 9/11 truth work? My training in analyzing narratives, especially the folk narrative categories of myth and legend, helps me understand how the official myth of 9/11, and its ongoing breakdown into legend, functions in American culture.

Such training offers an interesting perspective not only on the official story, but also on the alternative stories offered by skeptics and 9/11 truth activists. For many 9/11 truth activists, the story of 9/11-as-inside-job functions as a sacred myth, just as the official story is a sacred myth for the likes of Steve Nass. Many members of the 9/11 truth community grow angry when anyone questions their version of 9/11-as-inside-job. They are turning their own version of 9/11 into a sacred story—a myth.

Many 9/11 researchers, I have noticed, become irrationally attached to one particular element of their 9/11-as-inside-job story. There is a whole subculture of 9/11 truth-seekers—a cult, if you will—who are passionately attached to their conviction that no planes crashed into the World Trade Center, or that, at the very least, all of the extant footage of the plane crashes is fake. Not all of these people are irrational. Morgan Reynolds, the Bush Administration's former chief economist in the Department of Labor, argues from evidence that the footage of the plane crashes into the World Trade Center must be fake, because the footage shows no deceleration, no shearing of wings and tail sections, imprints that are too small for 767s, and so on. While Reynolds makes this argument on rational grounds, and understands that the whole question is marginal to the larger debate about the evidence for an inside job, many other "no planers" are not so rational. They have made the whole "no planes" issue a kind of religious icon, a shibboleth that determines salvation or damnation. If you believe in "no planes" you're in their cult; if you don't, you're an evil heretic who must be working for the Bush Mob, the Mossad, or the CIA.

Having studied literature, mythology and folklore, I am somewhat detached from the mythic thinking that goes on in the 9/11 truth movement, as well as from the much more widespread and pernicious mythic thinking that supports the official story of 9/11. I can look at the various alternative narratives of this or that aspect of 9/11—the "conspiracy theories" to use the pejorative misnomer—as legends that stage an explicit or implicit debate on belief. And I can tell the difference between a critical, empirically-based approach to 9/11, as exemplified by the rigorous work of Ahmed, Griffin, Thompson, Hopsicker, Hicks, Tarpley, and portions of the work of many other revisionists, and the mythic thinking that has produced the dominant discourse on 9/11 by accepting the official story on faith, and refusing to examine evidence that disproves it.

The interplay of mythic and empirical thinking, however central to any rigorous analysis of 9/11, was not really the focus of my work on Moroccan legend. My main concern was the *rhythm* of legend—the way repetition and novelty create patterns of meaning in the telling and reception of legends. For just as music communicates at deep emotional and spiritual levels by building patterns based on repetition, and then subverting the listener's expectations by changing the patterns, so too does storytelling. I discovered that in a great variety of Moroccan legends, ranging from contemporary legends about ghosts and spirits to the classic Sufi saints' legends of medieval times, a rhythm representing "the ordinary" is established and then suddenly and devastatingly subverted by the representation of a supernatural image or event. In the Sufi saints' legends, it is the miracle that subverts the ordinary. In contemporary legends, it is the amazing thing that may or may not have really happened to the teller, his friend, or a friend-of-a-friend (FOF).

My dissertation, which will *insha'allah* be published in book form as *Rapturous Ruptures: Reality Breakdown in Moroccan Legend,* develops this insight at length. The key term "reality breakdown" is a very loose translation of *khawariq al-ada'*, the most common Arabic expression for an apparently supernatural or miraculous event. Literally it means "ripping/shredding of habitualness." The expression carries the idea that ordinary experience is a tissue woven out of habits, and that this tissue may be rent or torn by extraordinary events that rupture habit in an astonishing way.

Again, the implications for the study of 9/11 are obvious. 9/11 has functioned in the American collective psyche in the way that a widespread report of an extraordinary religious miracle might function in another culture. 9/11 was a massive collective shock that shredded Americans' habitual lives. This "miracle," actually a spectacular human sacrifice, became the focal point of a new pseudo-religion of post-9/11 "patriotism" that was in reality a kind of idolatrous secular fundamentalism, a blind, rabid, murderous dogmatism that mirrors the worst kind of Christian tradition, itself based on the human-sacrifice image of the Crucifixion. By the grace of God, America's idolatrous 9/11 "religion," and the myth it is based on, never really took hold. Now, as the truth about 9/11 gradually comes to light, another massive collective shock is in store for us. This one, I hope, will trigger genuine religious sensibilities, not phony ones. (Genuine religion triggers expanded consciousness, compassion, and truth—not inculcated stupidity, arrogance, dogmatism, and murderousness.)

The stories I collected and analyzed in Morocco were supernatural legends, not spectacular myths. And they were organic outgrowths of a genuinely religious mythology, not false tales scripted to sell an imperial agenda. Thus they were life-giving, not death-dealing.

The most common kind of traditional saint's legend is the rain miracle, in which a saint's miraculous life-giving power, or *baraka*, ends a drought. In such a situation, each successive day of drought is a repetition, an expression of the death-dealing aspect of the habitual. When the saint elicits Divine intervention and brings rain, the habitual situation of endless drought is shattered; and consciousness, along with the desiccated earth, comes to life. Time dilates; each raindrop splashing on the face feels like the first raindrop you ever felt. The state of consciousness necessary to bring rain, the mystical state attained by the saint, becomes the common property of the group. The earth experiences rebirth, and in the community, a legend is born.

Ironically, the repetition of rain-miracle legends turns the miracle itself into another expression of the habitual. To re-create the habit-shredding effect of the miracle, it needs to occasionally be turned inside-out. That is what happens in the legend of Sidi Buzidi, a famous Moroccan Sufi saint whose anti-miracle is presented in the following story, collected from a young man who studies Sufism at al-Qarawayyin University in Fez.

Sîdî Bûzîdî and the Garden

As you know, Fez is famous for saints' legends. Wherever saints have alighted, miracles (*karâmât*) have descended, just as wherever prophets have alighted, prophetic miracles (*mu'jâzât*) have descended. In the case of Fez, if we speak about the miracles of its saints, we must realize that they are limitless and innumerable. One that occurs to me now is a well-known story here in Fez about one of God's saints named Sidi Bûzîdî. [26] Sidi Bûzîdî lived during a time in the history of Fez that is known as the age of the devout saints (*al-auliyât as-sâlih*).

There came to pass a time of drought and famine. The people called on him to bring rain, asking him to pray the rain prayer (*salât al-istisqâ'*) on their behalf. He refused the first time, and the second, and the third. After they had repeatedly begged, implored and demanded his help, he finally went with them to a walled garden and orchard. They knocked on the door to the garden. And lo and behold the garden's owner emerged and said, "What do you want?" Sidi Bûzîdî, with the others behind him, asked: "Do you water your garden?" The garden's owner answered, "What's it to you? Why should you care? The owner of things has the power to take care of everything."[27] The people realized that God, be He praised and exalted, can bring rain to his servants with or without prayers according to his wont. And they realized that saints who achieve this station of sainthood know that God's book comprises the destiny of all things, and that His power determines the fate of all things. (This tale is still told here in Fez.)

My commentary, adapted from my dissertation:

By opening the storytelling session with this well-known legend about Sidi Bûzîdî, Farid, the storyteller, is making a doctrinal statement about the miracle in Islam. The theological point of the story is that saints do not work miracles, God does. The saint is just the conduit. A human being who takes credit for preternatural events is not a saint but a magician. By rebuking the people who had asked for his intercession, Sidi Bûzîdî emphasizes the doctrinal insistence on absolute reliance on God that is the basis of the theory of *karâmât*, or religious miracles of the saints.[28]

But this story is not just a morality tale supporting orthodoxy and acceptance of God's will, but a shredding or rending of the ordinary pattern, based on the expectation that the saint will intervene and at least try to bring rain. (In a legend, the expectation is that he will succeed.) Instead of miraculously bringing rain, Sidi Bûzîdî undermines this expectation, and shatters the habitual pattern of the hagiographic notice, by demonstrating the necessity of absolute reliance on God, rather than on saintly intervention.

The "miraculous" nature of this anti-miracle lies in its smooth, seemingly pre-arranged quality. Sidi Bûzîdî leads his interlocutors straight to the right place where the right person, the garden's owner, will say the right thing at the right time. It is as if there were a telepathic link between Sidi Bûzîdî and the garden owner, allowing the former to act as straight man for the latter, whose punch-line merits a divine drum roll (of thunder, hopefully.) This preternatural relationship between Sidi Bûzîdî and the garden owner also stands as a double for Sidi Bûzîdî's, and the exemplary human's, relationship to God. Sidi Bûzîdî apparently placed complete reliance on the garden owner, knowing that he would be home and would say the right thing, just as the righteous human is supposed to place complete reliance on God. That reliance is then equated with the "miracle" of the gardener's preternaturally appropriate punch-line. The implication is that absolute faith and reliance produces this sort of knowledge, known in Sufism as *'ilm lâdûnî*—knowledge that comes directly from God when the ordinary human ego gets out of the way.[29] This kind of trust and submission on the part of vulnerable people during times of drought is itself a miracle of the human spirit.

Though the focus of my dissertation research was the Moroccan Islamic tradition allied to Sufism, I also came in contact with individuals and schools of thought usually categorized as Islamist, *salafi*, or "fundamentalist." In fact, I discovered, there is plenty of overlap between the supposedly opposing "Sufi" and "fundamentalist" categories. Many Muslim intellectuals who take their Islam seriously, whether "Sufi" or "Salafi," would like to see religion, rather than the secular state and capitalist consumer culture, play its natural role as the central pillar of the community.

I spent most of my 1999-2000 Fulbright year in Oujda, considered the most Islamist-friendly city in Morocco. Oujda is on the Algerian border, about 40 miles from the Mediterranean. Its language and culture are made up of a unique blend of Algerian and Moroccan elements; in fact, the Western (standard) Moroccan dialect I studied, itself radically different from Standard Arabic, is very different from what is spoken in Oujda. When you throw in French and Berber, both very common languages in Morocco and especially in the Oujda region, the result is a rich and tantalizing linguistic stew—and a challenge to the visiting scholar.

Though a Muslim myself, I arrived in Oujda with the usual prejudices against "Islamic fundamentalists." I thought they were violent, puritanical, and obscurantist—potential terrorists, maybe even would-be kidnappers of nice young Western scholars like myself. I had read in

American newspapers that Islamic fundamentalist fanatics had killed 100,000 people in Algeria's decade-long civil war, carrying out ruthless massacres that involved mass exterminations of whole villages and neighborhoods. The image of being seized and spirited across the border by such people occasionally rose into consciousness, only to be pushed back down into the recesses of consciousness where unwanted nightmares abide.

I guess I didn't really expect to be kidnapped. But I had been conditioned by the American media to carry subliminal images like these somewhere in the back of my brain, and being a Muslim didn't automatically erase them.

Once I got to know some of the scholars at Mohammed V University in Oujda, I was surprised to learn that they were unanimously convinced that the Algerian government, and not "Islamic fundamentalist terrorists," had murdered virtually all of the 100,000-plus Algerians whose deaths had been attributed to Islamists in the Western media. They explained that back in 1989 an Islamist coalition had been poised to win national and local elections and take control of the Algerian government. The corrupt, fascist, secularist junta, awash in oil money stashed in Swiss bank accounts and in bed with Western corporations and intelligence agencies, feared that the Islamists would put an end to their misrule. So a coup d'état was arranged, the elections were called off, and Islamist leaders were rounded up, sent to desert concentration camps, and in many cases tortured and murdered.

Since then, according to my sources, Algerian government death squads had been waging a near-genocidal war of extermination against segments of the population that supported the Islamists. These death squads did their dirty work not in the wealthy suburbs of the secularist elite, but in the rundown neighborhoods and poor villages whose people supported the Islamists. These government death squads would disguise themselves as Islamist guerillas, in the classic tradition of false-flag terrorism, and carry out their massacres under the noses of the army and police, who would remain safely locked in their stations and barracks until the massacres going on just outside their doors were over.

Since I had spent the entire 1990s reading that anti-government Islamic terrorists were responsible for the Algerian massacres, I regarded the false-flag reports with a degree of skepticism. Could the Algerian government really kill 100,000 of its own people using bogus "Islamist" death squads and get away with it? If these stories were true, wouldn't everyone know that the victims lived in Islamist-friendly neighborhoods and villages, and realize the government was lying?

But the more I learned, the more it became apparent that my sources, including a number of university professors, were telling the truth. Newspaper and television reports did often mention that the massacres typically occurred right under the noses of the soldiers and police, and that almost all the victims lived in Islamist-leaning neighborhoods and villages. Gradually the truth was seeping out—from the bottom up. Ordinary people spread the truth by word-of-mouth, while the government-controlled media spewed lies. Sound familiar?

As a folklorist, I found this pattern fascinating. Historically, folklorists assumed that the educated elite—the class from which folklorists themselves emerged—had a monopoly on "scientific" truth, while the rural, uneducated, popular classes they studied were prey to all variety of misinformation and superstition. Information transmitted through established channels, such as universities, publishing houses, and the mass media, was assumed to be reliable, while informal communications between ordinary people were unreliable "folklore." The reason? Established institutions had built-in filters that removed the noise and left the signal. Ordinary people's communications were mostly just noise—fascinating, emotionally-expressive noise, worth collecting and analyzing, but without much truth value.

Nowadays, folklorists have somewhat different assumptions. Some have even recognized that established institutional filters tend to screen out certain kinds of information not because it is necessarily inaccurate, but because it does not serve the purposes of the institution. A classic example is the Church's persecution of Galileo and its rejection of the accurate but institution-threatening information he brought. Even today, academic institutions have been notoriously impermeable to information that threatens dominant paradigms, both social and scientific. Research on the JFK assassination, the power of the Federal Reserve and its elite financial networks, false-flag war-trigger events, UFOs, and such alleged psy abilities as telepathy, clairvoyance and precognition has been systematically discouraged and under-funded in American academia, despite the fact that abundant evidence shows that these areas are of tremendous potential importance, whether or not particular claims turn out to be true.

What this means is that the people and their "folklore" may be far ahead of the institutional gatekeepers in their knowledge of at least some of these fields. Two centuries ago, the scientific community almost unanimously pooh-poohed reports that flaming rocks fell from the sky, despite the fact that every peasant in Europe knew about meteorites. More recently, folklorists have learned that "old hag" stories—reports of nocturnal attacks by evil spirits—are based on actual experiences that occur cross-culturally and share core features. And today, psy research has demonstrated far beyond any reasonable doubt that humans are capable of telepathy, clairvoyance and precognition, as the majority of the world's population knows from firsthand personal experience. Yet the dominant institutions continue to deny the scientific and anecdotal evidence for psy, just as they deny the obvious facts of the JFK assassination, which the great majority of Americans, indeed the majority of people worldwide, know was an inside job.

The people in Morocco knew the truth about the Algerian government death squads. They knew that the Algerian government had plenty of motives: Eliminate 100,000 potential enemies, demonize its opponents as "terrorists," frighten its people into running to the government for protection, legitimize its increasingly brutal fascist dictatorship, and convince the West to give financial and military support to its utterly bogus "war on terror." The Islamists, for their part, would have no motive for killing their own supporters—any more than anti-imperialist Muslims would have a motive for flying planes into the World Trade Center and triggering an angry expansion of American empire that would kill hundreds of thousands of Muslims and unleash the full terror of extremist-Likudnik Zionism on the occupied Holy Land.

My experience in Oujda showed me that a government could spend ten years massacring 100,000 of its people, falsely and even ludicrously attribute those massacres to its enemies, and convince the domestic and international media that black was white, up was down, and, as Orwell put it, freedom was slavery, war was peace, and ignorance was strength. This abject lesson in the amazing ability of governments to perpetrate false-flag terror attacks, and con people into believing absurd myths about those attacks, planted a seed of skepticism that would find fertile soil in the aftermath of 9/11.

Dead Calm Before the Storm (2000-2001)

I returned from my Fulbright year in Morocco in May 2000. My grandmother had just passed away at age 97, and my dad was hyper-competitive as ever as he fought a losing battle with a gall bladder cancer that had metastasized when the surgeon neglected to enclose the organ before removing it. The doctor hadn't intended malpractice; he was just an older physician who had never been trained in the newfangled "enclose the organ just in case" method of gall bladder extraction. Having removed dozens, perhaps hundreds, without finding a single one with cancer, he thought he could get away with it one more time before he retired. We could have sued that doctor and been set for life, but nobody in my family wanted to profit from my dad's misfortune, or make the doctor feel any worse than he already did.

I would have preferred to stay in Morocco and extend the Fulbright for another year, but with my dad nearing the end of his life, and my Moroccan wife once again yearning for America as she did when she was young, I had two compelling reasons to return to the USA. So we packed our many bags and flew from Casablanca to Chicago on the very day that Shaykh Yassin, the Moroccan Islamist leader, was released from his lengthy incarceration as Morocco's most famous political prisoner. My stay in Morocco had convinced me that Islamists like Shaykh Yassin were the Muslim world's best hope for a democratic future, so I was happy to see him go free. I loved the way Shaykh Yassin, like so many Islamist leaders from so many countries, fearlessly spoke truth to power and was prepared to suffer the consequences with equanimity.

When the new King Mohammad VI had offered to free him several months earlier, making noises about democratization and human rights, Yassin had replied: If you really want to do the right thing for your suffering nation, O king, first return the billions of dollars that you and your thieving family of Zionist-loving American-imperial stooges have stashed in Swiss bank accounts. Naturally the prison door slammed back shut in his face! But the newly-free print media reported his miraculously brave words, and a spirit of hope swept over Morocco like a spring breeze. And a few months later, the new king underlined his commitment to ending or at least moderating his father's legacy of human rights abuse by releasing Shaykh Yassin, despite the shaykh's outspokenness. As I left Morocco to return to America in 2000 c.e., the winds of political change seemed to be blowing in the right direction—at least in Morocco.

U.S. America, unlike Morocco, seemed stuck in the doldrums. I was annoyed when my antique hookah was confiscated by customs and apparently tested for drug residues before being finally returned to me a month later. After spending almost a year in an allegedly unfree country where half the cafés exude the sweet smell of hashish, returning to the Land of the Free, where you have to pee in a bottle to get a job and where a huge proportion of the population languishes in horrendous, rape-plagued prisons, was not without its ironies.

Back in the USA I set to work writing my dissertation and helping teach, grade and develop courses in Islam, Folklore, and African Languages and Literature for the University of Wisconsin. My dad passed away in December, 2000, right after the Bush Boyz stole the election that Gore had rightfully won, using the fascist goon-style tactics they would subsequently employ with 9/11, the anthrax attacks, the Wellstone assassination, the ongoing war crimes, and so on, till the American people were so brain-numbed and beaten down they would accept the theft of the next election with computer fraud even in the teeth of a clear 53%-47% landslide loss to Kerry. Maybe my dad was lucky he didn't live to see all that. He was such a rigorously ethical guy that the thought of lying and cheating on such a scale would never even have crossed his mind as a possibility. Forced to confront it—and I might well have thrust David Griffin's books upon him had he lived longer—it would have torn him apart. He would be too smart not to see the facts for what they were, yet too ethical to cope with the thought of such monstrous criminality overtaking the country he loved. He lived his life under the illusion that everyone else was nearly as ethical as he was, and he may have been lucky to die when he did, with that illusion still more or less intact. Now, I imagine him sailing the sea of stars, occasionally glancing down at our poor benighted earth to cheer me as I round the last mark and head upwind toward the 9/11 truth finish line.

~~~~~
## FALSE FLAG FACTS

There almost certainly were no 9/11 hijackers. No Arab names were on the passenger manifests, no Arab DNA was found on the Flight 77 FOIA request. Half the "hijacker" scapegoats had trained on military bases, but their flight skills were abysmal. Cell phones don't work at flight speed and altitude, so those reports are as fake as the hijacker's passport on the street. 9/11 followed an old pattern: Operation Northwoods was a false-flag plan using a drone and a passenger plane, back in 1962!

# Of UFOs and Reptile Armies (August, 2001)

I do not believe in UFOs. Neither do I disbelieve. My touchstone on these matters is Carl Jung, who brackets the question of whether or not these things physically exist and instead examines their psychic causes and consequences.

I do, however, have a UFO story to tell. Emotionally, the story is all intertwined with 9/11 in the deepest recesses of my mind. Many people who hear it tell me I must be crazy to tell it, because it suggests that I believe in UFOs. Others say I am crazy to have emerged from such an experience *without* a deep-seated belief in the reality of UFOs. As for me, I regard my experience as ambiguous, and draw no firm conclusions from it.

My family and I were visiting my mother and other relatives in Montana in late July and early August, 2001, seven months after my father had died. The day before we packed up our van to drive back to Wisconsin, the local newspaper headline caught my eye: CATTLE MUTILATIONS RESUME AFTER 20-YEAR HIATUS. The article reported that cattle were once again being kidnapped and mutilated— lifted into the air, drained of blood, their internal organs, lips, eyes and genitalia removed, then dumped out of the black helicopters or UFOs, take your pick. According to the article, this had not happened since around 1980. Local cattlemen were going bananas, and investigators were mystified. The consensus: "They're baaaaaa-aaaack!" Whatever *they* were.

I recalled reading about this sort of thing back in the late 1970s and up through the early 1980s. As best I could remember, it was never quite clear whether aliens, military Satanists, or coyotes were to blame.

We literally left Montana in a cloud of smoke—a statewide cloud of smoke from wildfires that were burning in many dozens of places across western and central Montana. It gave the magnificent landscape an infernal cast, a sort of John Ford meets Dante quality, as we traveled in and out of the burning areas. At midnight after our first day's journey I drove straight through a good-sized fire that was blazing on both sides of the freeway, an eerie scene that I still remember with a shudder. I had to drive all night to get out of the smoke.

On our third day, with the Montana fires safely behind us, we pulled into Keyhole State Park in eastern Wyoming, with the intention of visiting Devil's Tower—the location of the UFO landing in *Close*

*Encounters of the Third Kind*—the following day. The park ranger in the booth slowly and jerkily slid open his window. He was a creepy-looking fellow with a wizened, bony face and bizarrely clumsy stacatto movements. The sign told us that the camping fee was seven or eight dollars, so I thrust him a ten-dollar bill. He snatched it spastically, mumbling "we are back. We have been gone for a long time, but we are back. Yes, we are back. We were away, but now we are back." He kept mumbling like this and fumbling with the money, and with his cash box, for what seemed like several minutes, repeating the "we're back" refrain ad nauseam before finally succeeding in flailing my change through the open car window. My wife was visibly terrified. I was confused. Was the ranger retarded? Had the state just resumed its hire-the-handicapped program? Should I call an ambulance or a mental hospital?

As I pulled away from the booth and into the campground my wife started repeating "He's an alien. That man is an alien." Now she couldn't stop, any more than the wacky park ranger could stop saying "we're back." It seemed to me that she was as crazy as he was. I explained to her that the ranger was undoubtedly just a little off in the head, and that the Wyoming State Park system must have resumed its hire-the-handicapped program, which would explain the "we're back" thing perfectly.

She wasn't quite convinced, but at least she finally stopped repeating herself, which was more than I could say for the ranger. We found a lovely campsite next to a small natural rock bridge and overlooking the lake. I set up the tent while my wife made dinner. As a storm loomed across the lake, I took a late-afternoon hike through the sagebrush and thorn country that flanked Keyhole Reservoir.

After fighting my way through the thick brush for perhaps half a mile, I suddenly came upon a barren spot that gave me the creeps. It was in the form of an almost perfect circle, with the brush simply *stopping* for no apparent reason around the perimeter. And it was littered with bones. Animal bones, yes. But still...

I hurried back to camp as darkness fell and the storm approached. After dinner I told my children a bedtime story: the strange-but-true tale of the bone-littered barren circle I had discovered, embellished with UFOs and aliens just to spice things up. My wife was thoroughly creeped out when I left them in the van and went to sleep alone in the tent.

As I lay in my sleeping bag I watched bursts of heat lightning illuminating the tent's inner walls, rendering them translucent, strobe-like, for split-second burst after burst. Some of the heat lightning bursts were amazingly bright. And whenever a particularly bright burst of lightning occurred, the people at the neighboring campsite would start laughing hysterically—or were they screaming in terror?—and their dog would let loose with a horrific, unearthly howl. After a climactic chorus of screams and howls, I heard car doors slamming, an engine starting, and tires squealing. Then I heard my wife screaming hysterically: "Kevin, help! Au secours! Save us!" I extracted myself from the tent and raced to the van. The door was locked. Panicked, I yelled "Let me in!" My wife, even more panicked, screamed hysterically: "Are you Kevin? Are you sure you're not an alien? Speak French to me to prove you're really Kevin!" (We had always spoken French at the beginning of our relationship, and still used it to imbue conversations with intimacy.) I said "c'est bien moi cherie, qu'est-ce qui se passe?"

Convinced that I was my own French-speaking self, and not someone from a distant galaxy, my wife unlocked the van for me. She kept saying "Did you see them? Did you?" See what, I asked. "The aliens!" What aliens? "The lights? Didn't you see the lights?" She explained that what I had taken for heat lightning had really been moving lights in the sky that had been swooping down toward our campsite at incredible speed and then retreating just as fast, creating the illusion of a flash of light. She had been watching them through the van windows, too terrified to even scream. The neighbors had been watching them and screaming and howling whenever they swooped in, then finally decamping and fleeing at high speed in their car.

Intellectually, I thought my wife was out of her mind. But emotionally I was just as panicked as she was. "There's one now" she said with a shudder, pointing to what looked like a moving star going by overhead. It could have been a satellite. That light-in-the-sky definitely was not a normal airplane with flashing warning lights. It looked just like a star, except it was moving. The star-like object described about twenty degrees of arc before it disappeared behind a tree, never to reappear. The next day, we drove to Devil's Tower just in case they decided to reappear in broad daylight. They didn't.

Later, after we had returned to Madison and I had recounted the story to the general hilarity and amazement of friends and family, I couldn't decide whether the whole episode was frightening, uproariously funny, or somewhere in between. I tended to see a series of Jungian synchronicities, along with plain old suggestibility, as a more likely explanation than an actual UFO or alien encounter. (A year later, after reading John Keel's *The Mothman Prophecies*, I did have to admit that the park ranger had acted a bit like some of the Men in Black that Keel describes.) I guess I should have been afraid—whether for my wife's sanity or for the future of an earth under attack by flashing, swooping lights—but the part about "Speak French to prove you're not an alien" gave the whole thing an over-the-top surreal quality that prevented me from taking it too seriously. Besides, I'd always known my wife was a little... imaginative. That was part of the reason I'd married her.

Another disturbing premonition of weirdness to come hit me in the third week of August, 2001, not long after we had returned from our trip. The inspiration for a poem came over me, so I grabbed a pen and wrote it down before it left. The poem's title was Zahf al-Jafaf, an Arabic phrase that I translated as "Drought's Crawling Reptile Army." My poem used the drought that had been afflicting much of the Middle East for several years as a metaphor for the ravages of imperialism.

Here is the poem, preceded by the introduction I wrote about six weeks later, when I was submitting the poem for publication (it has since appeared in a book and two magazines):

### Introduction to *Zahf al-Jafáf (Drought's Crawling Reptile Army)*

"God give me the guts to change what can be changed, the patience to accept what cannot, and the wisdom to know the difference." This poem uses drought, which is an unavoidable catastrophe, as a metaphor for war—a catastrophe that is at least theoretically avoidable. If the American news media had been doing their job over the course of recent decades, the war that we are entering now could and would have been avoided. Specifically, if it had told the American people the truth—that the US government, in connection with certain private interests, has been systematically laying waste to the Middle East for 50 years, impoverishing and dispossessing the local people, stealing oil, stealing Palestine, and setting up puppet dictators as accomplices to the theft—the American people would have stood up and demanded a change in policy. And maybe September 11th never would have happened.

I wrote this poem in mid-August of 2001, less than a month before September 11th. It hadn't rained in weeks and my garden was drying up; I was following the progress of the terrible drought that had been devastating much of the Middle East for two or three years, and the terrible colonialism and imperialism that has been ravaging the region since Napoleon invaded Egypt 200 years ago. I felt something in the air, and wrote it down.

### Zahf al-Jafáf (Drought's Crawling Reptile Army)

It rained
 and rained
  and rained
And suddenly stopped.
The earth echoed for awhile.
Then was silence.
The static hiss of drought
Rattled its snaky husk,
Dragged its desiccated belly
Toward our town,
Wrapped itself around our throats
And plunged its fangs
Deep into a refreshing well of blood.
One drop escaped.
It trickled to the earth,
Tickling the parched grass with its red
And silver tongue.
Faint laughter from the dusty graves
Of our forgotten ancestors arose,
And segued into echoes
Of faint
Distant
Thunder.

After September 11th, roughly a month after the close encounter in Keyhole State Park and three weeks after I had been inspired to write *Zahf al-Jafaf*, the two events blended together in my mind as an ominous wind of warning—dry, snaky, rattling warnings of a reptiloid invasion, a dust-storm of things that drain blood from cattle and slice out their internal organs and blow up landmark buildings and launch aggressive wars and feast on human blood and tears and misery.[30]

# Thierry Meyssan (winter 2001-2002)

When I first heard about Thierry Meyssan's claim that a missile, not a jetliner, had hit the Pentagon, I thought he was crazy.

The e-mail directing me to Meyssan's *Hunt the Boeing* website came sometime during the winter of 2001-2002. At the time I was hard at work designing a log house I would soon build on some rural family land, while also working on the dissertation I would finally finish in 2004. (The log house was a great excuse for putting off the dissertation.)

I'm a little vague on the date, because that first Meyssan e-mail didn't much impress me. It was from a friend I usually consider a pretty smart guy, an artist and web designer named mIEKEL aND who co-founded Dreamtime Village, an avant-gardist permaculture community in Wisconsin's Driftless Zone.

I looked at the pictures at Meyssan's site. Sure enough, they seemed to raise questions about what really happened at the Pentagon. There was no jetliner debris, no damage to the Pentagon lawn, nothing but what looked like a 15 to 20-foot hole in only the first floor of the building with unbroken windows all around it. It sure didn't look like a hole that could swallow up an airliner that was over 150 feet long, 120 feet wide and over 40 feet high.

I later learned that the fifteen-foot hole was actually in the second floor, and that a larger first-floor impact area was obscured, in that particular picture, by water being sprayed by firefighters. In any event, the lawn was in pristine condition—impossible if a 757 had hit the first floor. Huge spools of wire sat untouched in the path of the alleged jetliner. There was no impact damage where the 757's engines and wings would have hit. And there was no 757 wreckage.

Upon first inspection, however, I drew no firm conclusions. There was enough water and smoke obscuring part of the façade to cloud my judgment. Maybe I'm missing something, I told myself. Photos can be misleading. Or maybe they're forgeries. And what do I know about plane crash forensics?

I shot off some e-mail replies to aND and others who were hyping Meyssan: "Yes, there seem to be some legitimate questions here, but these photos don't convince me." I hope I did not resort to vacuous arguments like "Duh, what happened to the passengers?" Obviously any covert operation sophisticated and ruthless enough to even attempt a

9/11 hoax would have no problem creating the appearance of disappeared passengers, whether by dumping a passenger plane over the ocean, landing the plane and murdering any non-complicit passengers, creating bogus "passengers" out of carefully developed aliases, or by other means.

For more than a year-and-a-half I considered Meyssan's claims implausible and backed by insufficient evidence. In short, I thought he was nuts. I didn't start taking Meyssan seriously until October, 2003, when I watched him debate a Pentagon flack on al-Jazeera's flagship program *Al-Ittijah al-Mu'aqas*. Meyssan sliced, diced, and re-spliced that unfortunate flack six ways from Sunday. He offered solid arguments, while the Pentagon guy could only reply with childish name-calling. That Pentagon flack came across as an arrogant American bastard, and when he insulted Meyssan as a "crazy conspiracy theorist" he was insulting the majority of al-Jazeera's audience, who came into the debate finding Meyssan's claims credible or at least plausible. At the beginning of the program, the running poll showed that 70-something percent of the audience thought the US government perpetrated the 9/11 attacks, while 20-something percent blamed al-Qaida. By the end it was 89% US government, 11% al-Qaida.

I realize that many of my American readers, brainwashed by decades of anti-Arab racism and Islamophobia in their corporate media, will not be impressed by what 89% of al-Jazeera viewers think about anything. Having lived in an Arab country, read Arab newspapers, and watched al-Jazeera regularly for years, I have a different perspective. I have found that Arab newspapers are, on the whole, at least as diverse and sophisticated as American ones—which isn't saying much. More importantly, I have learned that al-Jazeera is better than the BBC in terms of journalistic professionalism and independence. A recent article in *Foreign Affairs*, the mouthpiece of the conservative American establishment, admits that al-Jazeera is one of the most professional and reliable journalistic outfits in the world.

The al-Jazeera audience, like the channel itself, is relatively smart and sophisticated. Al-Jazeera viewers represent the educated elite of the Arab world, and it is safe to say that the average al-Jazeera viewer would outperform the average CNN viewer in any test of world geography, history, politics, economics, or philosophy.

So when Meyssan mopped the floor with that Pentagon flack, and 89% of al-Jazeera's audience said the US government was behind 9/11, I decided I needed to actually read Meyssan's books, rather than just skimming summaries of them on the internet. Unfortunately I was very busy with a class of 165 students for which I was grading three papers per student—a total of almost 500 essays for the semester—so I was unable to find time for Meyssan's books until early 2004. By that time I had learned that David Ray Griffin, a scholar for whom I had enormous respect, was taking Meyssan very seriously.

~~~~~

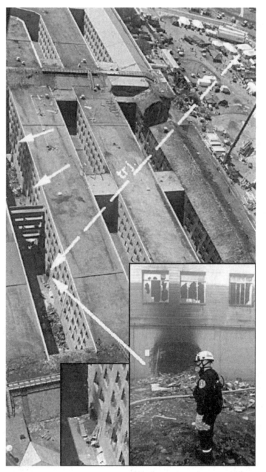

The first 9/11 Truth book of them all, Meyssan's *The Big Lie (L'effroyable imposture)* broke all sales records on its release in France in 2002. The French media have so mercilessly pilloried him ever since.

While not as clear-cut as the WTC7 demolition, there are plenty of holes in the story of the Pentagon "plane crash." This photo shows the impossible trajectory the "Boeing" would have had to take. No official report explained the "exit holes." It looks more like a bunker-busting missile than a jet-liner, which is only a hollow aluminum tube. The point of impact was flush to the ground, so the engines, which are slung lower than the fuselage, would have flown under the ground!

The Pentagon is defended by anti-aircraft missiles and a nearby fighter squadron; yet "Flight 77" meandered 90 minutes before the strike without being intercepted – standard procedure is about 15-20 minutes. 84 security cameras were trained on the spot, but only five frames of film were released – showing no plane. In *Pentagate*, Meyssan cites a ballistics expert finding that the white color in the fireball is from a missile armed with high explosives. Post-crash videos show little airplane wreckage.

David Ray Griffin

I had first heard of David Ray Griffin back in the 1980s when I was studying postmodern theory at San Francisco State University. After reading the too-often-opaque prose of such French philosophers as Lacan and Derrida, I found Griffin's lucid American English both pleasant and edifying. Though I had no interest in organized religion at that point in my life, I found that Griffin's theology—in reality an unusually sensible brand of philosophy grounded in universalist ethics— could make sense to anybody, whether Christian, Muslim, Jew, Hindu, Buddhist, or Nun of the Above.

Griffin became, for me, the epitome of that all-too-rare kind of scholar: the type blessed with uncommon common sense. Where other writers might blather on for dozens or even hundreds of pages without accomplishing anything beyond ever-increasing obfuscation, Griffin could be counted on to analyze a complex issue, whether theoretical or empirical, and quickly clarify what was really at stake. The classical French notion of *le mot juste*—the exact right word for a given idea— applies to Griffin's writing style, whose clarity of prose mirrors its clarity of thought. As Fenelon put it: "Genuine good taste consists in saying much in few words, in choosing among our thoughts, in having order and arrangement in what we say, and in speaking with composure." Though this kind of good taste is no longer *de rigueur* in academia, its rarity does not make it less valuable.

Though I always admired Griffin, I did not identify with him, nor did I always agree with his approach or his conclusions. I felt no urge to join his post-Whiteheadian theoretical school or to come down on his side of every argument. But I recognized an unusually clear thinker when I saw one; so when I heard that David Ray Griffin was working on a book compiling evidence that 9/11 was an inside job, I knew I had better take a long, hard look at the issue.

That was in late November, 2003. I started stealing slivers of time from my teaching duties and family responsibilities to peruse Paul Thompson's *Complete 9/11 Timeline*. I ordered Meyssan's books through interlibrary loan. I read Nafeez Ahmed's *The War on Freedom*—the seminal 9/11 truth book. I discovered seminal 9/11 truth websites including 911truth.org, whatreallyhappened.com, and globalresearch.org. I re-read Gore Vidal's powerful 2002 essay "Goat Song," which argues that when the Secret Service let Bush continue reading a children's story about a pet goat during an alleged surprise attack on America, and made no effort to protect the President or have him assume his Commander-in-Chief duties for over an hour, they pretty much gave the game away.

By the time Griffin's first 9/11 book *The New Pearl Harbor: Disturbing Questions About the Bush Administration and 9/11* came out in March, 2004, I had already done enough background research to know that most of the evidence he was citing held up under scrutiny, while the evidence for the official story did not.

Actually, I had figured that out by early December. And I had experienced considerable psychic pain as a result.

It wasn't that my faith in my government and its "war on terror" was punctured. For me, there had never been any such faith to begin with. It was always obvious to me that the so-called war on terror was a fraud and a farce, regardless of who was behind 9/11. Had the Bush Administration, more accurately termed the Cheney regime, been genuinely concerned about a terrorist threat after 9/11, it would have sealed the borders, toned down the imperialist aggression that provoked terrorism, and launched the mother of all investigations to determine who had really been responsible for the 9/11 disaster, including the dozens or even hundreds of US officials who had to be criminally negligent for such a ludicrous plan as the alleged 9/11 hijackings to succeed so spectacularly. Everyone responsible would have faced swift and merciless justice, and any military response would have been sharply focused on proven 9/11 perpetrators, not on gas pipelines in Afghanistan and oilfields in Iraq. Consider Bush's March 2002 statement about Bin Laden: "You know, I just don't spend that much time on him, Kelly, to be honest with you...
I—I'll repeat what I said. I truly am not that concerned about him."[31] That kind of talk pretty much pulls the rug out from under the 9/11 – war on terror hoax, whether or not you have bothered to inform yourself about how the WTC buildings were demolished.

Though I was not a government-worshipper, nor a fan of the Cheney regime, facing the fact that top US officials appeared to have orchestrated such a murderous attack on their own country hit me like a ton of collapsing rubble. It wasn't so much the mass murder of US citizens that got to me. Governments plan a mass murder of their own citizens every time they go to war. The moral difference between blowing up a couple of buildings full of mostly middle-age civilians, versus dressing a bunch of kids in uniforms and sending them off to die, is not all that obvious to me. And the idea that military strategists would balk at the strategic loss of a few thousand civilians, when their job description involves planning "acceptable" strategic nuclear exchanges that would leave millions of US civilians dead, always struck me as far less probable than the conventional wisdom would have it.

No, what got to me was not the murderousness of the 9/11 attacks—small potatoes by historic standards—but the mendacity. The level of lying necessary to carry out such a plan was almost beyond my comprehension. How could people care so little for the truth? How could they have that much contempt for their fellow human beings—and for the American tradition of Constitutional democracy?

I started reading up on the neoconservatives, and was horrified and nauseated by what I found. The cult followers of a demented philosopher-guru named Leo Strauss, the neocons advocated what amounted to a mentocracy—governance by systematic lying. They believed that people were too stupid and cowardly to face the truth, so leaders needed to feed them nonstop lies—especially simplistic black-versus-white myths, and the fabrication and demonization of "enemies." According to the neocons, lies—not the informed consent of the governed—were the basis of obedience to authority and social cohesion. These guys made the Party in Orwell's *1984* look like the League of Women Voters.

The worst part was that the neocons were now in control of the federal government. Led by Paul Wolfowitz, Richard Perle, Douglas Feith, Scooter Libby, and Karl Rove, the neocon extremists Colin Powell called "the f*ing crazies" had infiltrated and taken control of two key centers of power: The civilian bureaucracy at the Pentagon, and the Vice President's office.

These people were basically Nazis. Their whole worldview had been formed by Strauss, the psychotic refugee from Nazi Germany whose philosophy could be summed up as, "If you can't beat Hitler, join him." Though mostly Jewish and all extremist Likudnik Zionists, the neocons had apparently teamed up with the Bush crime family, which had helped finance Hitler's rise to power, to arrange the 9/11 Reichstag Fire and the destruction of Constitutional governance in the USA. In fact, Bob Dole's former chief advisor Stanley Hilton, who went to the University of Chicago with many key neocons, reminisced that they spent their college careers plotting the destruction of American Constitutional governance — and realized their aims on September 11th, 2001.[32] A key work that emerged from the neocon University of Chicago period was Edward Luttwak's *Coup d'Etat*, a virtual recipe for the neocon seizure of power following the 9/11 Reichstag Fire.[33]

The neocons are psychotic mass murderers in love with war, the most basic and pervasive form of mass murder. One of them, Michael Ledeen, approvingly cites Machievelli: "A prince must have no other objectives or other thoughts or take anything for his craft, except war." But how to provoke war, when most people desire peace? Ledeen explains: "In order to achieve the most noble accomplishments, the leader may have to 'enter into evil.' This is the chilling insight that has made Machiavelli so feared, admired and challenging... we are rotten."[34] Yes, Michael, you and the neocons *are* rotten. You guys make Hitler himself look like Mother Theresa. Now that you have shown your true faces, the whole human species—the whole universe—God himself—all of us *are* at war: With *you*. And make no mistake, we will rid ourselves of your blight. Hasten to the hell that awaits you, accursed satan!

My heart was shattered by this information. I was outraged, saddened, disgusted. I could not sleep. I lay awake nights imagining forms of resistance ranging from nonviolent protest to the most extreme forms of violence.

During those weeks of torment, it gradually dawned on me that all-out nonviolent resistance, in the form of seeking and telling the truth about the events of September 11th, was the right thing to do... the only thing to do, under the circumstances. I started a group called 9/11 Truth Squad and began distributing information. Thus my nonviolent truth jihad was born.

As I worked through my sadness and anger, I began to realize that 9/11 truth offered a rare opportunity to change the world for the better. The powerful emotional effect of the 9/11 television spectacular, intended as a force for evil, could perhaps be turned inside out and made into a force for good. A gigantic advertisement for war and hatred, 9/11 could, were the truth about it revealed, become an advertisement for peace and love. 9/11 truth would annihilate the war that 9/11 had launched, turn the USA away from the aggressive imperialism that was so at odds with our core values, and create a new era of peace and prosperity. The utterly antiproductive military budget could be not just slashed, but virtually eliminated, and our resources could be turned toward saving our endangered planet. America could once again become a democracy and a moral leader. With environmental and energy crises on the way, such moral leadership could make the difference between leaving a green and living planet to our grandchildren, versus turning the earth into a charred cinder.

Unfortunately I had a dissertation to finish and a family to feed, so

9/11 Truth Squad got off to a slow start. My first big event was the University of Wisconsin Marathon 9/11 Truth Teach-In on September 11th, 2004, the third anniversary of the attacks. I had defended my dissertation just a few days earlier, so conducting a fourteen-hour teach-in at that point was an exhausting enterprise. I remained beside a 2 foot by 8 foot banner at the center of Library Mall at the heart of the University of Wisconsin campus from 9 a.m. to 11 p.m. —fourteen hours, minus a few bathroom breaks— distributing literature, haranguing crowds, and participating in spontaneous conversations. Most of those who stopped to listen were polite and interested, and more than a few said they had long known that 9/11 was an inside job.

The worst moment was my encounter with an angry, hysterical woman who had lost her husband in the World Trade Center, and who blamed Muslims—all Muslims—for his murder. She wanted the world's entire Muslim population exterminated, and she was furious with me for questioning her core beliefs. I stopped my 9/11 truth comrades from screaming back at her, and did my best to calm her down and re-open her heart, which had obviously been injured by the loss of her husband far more than my own had been by facing the likelihood that 9/11 was a neo con job. She left less angry than she had arrived. I hope the seed I tried to plant has since blossomed into some serious healing for that poor suffering woman. In the end, that is what 9/11 activism is about.

In fall 2004, with the Ph.D. and Marathon Truth Teach-In accomplished, my career as a 9/11 activist was off and running. I ordered dozens more wholesale copies of *The New Pearl Harbor* and gave them away at cost—sometimes gave them away free. I photocopied the first couple of chapters and distributed them in campus mailboxes with a scrawled note, "Welcome to the American samizdat era." I called talk radio and mentioned the book.

In November 2004, after witnessing scenes from the Fallujah massacre on al-Jazeera, I started oscillating wildly between anger and depression. (See my essay "Ramadan Reflections" in this book.) Anger makes you do stupid things, and depression stops you from doing anything. I decided to engage in some reality-based therapy. I worked on letting go of the bad emotions and focusing on trying to find a way to make a significant contribution to ending the madness of the 9/11-triggered crusade-jihad. And suddenly it came to me: The world needed an interfaith 9/11 truth group. It needed to witness Muslims inviting Jews and Christians to join them in honest dialogue in search of truth.[35] If 9/11 had been designed

My truth jihad, like David's truth crusade, is a win-win situation. If they take me out, I will have achieved the highest form of martyrdom—the self-sacrifice of a peaceful truth-warrior at the hands of ultimate evil. Martyrdom doesn't get any better than that. And if they don't, God willing, I could very well live to a ripe old age and achieve my literary ambition of becoming the Muslim Dostoevsky... or, failing that, at least enjoy watching my kids grow up and start families of their own. I'd also like to continue doing permaculture work, and help my Muslim and American compatriots figure out how to build locally-based sustainable communities. I cannot do any of this, in good conscience and with peace of mind, as long as the 9/11 Big Lie stands.

How did I get to this impasse? Why did a fairly normal Midwestern kid end up converting to Islam and launching an all-out, balls-to-the-wall truth jihad? Sometimes I wonder about that myself.

~~~~~ **FALSE FLAG FACTS** ~~~~~

SMOKING GUN No. ONE: IMPLOSION of BLDG. WTC7

It was not hit by a plane, yet Bldg. 7 suddenly collapsed into a tidy pile of rubble at 5:20 pm on 9/11. This fact was blacked out by the media, not mentioned in the *9/11 Report*, and never explained by the government.

Its fall had all the characteristics of a demolition by pre-set explosives:
* Collapse inwards and straight down into its own footprint
* Puffs of dust shoot out from the façade before floors collapse.
* Steel beams chopped into short pieces; 47-story structure demolished into rubble pile about 3 stories high.
* It's all over in 6.5 seconds, about the speed of a free fall through air.

Films like *9/11 Mysteries, Painful Deceptions, Improbable Collapse* are available on DVD, or viewable online on trutube, youtube and google video. *9/11 Revisited* has lots of audio footage of explosives detonating too.

9/11 Synthetic Terror has some official photos of demolitions to compare to.

to trigger a barely-disguised war on Islam, as most Muslims and many non-Muslims were beginning to realize, an interfaith 9/11 truth dialogue might be the best way to stop the war before it reached genocidal proportions.[36]

I e-mailed a proposal to David Griffin, Dr. Faiz Khan, and others. Dr. Khan, a medical doctor at Long Island Jewish Hospital, was America's leading Muslim 9/11 truth activist. He had performed a vast amount of interfaith educational work even before 9/11, and had been chosen by BeliefNet to write "An American Muslim Responds to 9/11" in the immediate aftermath of the attacks. When I received extremely enthusiastic responses from Dr. Khan, as well as from David Griffin, former Bush-père official Catherine Austin Fitts, and many others, I knew that I had no choice but to make MUJCA-NET—the Muslim-Jewish-Christian Alliance for 9/11 Truth—a reality.

I checked out a web-design book from the library and built the website mujca.com. Faiz Khan wrote our inaugural essay, and MUJCA quickly garnered endorsements from some of the world's foremost Christian theologians including John Cobb, the founder of process theology, and Rosemary Reuther, widely viewed as the world's leading feminist theologian.[37] Amber Haque, a visionary Australian Muslim who had developed the ideas of Teilhard de Chardin into a movement called Planetization, volunteered as MUJCA's webmaster. (I spent our first year of constant interaction assuming that Amber was male, having googled a male Amber Haque who fit the bill, and was later surprised to learn that she was actually MUJCA's web-*mistress*.)

One of our endorsers, Dr. James Goulding, suggested bringing David Griffin to speak in Madison. Jim had first learned about the 9/11 truth movement from my friend Salih Erschen, a local Muslim community-outreach activist. Jim had invited Salih to speak to his World Religions class at Edgewood College in Madison. Salih had mentioned to Jim that most Muslims thought 9/11 was an inside job, and that David Griffin had written the best book on the subject. Jim's response: "This Griffin guy must be some kind of kook. Wait a minute—did you say *David* Griffin?"

Jim was an old seminary-school classmate of David's, and knew of David's formidable reputation as a sensible, accomplished philosopher-theologian. He reacted with incredulity at the prospect that *the* David Griffin could be the same person as the nutty conspiracy theorist Salih was citing.

Though completely dismissive of the inside job hypothesis, Jim's curiosity was aroused. After reading Griffin's *The New Pearl Harbor*, he was no longer dismissive. He contacted me, endorsed MUJCA, and brought me on board as a co-course-designer and co-instructor for the community-based Islam course he was creating at Edgewood College.

In winter 2004-2005 David accepted Jim's invitation to speak in Madison. We were off and running toward what would become the 9/11 truth event of the year—a nationally-televised masterpiece of a speech that helped revive the moribund 9/11 truth movement and set it on its present course toward ever-increasing prominence and eventual victory.

We were not expecting anything quite that magnificent. Originally Jim was thinking in terms of an audience of several dozen people at most. I hoped for more, though I did not expect to see those hopes fulfilled. But after I talked to Norm Stockwell, the venerable Madison activist who helped build Madison's community radio station WORT into one of the best in the country, I started thinking bigger. Norm suggested holding the event at a local theater that holds something like 800 people, and charging admission to cover the cost of renting the space. That was impossible, since I didn't have the necessary two thousand dollars in front money. But if Norm really thought we could get 300 people—the break-even point—to come out and pay to see David, maybe we should at least be thinking in terms of a few hundred, not a few dozen.

I told Jim, my co-organizer, "If we're going to do this, let's do it right." I sent out the first round of press releases almost three months in advance; posted stories at Indymedia outlets; arranged for promotion on WORT community radio; called in to talk shows and mentioned the event; got on the phone with local media people; and generally made a nuisance of myself.

Jim, for his part, had planned to organize the event through the leading local peace group. But a certain left gatekeeper there, an obnoxious dinosaur-communist blowhard and bully who had made it his business to work tirelessly against 9/11 truth, mobilized his small cult following and blocked the Griffin-sponsorship resolution by one vote.

That left me to arrange the whole thing on no money, no resources, and no sponsorship from any local group. I contacted dozens of student groups by e-mail and telephone. Some of the individual members were enthusiastic, but few of them could convince their groups to lend their names as sponsors. The problem, as always, was that those who had examined the 9/11-revisionist case were a knowledgeable minority, while those who opposed "conspiracy theories" on *a priori* grounds, without ever having examined them, were an ignorant majority. When ignorant people are in the majority, proud of their ignorance, scornful of those who possess knowledge, unwilling to even consider the possibility that knowledge could exist, and unconsciously terrified that knowledge *might* exist, the educator's job is very difficult. As a Muslim, I was emotionally prepared for this difficult situation by my understanding of the lives of Muhammad and the other prophets, who had faced the same kind of willful ignorance at the beginning of their prophetic careers. The story of Muhammad in particular is a moving testament to the power of truth to overcome apparently insurmountable odds and win a clear victory over lies, denial, and ignorance.

To get a campus room for Dr. Griffin's speech, I needed at least one student group to serve as main sponsor. But none were forthcoming, even after dozens of hours spent calling and e-mailing their members and leaders. Unable to bring Muhammad to the mountain, I tried bringing the mountain to Muhammad by asking friends to start a student 9/11 truth group. Two quickly agreed—but I could not find a third. Several people I had thought of as friends were too cowardly to allow their names to be listed as members of a Griffin-sponsoring 9/11 truth group.

Finally I found a student group, the Wisconsin Union Directorate Current Issues Committee, willing to book a campus room. Interestingly, this group had no political ax to grind—they were simply willing to hear what Dr. Griffin, one of America's leading philosopher-theologians, had to say. I thought it very strange that all the dozens of groups rabidly opposed to Bush Administration policies ushered in by 9/11 refused to sponsor Dr. Griffin's talk, while a neutral, apolitical group was willing.

We booked a room holding a little under 300 people, which seemed a bit large given the likelihood of a media blackout on the event. At the time, no US mainstream media outlets had covered 9/11 truth events, and there was no reason to believe this event would be any different.

On or about April Fool's Day, a few weeks before the April 18th talk, a C-Span representative called my house and got the answering machine. Unfortunately, my children had been playing with the outgoing message, so what the caller heard was something like, "Hello, this is outer space!" followed by thirty seconds of mad laughter.

C-Span called again the next day. Fortunately I was home to pick up the phone before the answering machine kicked in. Nik Raval of C-Span told me they wanted to put Dr. Griffin's speech on national television, and *The New Pearl Harbor* would be the subject of their Book TV program.

I quickly sent out yet another round of press releases announcing that C-Span would be in Madison to cover the talk. My earlier press releases had been mostly ignored. This time I got a huge, incredulous response. Bill Lueders, the lead columnist for *Isthmus*, the local alternative weekly, mentioned that C-Span was coming to cover Griffin in his column. Amazingly enough, a columnist for the Republican daily, the *Wisconsin State Journal*, wrote a nice piece for the Sunday paper preceding the Monday event. We also got write-ups in the local minority paper, *The Madison Times*, and interviews of Griffin and me on WORT community radio.

C-Span came to check out the lecture hall and informed me it was unsatisfactory. They needed a room with a decent sound board. So we moved at the last minute, with the University's permission, to the largest classroom on campus, which held almost 500 people and boasted an excellent sound system.

That seemed like a huge room for an event that we had originally thought might draw a few dozen people. I didn't want Griffin speaking on national television to a mostly-empty room. I fervently hoped the C-Span publicity would draw a bigger-than-anticipated crowd.

When David and his wife arrived at the pre-talk benefit dinner we had arranged in his honor, I found him every bit the kind, gracious, thoughtful man I knew from his work. His dry sense of humor, which is barely evident in his books, comes across better in person. I felt privileged to meet this man whose work was central to a movement that seemed poised to change history more radically than kings, conquerors and armies ever had.

When David and I stepped into the lecture hall and found it packed with a capacity crowd, it literally took my breath away. I was so happy that it didn't faze me at all when the aforementioned left gatekeeper and anti-truth fanatic approached me just before I was to introduce David and snarled, "What are you trying to accomplish with this? We've been keeping a file on you! THAT'S RIGHT, WE'VE BEEN KEEPING A FILE ON YOU!" The poor guy's eyes were bugging out and his face was twitching. His grotesque expression was so hilarious, and his words so ridiculous, that I almost collapsed in laughter. Still, I somehow managed to pull myself together and give my prepared introduction.

David's talk was a masterpiece. Halfway through it, church chimes began pealing from the carillon next door. It was ethereal, unearthly—like a blessing. The chimes wouldn't stop. At first I was afraid they would be a distraction. But David just kept talking, and the chimes kept pealing, and I knew that this had become a blessed, holy event—a moment when history turns away from the path to hell, toward the garden that is our true home.

By the time it was over, I knew that this nationally-televised event, broadcast from one of America's leading universities, would kick the 9/11 truth movement into overdrive, guaranteeing that sooner or later the mainstream media would have to take notice.

They took notice sooner rather than later. Both mainstream daily newspapers carried excellent, balanced stories about Dr. Griffin's talk—the first breath of 9/11 truth in the news pages of any American daily newspaper. I was deluged with e-mails and phone calls of appreciation from 9/11 truth activists, who had been fruitlessly struggling to get this kind of event, and this kind of media coverage, for years. What was my secret? they asked. How had I convinced C-Span to cover the talk? I had no idea. My only word of advice: If your kids have been playing with the answering machine, make sure you pick up the phone when it rings.

~~~~~

FALSE FLAG FACTS

In his book *The 9/11 Commission Report: Omissions and Distortions*, as mentioned on p. 41, David Ray Griffin counted 115 lies that make up the Big Fat Lie we like to call the "9/11 Omission Report." Indeed, most of them are omissions of facts that give the lie to the Official 9/11 Lie. He lists all 115 of them in an article entitled "The 9/11 Commission Report: A 571-Page Lie" on 911truth.org.

Griffin finds major omissions of fact in all aspects of the official story: the alleged hijackers, the construction of the WTC towers, contradictions of the Pentagon story, actions of Bush and other "leaders," forewarnings, 9/11 financial scams, bin Laden and the Saudis, FBI whistleblowers, the ISI (the CIA's Pakistani arm), the expressed motives of PNAC neocons and defense intellectuals on domination of Central Asia, Iraq and other oil regions, the failure to intercept "hijacked airliners" according to standard procedure, prevarications in the timelines of the day, war games and drills, Operation Northwoods, and the commission's own conflicts of interest; Bush first nominated the war criminal Kissinger to head it.

Casablanca Deli (Summer 2005)

After the amazing success of David Griffin's U.W.-Madison/C-Span talk of April 18ᵗʰ, 2005, which garnered breakthrough media coverage for 9/11 truth, I was almost ready to hang up my 9/11 activist's hat. The Griffin event had been mind-bogglingly rewarding, but also exhausting. I was never really cut out to be an activist. I'm not exactly a logistical genius, nor am I a people person. Sure, I loved peace, love and understanding as much as the next guy. But I liked my family, literature, canoeing, swimming, teaching, and a few thousand other things a lot more than I liked political organizing.

My wife agreed with that assessment. She had never really taken to the 9/11 truth thing, and being a brown-skinned Moroccan Muslim in post-9/11 America was already hard enough without having a husband who was spending his life trying to convince Americans that their own government officials, rather than foreign terrorists, were responsible for the most horrific attack in their nation's history.

If my 9/11 activism was hard on my wife, it was even harder on my two elementary-school-age sons. They were Muslim kids in a small-town school infected with war fever. Some of their classmates' fathers, brothers, sisters, uncles and aunts were fighting in Iraq. That war had been sold to the American people as the only way to disarm Saddam Hussein's WMDs before Iraq inflicted another 9/11, or worse, on the USA. That this notion was beyond preposterous was obvious to me, but not to everyone. Why would Iraq attack America, a nation with enough nuclear weapons to incinerate Mesopotamia hundreds of times over, even if they really did have a few WMDs—which they almost certainly did not? Only the fear-addling effect of 9/11 could have turned the American people into such a bunch of bleating, cowering morons.

That was the sort of thing that my boys heard at home—that and endless discussions of how the Bush-Cheney administration had blown up the Twin Towers and murdered thousands of Americans in order to turn the whole country into a drooling mob of homicidal Islamophobic idiots. At school, of course, they heard something else entirely. Soldiers came to lecture at their elementary school, telling stirring tales of brave service in Iraq and Afghanistan. Every morning, the whole school "froze and rose" to sing along with the Star Spangled Banner and recite the Pledge of Allegiance. In short, talk about war and terrorism at their school was closer to the Dr. Goebbels style Nazi propaganda that Fox

News was vomiting forth nightly than to the outraged and appalled truth-telling they were hearing at home.

My wife had not enjoyed my frenzied run-up to the Griffin C-Span talk, nor was she shy about expressing her feelings. Additionally, she was having difficulties adapting to rural America, especially in the fascist-Islamophobic post-9/11 era. A Moroccan city girl, she didn't especially appreciate the foodways and folkways of Wisconsin country life.

She appreciated my 9/11 work even less, especially when it seemed to be driving our children crazy. One of our sons developed an obsession with politics during the 2004 election season, and took a cue from my 9/11 work to demonize Bush and lionize Kerry. That was okay as far as it went. The trouble was, the stuff he was hearing at home was so different from what he heard every day at school that he developed a sort of schizoid ability to flip-flop—good practice for a future politician, maybe, but very disturbing to listen to. One minute he was ranting about how Bush did 9/11, and the next moment he was loudly and aggressively mouthing pro-Bush slogans and denigrating Kerry. Though he understandably tended to be pro-Kerry when he was in a good mood, and pro-Bush when annoyed with his father, he sometimes flip-flopped several times in the same minute for no apparent reason. Often he would go on for hours like this, driving everyone around him batty and leading his parents to fear for his sanity.

Under great pressure from my wife, and concerned about my son, I decided to retire from 9/11 activism after the Griffin event. During the last crazy month leading up to David's talk, I had assured my wife that if she could put up with my activism for just a little longer, and let me finish organizing this one event, I would take a long rest from 9/11 activism and do something completely different in the post 4/18/05 era.

The stunning success of the David Griffin talk, however, brought a whole new set of pressures: Suddenly MUJCA was a leading 9/11 truth group, and I was the magician behind the miraculous C-Span event. "You have managed what no one else has been able to accomplish," David e-mailed me. Suddenly I was surrounded by fans and followers who were counting on me to work more miracles.

Who was I going to disappoint, my wife and kids or my new 9/11 truth comrades? I thought hard—and said to hell with the comrades. I unofficially retired from the 9/11 truth movement and started a restaurant.

A *restaurant!?* That was my reaction too. I was one of the few people I knew who had never, *ever* dreamed of starting a restaurant. My wife, however, had so dreamed. She is a fine cook and a personable hostess. And she badly needed a more active social life. Our corner of western Wisconsin was home to the American Players Theater—a world-class Shakespeare company—as well as Frank Lloyd Wright's Taliesin architecture school. It also was the home of an unusual number of free-thinking people of widely varying outlooks. We hoped that a Moroccan-Mediterranean restaurant beside the highway would draw the hippest people from our area and fulfill my wife's dream.

And it did—for about a month. Then the insanely unlucrative grind of a two-person operation selling gourmet food at McDonalds prices wore us down.

Our two-month restaurant was called Casablanca Deli, and our slogan was "here's cooking at you, kid." We hung Bogart and Bergmann posters on the walls beside the Moroccan bric-a-brac we hoped to sell along with the food. (Buy a plate of couscous, get a free hand-made brass lamp!) I saw myself in the Bogart role of a fascism-fighting café owner who wasn't really cut out to be an activist, but who made a small but impor-tant contribution when forced to by events. The problem was, I was no more cut out to be a café owner than an activist. Quite a bit less actually.

If the whole point was to do our young sons a favor, it wasn't working. We had pulled them out of school in mid-year and started a home-schooling program, but now, with the restaurant demanding an 80-hour workweek from both parents, there would obviously be no time for that. And while they sometimes enjoyed hanging around the restaurant and helping out, it got old for them very quickly.

It got old for me too, even before it was young. And 9/11 truth was beckoning me back. With a recommendation from David Griffin, I landed a job as co-editor of *9/11 and the American Empire: Christians, Jews and Muslims Speak Out* alongside process theologian John Cobb and Jewish Studies professor Sandra Lubarsky. (For more information, see the book's interactive website, http://mujca.com/newbook.htm.)

My wife could handle me doing a book. But she couldn't handle any more activism. Things came to a head when I was invited to the Washington, D.C. Truth Convergence in July, and couldn't bring myself to turn it down. My wife was not pleased. Exhaustion from long days and lack of sleep was making us both irate, and I undoubtedly harbored deep resentment of my wife, along with enough self-loathing to last a lifetime, for abandoning my truth jihad—my commitment to pursue 9/11 truth till victory or death.

As the time for my D.C. trip approached the domestic disharmony intensified. The last several days before my trip seemed peaceful enough, but that was only on the surface. I was fooled by my wife's placid demeanor. Inside, she felt deeply betrayed. She did not want me to go. For her, it was a sort of a test: Would I cancel my trip, stay home, and put all my energy into repairing my damaged relationship with her and making a go of the restaurant?

I failed the test, from her perspective at least. I traveled to Washington D.C. for my first 9/11 truth conference, the D.C. Convergence, where I gave a talk and met several of my heroes including Nafeez Ahmed, Paul Thompson, Ray McGovern, Morgan Reynolds, Webster Tarpley, Bob Bowman, and Barbara Honegger. I also made several new friends— notably the indefatigable 9/11 activists Gabriel Day and Janice Matthews, two key figures behind 911truth.org. And I got to briefly see my new old friend, David Griffin.

When I returned from Washington, D.C., I found an empty restaurant—and an empty house. My wife had moved out of both, taking our two children with her.

~~~~~

FALSE FLAG PHYSICS

The photo shows a woman looking out of the gash in the North Tower. Many people were alive in the Twin Towers when they exploded, like the firefighters who radioed that two hoses were enough to put out the fire. The jet fuel had  burned off in the first few minutes. It was room temperature inside, except for a few oxygen-starved fires, whose black smoke showed their low heat. It was not hot enough to crack window glass or kill people – so how could it weaken structural steel? No steel frame building has ever collapsed from fire, before, on or after 9/11. At right, in 2005 the Windsor Hotel in Madrid burned out completely – yet the steel frame remained intact. And even if it *could* weaken, a building would sag, not erupt like a volcano in a pyroclastic dust cloud, and plunge in a free fall to the ground.

Interlude: God's Dream

Richard Linklater is my favorite living American filmmaker. In his movie *Waking Life*, Linklater gives us a Dostoevsky-meets-Philip K. Dick vision worthy of those two brilliant authors: A protagonist goes about his day, running into various brilliant, obsessive characters. After meeting each character and discussing life's ultimate questions, he awakens and realizes that the encounter was a dream... and then goes about his day, meets another such character, and awakens yet again from *that* dream, ad infinitum.

Waking Life inspired me to dream up a metaphor for the human relationship with God. Remember, it is just a metaphor... or just a dream, if you will.

My metaphor is *God's dream*. Imagine for a moment that you are just a character in someone else's dream. Now imagine that this someone else is God.

What should your attitude be? Imagine that deep down inside, you *know* that you are not master of your fate and captain of your soul, but that your very existence depends on something so much bigger, so much vaster than you, that compared to it you are very puny indeed. You even have a sneaking suspicion that all the world's a stage, and that you are just one of innumerable little characters—you are probably not even a main character, a Shakespearean hero or lover, but one of the servants or groundlings who are only there for comic relief.

What is your reaction to your own cosmic insignificance? Does it frighten or anger you? Are you unhappy about being just a character in the dream of a much greater someone or something? Does the knowledge that your entire existence depends on this larger consciousness, and that your puny flame will go out the second it awakens, fill you with dread? Does the notion that your whole life is just an ethereal, ephemeral dream of a brief midsummer night, and not the rock-solid reality you would like to imagine, disturb you?

How *should* you react? You could get angry and rage at the Dreamer who gives you your very existence. But a dream character who rages at his or her dreamer is a force for psychic degradation, a bringer of nightmares. Or you could erect a hard shell of denial around your little split-off self, insisting that *you* are real, and the dream-stuff around you is real, and that anybody who suggests otherwise is crazy. Though not as nightmarish as hating your own Creator, this too would be a recipe for unpleasant dreams and psychic disintegration.

The sanest response, paradoxically enough, would be to surrender to the Reality... that you are dreaming. The moment a dreamer realizes that he or she is dreaming, the possibility of a lucid dream arises, one in which you know you're dreaming, and can control much or all of your dream experience.

Once you have surrendered to Reality, to the Dreamer in whose dream you are swimming, you are floating toward lucidity, toward light. Your surrender to the dreamer is, of course, a loving one. You love your Creator with all your heart with a primary love whose corollary is a secondary love for all His creatures. Your little dream expands as your consciousness slowly merges toward that of the Dreamer who loves His dream-characters, giving you insight into the dream-bits and roles of the myriad of other puny dreamers around you. You are becoming a Shakespeare character who loves Shakespeare, and by so doing gains a Shakespearian view of the characters and plays around you. And though you look forward to the eventual awakening that will snuff out your own puny dream-flame, and replace it with the clear and brilliant light of day, you are in no particular hurry to get there—not only because your dream is relatively pleasant, but also because you have been charged with the important task of informing your fellow dream creatures that they, too, are dreaming, and that they too ought to adapt an attitude of loving surrender.

This act of existential surrender—this *islam*—makes you a force for psychic integration. It ensures that the part of the larger dream-world you experience, and especially the awakening you participate in, will be a relatively pleasant one.

~~~~~

FALSE FLAG FACTS

According to Tarpley, Gen. Frank Kitson created the Kenyan Mau Mau, who killed a token 22 whites while annihilating tens of thousands of "rival nationalists," defeating and discrediting the independence movement, as Kitson wrote in *Gangs and Countergangs*. Zarqawi and Al-Qaeda are fake countergangs. Historian Antony Sutton claimed Wall Street created both the Nazis and the Bolsheviks. Were these countergangs that destroyed and discredited Germany and Russia, the chief rivals to Anglo world domination? Are the neocons a countergang set to take down the US? Such gangs are more efficient than false flag operations, because they can work by themselves for generations. A powerful concept.

Chicago: June 2nd-June 4th, 2006

I spent the rest of 2005 repairing the marriage and teaching two part-time courses that together added up to something like a full-time job. I continued to edit and write for e-newsletter of the Muslim-Jewish-Christian Alliance for 9/11 Truth, which I have sent out (and continue to send out) about once a week since January, 2005. Most of the pieces collected later in this book were first published in MUJCA News. (To subscribe, e-mail Kevin@mujca.com with "subscribe" in the header.)

By winter I was back in the thick of 9/11 activism. My wife wasn't exactly overjoyed, but since our sons were doing so well in their newly cosmopolitan surroundings she was able to handle it.

Soon I was helping plot a Chicago 9/11 conference with Gabriel Day and Janice Matthews of 911truth.org—both smart, hardworking 9/11 activists who had been doing 9/11 truth years before I knew such a thing existed. Gabriel is a shrewd, affable guy from Santa Cruz whose oversize head and eyes make him look unusually intelligent, which he is, while Janice is a sharp and indefatigable organizer from Kansas City, a mother of many with a heart several sizes too big who is not about to let it get broken by her country's continuous descent into fascism. Janice and I had chatted at length on the phone after the David Griffin C-Span talk, and I found her a kindred spirit, a fellow truth jihadi who felt pretty much as I did: Give me 9/11 truth or give me death!

Gabriel flew to Chicago in January, where I met him, along with Chicago activists Hal Snyder and Geraldine Perry and Peoria's prime lefty politico, Jim Senyszyn, to find a hotel.

Preparation for the Chicago conference included weekly and sometimes bi-weekly conference calls, usually involving six to eight voices. I met some great folks on those calls. Ian Woods, publisher of the terrific 9/11 truth magazine Global Outlook, was a steady, sensible presence, and we intermittently brought in such talented and knowledgeable 9/11 truth luminaries as Roger Peters of 911blogger.com, Michael Wolsey of Colorado 9/11 Truth, David Kubiak, Kyle Hence and Mike Berger of 911truth.org, Les Jamieson of New York 9/11 Truth, Mia Hamel of Tampa, and Carol Brouillet of Northern California 9/11 Truth. By the time the run-up to the conference was in full swing, Les and Carol were full-time participants, and Carol's positive energy and previous experience organizing 9/11 conferences were especially helpful.

Normally I don't like talking on the phone, but I actually found myself looking forward to those sometimes-frustrating Chicago Conference calls. As a folklorist, I have studied many folk groups—made up of people with a common interest or identity who preserve and transmit expressive culture—but I don't think I'll ever run into a better one, with more genuinely first-rate human beings, than the 9/11 organizers I encountered en route to Chicago. (Well, come to think of it, some of those Moroccan Sufis were pretty cool, too.) To become a 9/11 activist, you have be smart enough to see through the cover-up, sound of heart enough to care, and brave enough to risk social opprobrium or worse. Those who aren't yet brilliant, brave and compassionate, like the scarecrow, tin man and lion at the beginning of *The Wizard of Oz*, self-select themselves out. Being in regular contact with such people was and remains a privilege. The moral: If you want to meet really great people, forget the bowling alley, forget the church social, forget the personal ads. Become a 9/11 activist.

Organizing a conference with all those great people, however, was time-consuming and often frustrating. The 9/11 truth movement sometimes seems like it is made up of all leaders and no followers—strong personalities whose strength is original thinking and self-directed action, not cooperation, self-subordination, and willingness to serve someone else's agenda. It reminded me a bit of a housing co-op I used to live in where every decision had to be unanimously affirmed by all 29 people. The weekly meetings in that household, like the weekly phone calls of the Chicago conference organizers, sometimes kept me up past my bedtime.

In May, 2006—a month before the Chicago conference—I brought Morgan Reynolds, the Bush Administration's former chief Labor Dep't. economist, to the University of Wisconsin-Madison's State Historical Society. Morgan is a witty, charming, raffish guy whose disgust with politics in general and the treasonous Bush Administration in particular has apparently elicited an inner vow to tell the truth, the whole truth, and nothing but the truth, exactly as he sees it, and to hell with what anybody thinks. He has coined some magnificent sound-bites; he says his ex-Bush Administration bosses "blew the Twin Towers to kingdom come," so as to produce "two hours of gripping television, just right for the American attention span, showing people-eating pyroclastic mushroom clouds chasing fleeing crowds through the streets of Manhattan" in order to traumatize Americans into giving up their liberty and prosperity in favor of costly, bloody, strategically-foolish wars of aggression.

The Reynolds talk went splendidly, drawing an enthusiastic overflow crowd to the Historical Society to hear one of the most outspoken performances ever offered by a former member of any American administration. No doubt that's why the event was censored, subjected to a total blackout that covered all the media, local, state, national, radio, TV, and the newspapers.

Two weeks before the Chicago conference, my wife, our two children and I, unable to pay rent on our house after a roommate had broken the lease and moved out, were forced to move into a one-bedroom apartment. The logistical hassles surrounding the move added to the complications of organizing the conference, and almost brought me to my wit's end. Fortunately, at the moment of maximum stress I got an e-mail out of the blue from a deep-muscle massage therapist offering me free treatment. Bestowing her treatment on preferred activists was her way of supporting the causes she believed in. The treatment not only relieved tension, it turned out, but also eased the chronic pain in my knee and hip joints from old basketball injuries. Rejuvenated, I pulled myself together and finished helping organize the conference, arranging last-minute bookings for former Star Wars Chief Col. Robert Bowman, along with the "Ayatollah of Comedy" and candidate for World's Funniest Muslim, Azhar Usman.

The Chicago conference was a huge success. We had expected a minimum of 200 people, and hoped to break even financially with 300. The official attendance figures turned out to be more than 600, and the actual attendance the first night may have been considerably more. Friday began with 9/11 truth pioneer Alex Jones leading a march and rally in downtown Chicago. On the train ride back to the hotel I got to chat with New York Times journalist Alan Feuer, who was covering the conference for what passes for America's newspaper of record.[38] That was my first contact with America's major mainstream media, but it would not be the last.

MUJCA colleague Khalil York and I were too busy working the literature table and helping with conference logistics to see more than a few of the events, but the ones I did see were terrific. Alex Jones the feisty, freedom-loving radio rabble-rouser, and Steven Jones the calm, pious Mormon physicist delivered a terrific one-two punch on Friday night. Alex covered the history of false-flag terrorism leading up to 9/11, while Steve discussed the evidence for controlled demolition of the WTC by way of a discussion of solar cookers—the kind of appropriate technology humanity could be working on if we weren't so busy lying to each other in order to kill each other en masse. MUJCA co-founder Faiz Khan[39] gave a great talk with me the next morning. Jim Fetzer was a founder of Scholars for 9/11 Truth (st911.org), to which I belonged, and I had been anxious to meet him. I was not prepared for the passion and eloquence of his talk, which lucidly laid out the best evidence that 9/11 was an inside job, and called for a popular uprising to restore the Constitution. I was overjoyed that Jim had chosen the Madison area as his new home, after retiring from his teaching job at the University of Minnesota to devote himself to 9/11 truth work. He and I would clearly be working closely together in the future.

Though I unfortunately missed William Pepper, the attorney who had convinced a jury of US government involvement in the assassination of Martin Luther King, I loved the fiery and dryly humorous talks by former British intelligence agent and whistleblower Annie Machon and radio host Maria Heller Saturday night. Both of these passionate, witty women had more cojones than 99% of the men in America, who had allowed their nation's Constitutional system to be destroyed by an act of high treason and mass murder with nary a whimper of protest. (A roster of the more than forty 9/11 truth luminaries who spoke in Chicago is at the Conference archive, http://911revealingthetruth.org.)

As the leader of the Muslim-Jewish-Christian Alliance for 9/11 Truth, co-sponsor of the event along with 911truth.org, the Chicago conference's smashing success once again made it impossible for me to quit my truth jihad even if I had wanted to. After the Griffin C-Span talk at the University of Wisconsin, the Morgan Reynolds event at the Wisconsin Historical Society, and now the Chicago conference, I had now helped organize three 9/11 events, and all three of them were triumphant, expectations-smashing landmarks. Not bad for a guy who normally can't even organize his desk. My wife's chances of retiring me from 9/11 activism had gone from slim to none.

~~~~~

FALSE FLAG FACTS

Translator Sybil Edmonds was silenced by a gag order when she found out the FBI was running a terrorist cell it was supposed to be monitoring. Massive short-selling of airline stocks proving foreknowledge of the 9/11 attacks was traced to CIA Executive Director Buzzy Krongard's old bank. Many witnesses reported explosions in the WTC Towers, and that WTC 7 was set to collapse - BBC and CNN reported it up to an hour before it fell!

Fame without Fortune (Summer 2006)

There's a song that goes something like "Don't want to be rich and famous, I'd rather be rich and obscure." Now that I am poverty-stricken, in debt way up past my eyeballs, and world-famous for no good reason, I can testify that being poor and famous is not all it's cracked up to be.

What did I do to deserve this? I picked up the phone when Jessica McBride called.

Back in my pre-married, pre-Islam *jahiliyya* days, when a woman as attractive as McBride rang, I could be counted on to pick up. But now, Muslim and married, I wasn't particularly interested in hot-looking women. Especially if they were Republicans. And *especially* especially if they were married—to an ambitious Republican District Attorney no less who was running for State Attorney General. (And besides, how did I know she was hot-looking?)

I should have known from her flirtatious voice that Jessica McBride spelled trouble. But when she asked "Hey, what are you doing tonight?" and sweetly invited me on her radio show on WTMJ, the biggest radio station in Wisconsin, I went ahead and made a date. She even charmed me into sending her the syllabus for the Islam 370 class I would be teaching in the fall.

That evening, my phone rang at the appointed time. I answered. It was WTMJ. I waited... thirty seconds... one minute... two minutes... and the Jessica McBride show began. She introduced me with a harsh and lengthy diatribe, calling me "Wisconsin's Ward Churchill" who would be corrupting the youth of Athens with my "conspiracy theories." I responded as politely as I could... but the politeness soon wore thin, and I ended up giving it back to her as good as she could dish it out, while stating in no uncertain terms where I stood on 9/11 truth. (The show has become a cult classic in 9/11 truth circles, and is archived at www.911blogger.com/2006/07/jessica-mcbride-interviews-kevin.html.)

The next day Wisconsin Assemblyman Steve Nass issued a press release calling for the University to fire me from my $8,000 job as a part-time instructor. The opinions about 9/11 that I had expressed on McBride's show, he said, made me unfit to teach. "Not one dime of the taxpayers' money for Barrett" became his slogan.

During the ensuing media circus, the University reviewed my teaching record and syllabus, concluding that I am as professional an instructor inside the classroom as I am a passionately committed truth jihadi outside of it. They decided that firing a college teacher for expressing controversial political opinions on a radio show would be a senseless rollback of the prevailing norms of academic freedom. I was deemed fit to teach. Nass responded by going ballistic. He rounded up 61 Wisconsin state legislators who demanded that I be fired, threatening the University with budgetary mayhem if they refused. But the decision had already been made; I would be teaching, and that was that.

Not everyone was pleased with the decision. Fox "Far Unbalanced" News commentator Sean Hannity invited me on his show to call me a "nut" who had no business teaching, while his evil twin Bill O'Reilly seemed to suggest I ought to be murdered, tossed in the river and found floating in the harbor. Asked to respond to O'Reilly's statement, I said, "I'm not going on any hunting trips with Cheney... and if O'Reilly invites me to an Italian restaurant I'm going to turn him down, too."

Thanks to McBride and Nass, with some help from Fox News, I am now one of the world's most famous "conspiracy theorists," a wide-open field now that Oliver Stone is out of the running. Stone, who knows what it's like to be the whipping boy of the psy-ops psychopaths, is back in the good graces of the misnamed "intelligence community" thanks to *World Trade Center*, a film about 9/11 that does not overtly question the official version—though in the background on the soundtrack the audience can hear some of the explosions that prepared the way for demolition.

What will the future bring? 9/11 truth, I hope. The 9/11 skeptic's movement is very near the tipping point—the moment when the media can no longer ignore the fatal flaws in the official story, and a Watergate-style scandal forces a new investigation followed by treason trials. A recent Scripps-Howard poll showed that 36% of the American people think it either "very likely" or "somewhat likely" that top US officials orchestrated or facilitated the 9/11 attacks to trigger war in the Middle East. That is almost 100 million people—far more than voted for Bush in either the 2000 or 2004 elections, even if we accept the dubious numbers from the Diebold voting machines.

Compared to the future of the nation, and the world, my own future is a non-issue. As a "colleague" who boasted of his intelligence connections e-mailed 9/11 truth physicist Steven Jones, in what seems to have been a thinly veiled threat: One person's future is insignificant compared to the larger issues at stake.

I do hope to keep teaching and writing, my two main vocations. I hope to see my children grow up and build lives of their own. I hope to continue working with Khidria, a nonprofit corporation that sponsors a Sufi retreat and permaculture center in western Wisconsin. I hope to keep working with Planetization, a group working for a peaceful, spiritually-based unification of the planet by the people, not by the current government-corporate-bankster regime (see planetization.org).

But I have no desire whatsoever to do any of these things in the shadow of the 9/11 Big Lie.

Let truth prevail or the heavens fall.

Lone Rock, Wisconsin
Tuesday, August 22nd, 2006

~~~~~

False Flag Physics: The Twin Towers of Terror

See for yourself: this is a test of perception. Can you see a tower toppling on the left, and one exploding on the right? What should happen to the upper stories of the South Tower on the left? Keep tilting, break off and fall to the ground – but they didn't. A second later they were pulverized and disappeared in a cloud of dust. They were blown up in mid-air. On the right, the South Tower explosion continues. Huge pieces of steel fly 70 feet outward and upward, concrete and building contents are turned to fine dust. In a real collapse from weakened columns, a building sags to one side and sinks slowly *downwards* – not at free-fall speed. The arrow points to puffs of smoke from rows of charges that cut supporting columns, followed by blasts that pulverized the insides of the tower.

Part 2: Selected Screeds

A. Religion, Islam, and 9/11 Truth

Ramadan Reflections: MUJCA-NET's First Year

By Kevin Barrett, Founding Member, Muslim-Jewish-Christian Alliance for 9/11 Truth: MUJCA-NET: http://mujca.com

As MUJCA-NET's first birthday approaches, I find myself in the middle of the sacred month of Ramadan, the Muslim month of fasting. It is an ideal time for reflection and contemplation. Going without food, drink, drug, or sex during daylight hours changes your whole outlook—indeed, changes the quality of consciousness on which your outlook is based. Fasting, Aldous Huxley wrote, is the royal road to religious experience: It induces compassionate contemplation, a purity of focus that Muslims call *taqwa* or God-consciousness, and sometimes (especially when taken to a usually inadvisable extreme) even visions and paranormal phenomena.

This change of consciousness is not just a private individual matter. During the month of Ramadan, about one sixth of the world's population is fasting for religious reasons. Those who are attuned to subtle perceptions may notice that the world takes on a special fresh, clean quality during the sacred month. While we Muslims have our own scriptural reasons for believing this, non-Muslims who are aware of the work of such scientists as Rupert Sheldrake and Dean Radin (google them), or science-savvy theologians in the mold of de Chardin, might agree that a billion people fasting at the same time could have a profound effect on the collective consciousness of humanity.

The Birth of MUJCA-NET

The idea for MUJCA-NET was born almost one year ago during Ramadan—on the sacred night, the Night of Destiny, the night that the Qur'an descended on the Prophet Muhammad, peace and blessings upon him. On the 27th of Ramadan last year, I was glued to the al-Jazeera news channel as US troops launched their long-dreaded assault on Fallujah. The shock of that event, compounded by the special sensitivity that is the product of fasting, and the awe induced by the Night of Destiny, almost drove me insane. I simply could not believe that someone, somewhere, had decided to conduct what was bound to be a bloody, near-genocidal assault on Iraq's City of Mosques... on the Night of Destiny! That would be like trying to win Christian hearts and minds by laying waste to the Vatican, gang-raping the nuns, and cutting the Pope's throat... all on Christmas Eve. Invading Fallujah was an absolutely lunatic idea on any day of the year; it could only result in a holocaust for the city's civilian population as well as some of the most important religious architectural heritage in the world. Every single one of the world's 1.2 billion Muslims would have to seriously consider taking up arms upon hearing of such an assault. At the very least, it would demolish any US claim to legitimacy in Iraq. And on the Night of Destiny!? No sane occupation force would even dream of picking the Night of Destiny to invade Fallujah. It had to be a mistake. It couldn't really be happening.

On the Night of Destiny, one is supposed to stay up all night if possible, praying, contemplating, and reciting Qur'an. One is supposed to focus on the peace that passeth understanding, "peace unto her (the night/ the descending angel) until the rising of dawn" (Quran, Surat al-Qadr). Last year I certainly didn't get much sleep—but it wasn't because I was spending the night in Qur'an-inspired inner peace. Instead, I was horrified at the wrong that was being done in my name, and desperately imploring God to make it right. And there emerged in me the realization that if it was to be made right, I was going to have to do my part. I would have to give everything I had—my life, if necessary—to stop this madness.

During the next few days it only got worse. Reports emerged that US soldiers had gotten juiced up for the Fallujah slaughter through headbanging "Christian heavy metal" sessions. They had perpetrated innumerable atrocities, starting by going room to room in the hospital slaughtering patients and any medical personnel who resisted, then taking up sniper positions on rooftops and randomly murdering women and children in the streets, shelling mosques and living quarters, and executing the wounded with point-blank shots to the head. One such execution-style murder—of a helpless, badly-wounded old man in a mosque—was broadcast repeatedly on al-Jazeera.

The root of this evil, I saw, was the hatred whipped up by 9/11, which I had already investigated and found to be a probable inside job. But even if it weren't—whether you blame Osama Bin Laden or Osama Bin Cheney—the event was obviously intended to incite hatred and violence and bigotry between the faiths. I wrote to various religious scholars and 9/11 truth activists outlining the idea of MUJCA-NET, and quickly garnered support, endorsements, and advice from many quarters. David

Griffin was especially helpful, and Faiz Khan signed on as a co-founder. I quickly learned the bare basics of website design and put mujca.com on the cyberspace map...

It has not been an easy year for me personally. The emotional and financial stresses of 9/11 activism have taken their toll on me, and on my family. I have had to negotiate an endless compromise: how much time and energy can I devote to my children in the here-and-now, and how much can I devote to trying to build a world that will be worth growing up in? Under normal circumstances, the answer would be easy: To heck with the world, I'll take care of my children. But these are not normal circumstances. An America (and thus a world) run by the perpetrators of the 9/11 Big Lie would not be worth living in—not for me, not for my children. As David Griffin put it in the conclusion of his "Destruction of the Trade Towers" talk: "The welfare of our republic and perhaps even the survival of our civilization depend on getting the truth about 9/11 exposed."

For guidance in this struggle I look to the example of the Prophet Muhammad, peace and blessings upon him, who was entrusted with a far more powerful and frightening and important truth, and who endured far worse hardships than I have. On the Night of Destiny, in this same blessed month of Ramadan nearly 1400 years ago, the Qur'anic revelation descended on him, almost crushing the breath out of him as it demanded that he recite the divine message. He and his wife Khadija, the first Muslim believer, along with their small but growing band of companions, endured a decade of scorn and persecution, and another decade of all-out warfare aimed at their extermination.

Muhammad's message was much scarier than the 9/11 truth message. Through the Qur'an, God made it clear that the stakes we are playing for in this life are almost unimaginably high. To give even a faint taste of the different outcomes of righteousness and unrighteousness, it offered images of the pleasure garden versus cataclysm and hellfire. Your behavior —in conjunction with the quality of your heart—makes all the difference.

Like many prophets before him, Muhammad set an example for good people everywhere by persisting in speaking an unpopular but necessary truth. He and his companions suffered much, and risked their lives, as the faithful custodians of that truth.

All of us in the 9/11 truth movement, of whatever faith, are the custodians of a lesser, but still extremely important, truth. The Qur'an makes it clear that whole civilizations can be killed by unrighteousness, their ruins left as warnings to those who come after. David Griffin argues that however devastating 9/11 truth would be for America's self-image, "Far more devastating to the American psyche, the American form of government, and the world as a whole will be the continued rule of those who brought us 9/11, because the values reflected in that horrendous event have been reflected in the Bush administration's lies to justify the attack on Iraq, its disregard for environmental science and the Bill of Rights, its criminal negligence both before and after Katrina, and now its apparent plan not only to weaponize space but also to authorize the use of nuclear weapons in a preemptive strike." These evils, all stemming from the 9/11 Reichstag fire, have pushed the USA closer to economic, environmental and social collapse.

I hope that by next year's Night of Power, insha'allah, we will have taken even more small but persistent steps toward the truth that will set us free.

~~~~~

FALSE FLAG FACTS

Authors like Tarpley and Wisnewski have underlined the instilling of "enemy images" or "demonization" as a key tactic in psychological warfare or war propaganda. Bush's Axis of Evil is the successor to the Red Threat, the Yellow Peril, or the Judeo-Bolshevik Conspiracy of past decades. By getting two sides to demonize each other, the game of divide and conquer is played. The United States is now called The Great Satan by Islamic fundamentalists like Osama bin Laden, himself the favorite icon of the demonologists of the war on Islam.

Osama's biography in Felton's *Enemies by Design* depicts him as a pious youth, strongly influenced by the fundamentalist Saudi-Wahhabi sect the British installed in Arabia 200 years ago; Tarpley writes that Islamic fundamentalism was fostered by the British to isolate the Muslim world. The CIA then used Osama's religious fervor to expel the Red Army from Afghanistan. According to the BBC *Power of Nightmares*, he and Zawahiri later issued a call for an Arab Jihad that fell on deaf ears, so they turned to terrorism. Tarpley thinks Zawahiri was his MI-6 handler, and that Osama was a simple man used in a double play: to popularize self-destructive terrorism among Muslims, while scaring the West. Osama was visited by the local CIA agent in Dubai's American hospital in July 2001, and not arrested, in spite of being the FBI's " most wanted man." The videos of him confessing to 9/11 are fakes. Like so many useful idiots and patsies before him, the reward of Osama, the CIA's "Tim Osman," for services rendered to the American empire was to be scapegoated.

Truth is Our Trench

Two Profound Stories: and a Humble Strategic Anecdote

The 9/11 truth movement poses a unique spiritual challenge. Are you going to go on living a comfortable lie? Or can you handle an uncomfortable truth? If so, what are you going to do about it?

The great monotheistic wisdom traditions— Judaism, Christianity and Islam—offer a guide to the perplexed. Since the 9/11 attacks were designed to stir up hatred between these three great faiths, it is only fitting that we turn to them for advice in our dilemma.

In this essay I will consider two profound stories from the Jewish and Christian traditions, and a humble strategic anecdote from the early annals of Islam. I do so not because the Jewish and Christian traditions are more profound than Islam, but simply because these three stories fit together nicely, and the humbler Islamic tale forms a fitting coda for the symphony of the other two.

Job

The first story I turn to recounts the trials of Job, a good man forced to confront apparently gratuitous suffering. Job had a good life—a huge, happy family, plenty of the goods of this world, and the even deeper pleasure of serving his God faithfully. But one day God decided, for reasons known only to Him, to allow Satan to unleash the torments of hell on Job for no particular reason. Bit by bit, Job lost everything he had—his property, his family, and finally his health. Tormented by painful boils, Job finally cried out to God, "Why?" God answered him in an awesome theophany, saying "Where were *you* when I created the universe?" To rationalists, God's answer is most unsatisfying. To the faithful, it is most satisfying—especially because God gave Job back most of what he had lost. To mystics, it is God's appearance at the end, giving Job a taste of the direct experience of a brush with God—an experience that makes all the suffering seem insignificant and ephemeral by comparison—that is the real point of the story.

The story of Job restates, in monotheistic terms, Buddhism's first noble truth: Life is suffering. It also offers the same solution, but in mono-theistic terms: The endurance of suffering, acceptance of its truth, and a kind of non-attachment to the things of this world (i.e. faith in the One eternal entity, God) can provoke theophany and the direct experience of something much greater than the ordinary concerns of life, something so stupendous it makes the suffering seem an insignificant prelude.

Coming to terms with 9/11 truth does not cause boils to break out all over your skin—though in some circles it can make you a social leper. Unfortunately, facing the truth does entail significant psychological and spiritual suffering. Most people, in their state of ordinary happiness, which doubles as quiet desperation, see their government and its leadership rather the way a child sees its parents—as all-powerful and, hopefully, at least somewhat benevolent. A child who learned that her apparently normal father was a serial killer and sadistic rapist would have a hard time coping with that information. She would probably try to repress it, forget about it, avoid thinking about it, and enter a state of denial. If she did ever come to terms with such a horrific truth, it would be at the cost of a great deal of misery.

Since September 11th, 2001, we have been like children given more and more evidence, more and more increasingly obvious clues, and finally irrefutable proof that our national family is headed by psychotic serial killers who, on that dark day four and one half years ago, devoured almost 3000 of their own children—the very citizens they had sworn to protect. The process of being pummeled by more and more evidence, of being bludgeoned into submission (to truth, or to denial, as the case may be) parallels the sufferings of Job, who first loses his property, then his family, and finally is reduced to sheer physical agony. Our faith in the benevolence or at least non-malevolence of our government has also been shaken bit by bit, first by scandals like Enron, then by the uglier matter of Abu Ghraib and the global sex-torture gulag, followed by the dawning realization that we were led into the Iraq quagmire by inept, murderous liars, and finally by the weight of the accumulated evidence— which we may accept or deny as we choose, but which will not go away—that 9/11 was an inside job.

Jesus Tempted by Satan's Offer of Global Empire

If the story of Job speaks to our pain as the gradually disillusioning victims of the 9/11 swindle, the temptation of Jesus on the mountain speaks to the 9/11 perpetrator within us all. Jesus was invited to join Satan and lord it over a world empire—and just like us, he almost fell for it. I realize that this observation may make some readers *really* uncomfortable. What—me?! A 9/11 *perpetrator?* I can hardly fathom how anybody associated with the US government could do something so heinous—much less me! And *Jesus*! How dare you suggest such things!

The fact is, we are all potential 9/11 perpetrators. We all went along with the obvious fraud—some of us longer than others—and we all derived psychological benefit from accepting the lie. Most of us imagined ourselves part of a benevolent nation attacked by psychotic nihilists, and enjoyed the patriotic feeling of national unity that followed, and has since evaporated. A few of us—those who already knew that the US empire is basically a criminal enterprise—did the same thing in reverse, by enthusiastically embracing the "blowback" thesis, according to which the US got pretty much what it deserved on 9/11.

Interestingly, people from the latter group are often more resistant to 9/11 truth than the former. The reason is simple: These folks took pleasure in the 9/11 spectacle and are resistant to giving up that pleasure, just as neurotics, according to Freud, are unable to give up earlier fantasy pleasures in order to enter the cold hard world of factual reality. The diehard defenders of blowback, of course, are not the only ones who reveled in the 9/11 spectacle. The unpleasant truth is that we all did. The sight of huge jetliners smashing into gargantuan buildings, and those buildings exploding into powder and shards, is an awful yet ecstatic sight, especially when witnessed from the safe distance of a television screen. Ecstasy is the state of being temporarily outside oneself, and in beholding 9/11 we all experienced it. Most of us, however, were so overwhelmed by the horror and suffering, and the moralizing, sentimental, patriotic discourse that yapped incessantly from the military-contractor-owned TV networks, that we refused to admit that the experience had been ecstatic. We built a wall in our minds to separate ourselves from the memory of that unspeakable ecstasy. That wall prevented us from facing the soul-shattering truth: *We*—our nation—our government—had done this horrific, ecstatic thing.

The blowback diehards, however, embraced the pleasure of 9/11 in a different and perhaps uglier way. Their self-image and self-esteem are based on a feeling of moral superiority to other Americans who do not realize that their empire is a criminal enterprise—or that they even have an empire, for that matter. The small minority of Americans who have embraced the ideas of people like Noam Chomsky realize full well that the US empire is evil—and this realization would destroy their self-esteem... *unless* they replace it with another source of self-esteem: The feeling of moral superiority over other, ordinary Americans that comes from having read Chomsky. The 9/11 attacks, for these people, greatly bolstered their self-esteem. "See?" the blowbackers gloated. "The US empire is so evil that its victims are willing to cunningly and elaborately immolate themselves to get back at us! If you poor ordinary schmucks had just listened to us... " For these folks, the 9/11 attacks—provided that they were carried out by victims of the evil US empire—supplied the pleasure of vindication, even revenge. The 9/11 truth movement, and the mountain of facts toward which it incessantly gesture, threatens to take away that pleasure—and with it the last shreds of self-esteem of those who know their nation pursues an evil foreign policy, a fact that would be impossible to bear without a sense of moral superiority fed by self-satisfied gloating over the terrorism of 9/11. (Here I am exaggerating the psychological processes of the diehard blowbackers in order to make a point, not condemning the whole notion of blowback, which gestures towards an eternal truth: we reap what we sow.)

Whether pre-ex-patriots, blowbackers, or 9/11 skeptics, we have all tasted the unspeakable pleasure of the 9/11 spectacle, just as Jesus tasted the ecstasy of that view from the mountain, tasted the power that would be his if he said "yes" to Satan and bestrode a global empire. And, like Jesus, we are faced with a choice. Will we embrace that empire and, in so doing, accept Satan as our lord? Or will we say "get thee behind me, Cheney" and give up the pleasure that 9/11 delivered, and the power that it promises, by clinging tenaciously to truth? Will we follow Jesus, or the Lord of Lies?

In contrast to the grandiose, soul-wrenching stories of Job and the temptation of Jesus on the mountain, the Muslim story of the Trench is rather down-to-earth, and, in this context, almost anticlimactic. I could have chosen to end with the larger story of Muhammad's reception of the divine Truth and his sufferings and ultimate triumph in professing it. But the story of the Trench, a minor episode in that larger story of a man holding fast to Truth, offers 9/11 truth activists a solid bit of practical advice.

The Trench

Here is the situation as summarized by an Islamic website (http://www.iberr.org/salmaan.htm):

Twenty-four thousand fighters under the command of Abu Sufyaan and 'Uyainah Ibn Hisn were advancing on Al-Madinah to storm it and to lay siege to it in order to get rid of Muhammad, his religion, and his

Companions. This army represented not only his opponents the Quraish, for they were in alliance with all the tribes, and all had vested interests that were threatened by Islam. It was a last and decisive attempt embarked on by a coalition of all the enemies of the Prophet, based upon individual, collective, and tribal interests.

Today, many Muslims feel that they are in a similar situation, and that the 9/11 frame-up was aimed at inciting Americans to use their unrivaled global power to destroy Islam. The awesome military, financial and technological power of their enemies seems to present Muslims with an unequal fight against overwhelming odds—just as the overwhelming military, financial and media power of the anti-truth forces seems to present 9/11 truth activists with a hopelessly unfavorable fight.

What neither the Muslims nor the 9/11 truth activists fully realize yet is that truth is their trench—the invincible weapon that will demoralize the enemy and send him home with his tail between his legs. Here is the rest of the story:

The Muslims found themselves in a precarious situation. The Prophet assembled his Companions for consultation. Certainly they were gathered to reach a decision on defence and battle, but how could they put up a defence? And then a long-legged man with flowing hair for whom the Prophet bore great love, Salmaan Al-Faarisiy, held up his head and took a look at Al-Madinah, which was surrounded by hills, mountains, and exposed open country which could be easily broken through by the enemy.

Salmaan had much experience in warfare and its tactics in his native Persia. So he proposed to the Prophet something which the Arabs had never seen before in warfare. It was the digging of a trench in the exposed places around Al-Madinah.

And Allah knows what could have been the position of the Muslims in that battle had they not dug the trench, which was no sooner seen by the Quraish than they were stunned by despair. The forces of the enemy still remained in their tents for a month, unable to take Al-Madinah, until Allah sent them one night a storm which devastated their tents and tore them asunder.

Then Abu Sufyaan announced to his forces that they should return to whence they came. They were despondent and frustrated.

The truth is our trench. It is a line that the enemy cannot and will not cross. When we speak truth from the heart, and point to simple, verifiable facts, the Empire of Lies cannot engage with us, because to do so would be to admit the lie. They can only stand helplessly on the other side of the trench, calling us names, appealing to irrelevant truisms and emotional shibboleths, and growing increasingly paralyzed and hysterical as the truth gradually spreads. 9/11 Coverup Czar Philip Zelikow, driven to the brink of inanity by the chorus of voices pointing toward truth, famously sputtered that shooting down 9/11 truth activists and their evidence is like playing whack-a-mole—shoot one here, and another pops up there. Since his Commission had never bothered to even try to refute the vast majority of the evidence cited by the truth-seekers, some wondered whether he was comparing the activists themselves to moles (a term for an enemy agent who has penetrated one's agency, in intelligence jargon) and admitting that he thought they ought to be shot, but that it would probably be hopeless since for each one shot, several more would pop up elsewhere.

Whack a mole, and ten more pop up. Use your overwhelming superiority in lethal force to silence a voice of 9/11 truth, and the ripple of attention will bring ten more voices into the chorus. Kill Senator Wellstone, and not only will you be disinvited from his funeral, but you'll generate lingering, principled animosity that will eventually create ten new Wellstones.

When David Griffin published *The New Pearl Harbor*, he was asked if he feared for his life. "Not really," he said. "It's a win-win situation: If they kill me my book will go to the top of the New York Times bestseller list. And if they don't, I'll get to finish my *Summa Theologica* in peace." Griffin's brave comment reveals more than might meet the eye: had he not decided to speak out as forthrightly and effectively as possible on 9/11, he would not be at peace with himself when he sits down to write his *Summa Theologica*. The possibility that he would be violently silenced was real—but he knew, and hoped that they knew, that whacking this mole would just make ten more pop up elsewhere.

The moles will keep popping up, whether you whack them or not, and each new voice of 9/11 truth that appears makes the task of silencing the existing voices, or staging another bogus attack, that much more hopeless. One of the reasons I decided to devote significant time and energy to 9/11 truth activism was to run interference for people like David Griffin, Nafeez Ahmed, and Cynthia McKinney so that if somebody wanted to get to them, they'd have to go through me, and people like me. Another was so that if indeed another 9/11 did happen, and the US completed its descent into hell, at least I could go to my grave knowing I tried to stop it. This, I think, is not just self-sacrificing bravado, but smart strategy. It puts the Empire of Lies in a totally demoralizing lose-lose situation.

Zelikow's "whack-a-mole" comment was an admission of defeat by a man driven to despair by the power of truth—a man condemned, a dead man walking, a man who must feel that he is only biding his time till the inevitable treason trial. The truth was the trench he could not cross, and it left him paralyzed and sputtering like a Quraysh leader facing the stratagem of Salman al-Farsi.

The rest of the Bush Administration's 9/11-complicit secret government is in the same position. They have overwhelmingly superior power, but cannot use it—because they stand, deflated and helpless, before the trench of truth. The hot gust of 9/11 wind is gone from their sails, and they float aimlessly in the horse latitudes of the voyage of empire, becalmed almost as soon as the doomed voyage set out. The Captain is disoriented, cut off from reality, perhaps even at the brink of madness. Asked if he could point to a mistake he's made, something he'd do differently had he but known, his beady little eyes glaze over with deer-in-the-headlights fear, and he fails to speak.

Will our painful story, like Job's, have a happy ending? Only if we can learn non-attachment from temporal matters (like governments and material standards of living) and put our faith in truth, the Eternal. Will we follow the wisdom of Jesus and reject Satan's temptation to become the foul and lying rulers of a tyrannical global empire? Only if we follow the real teachings of Jesus, not the mad fantasies of those who yearn to rule—or destroy—the world. Will we, like the Muslims of Medina, succeed in defending the truth, and finally making it prevail? Only if we can overcome not just our fear of failure, but also our fear of success. The Muslims had to decide whether their cause was hopeless, or whether faith, courage, and smart judo-style tactics might, God willing, bring them victory. In the end, they chose wisely, and showed mercy at their greatest moment of triumph.

The 9/11 truth movement has everything it needs—so many smart, creative, caring people armed with an invincible array of facts. 9/11 truth is the trench that all the Pharaohs of this world with all their armies cannot cross. We simply need the courage to win, and the wisdom to show mercy in our victory.

Andalusian-Americans?
One Muslim's Vision of Deep Pluralism in the New World

"Andalusia with fields full of grain
I have to see you again and again
Take me, Spanish caravan"
—Jim Morrison

"Andalusia, when will I see her?"
—John Cale

GIFT OF A MIRROR

I send you this marvelous mirror:
let your face rise
over its far horizon
like a moon of good fortune.
Then you will have to admit
how beautiful you are
and will forgive me
the passion I feel for you.
And though your image is elusive,
it is still more accessible,
more benevolent,
and a better keeper of promises
than you are!

Ibn al-Sábúní (13th century Seville)[40]

Islam's view of diversity is colored by its cosmology, which mirrors the American motto *e pluribus unum*, out of many, one, as *e unibus plurum*: out of one, many.[41] Muslims view the cosmos as an unfolding process that flows from, and ultimately returns to, divine unity, which is the only reality that is absolutely Real; all else is relative and largely unreal or illusory, partaking of what Buddhists call *maya*.[42]

The Islamic cosmos is ranked hierarchically, with the beings that are closest to God/the Real/Divine Unity at the top or center, and those furthest from God at the bottom or periphery. Prophets and other pious and saintly persons are viewed as being ontologically closer to God than ordinary folks. In this scheme of things, piety becomes the most important personal characteristic ascribing social identity. In many parts of the Islamic world today, especially in a religious milieu, the first thing people wonder is not "what do you do?" meaning "what job do you have, and at what level of the occupational hierarchy are you ranked?" Piety and personal and family character are more important.

This hierarchy of piety becomes, in a certain sense, an invisible governing hierarchy that has far more influence on most people's lives than the official hierarchy of caliphs, sultans, parliaments, and the rest of the bureaucratic apparatus. When a conflict or problem arises, say, between two individuals or two families, they will probably find a pious, respected person—a family member, a neighbor, perhaps a local scholar with a reputation for God-consciousness[43]—to serve as arbiter. Only in extremely rare, intractable cases would anything resembling a government, defined as a bureaucratic network that claims and enforces a monopoly of legitimate violence in a given territory, get involved. This relative independence of governance from formal government is what allowed the Islamic world, in Hodgson's formulation, to reach its highest level of cultural achievement during the "Middle Period" when formal government was extremely weak.[44]

Keeping the above cosmology and its social implications in mind, we can see some of the parallels and differences between the ways that Islamic tradition, and U.S.-American tradition, embrace diversity. I would argue that both the Islamic and U.S.-American traditions fall at the extreme pro-diversity end of the world-historical scale, with Islam being an extremely diversity-friendly religion, and the United States of America being an extremely diversity-friendly nation, at least up until the September 11th attacks. But whereas the U.S. embraces diversity under an economic and governmental hierarchy that has grown ever stronger, despite Constitutional and Revolutionary traditions that are supposed to limit it, Islam embraces diversity under a relatively informal religious hierarchy.

In the Islamic view, the basic force holding society together is religion and family, not government. Thus diversity emerges, in an Islamic system, in the form of hierarchies of piety. The Qur'an, which Muslims regard as the ultimate divine revelation, states:

> For each of your several communities
> We have appointed a law and a lifeway.
> Had God so willed,
> He would have made all of you one community,

But He has not done so
That He may test you in what he has given you:
So compete in goodness.
To God is your return, and He
Will reveal the truth about what you dispute. (5:48)

The ideal social fabric, in an Islamic system or worldview, consists of diverse individuals and groups competing in goodness. Minority religious communities, or *dhimmis*, are supposed to be given nearly complete autonomy so that they may be free to inspire piety according to their own religious systems. They must not, however, challenge the over-arching Islamic system that protects them; the rationale would be similar to the one used by advocates of democracy, who argue that there is a limit to how much power democracies can allow the enemies of democracy to accumulate, lest democracy itself be destroyed. Likewise, were a relatively tolerant system like the Islamic one to allow its Christian *dhimmi* communities to seize power and overthrow the over-arching Islamic system of tolerance and autonomy for minorities, the Christians would (in theory) impose their fanatical notion, that everyone needs to be converted to Christianity, on all the other communities, and the tolerant, diverse Islamic system would be destroyed. This is, in the Muslim view, precisely what happened to Islamic Spain, or Andalusia—though exactly who was to blame and in what way is still debated.[45]

How should Muslims act when religious communities come into conflict? First, there is the Qur'anic precept, "There is no compulsion in religion" (2:256). Forced conversion, of any kind, is anathema. Another oft-cited Qur'anic verse states, "Say to the unbelievers: I do not worship what you worship; you do not worship what I worship; nor will I ever worship what you worship; nor will you ever worship what I worship. To you your Way, and to me mine" (109: 1-6). The word for "unbelievers" here is the pejorative *káfirun*, which could also be translated as "the ungrateful ones," "the God-deniers" or "the truth-concealers."[46] Thus the verse refers not to people from other faiths who are God-conscious, of whom the Qur'an tells us "they will have their reward from their Lord, will have nothing to fear, neither will they grieve" (2:62), but to those who actively resist God, or come into conflict with Muslims in a way that suggests they are resisting God (one can see why the two would be telescoped in practice). The verse urges Muslims to turn away from those who initiate conflict or actively oppose what seems to Muslims to be the good, and to take a "you do your thing, I'll do mine" attitude insofar as possible.

In situations where Muslim communities are under serious threat, the Qur'an urges *jihad*, or struggle, which includes but is not limited to armed struggle. The word is often misunderstood; the first meaning of jihad, i.e. the "greater jihad," is the inner struggle to be a good person, or to otherwise exert effort on behalf of the good, while armed struggle in defense of the faith, the "lesser jihad," is a secondary meaning. Islamic thought on lesser jihad or armed struggle in defense of the faith is roughly parallel to the theory of the just war in Christianity; and much as the theological niceties of what makes a war just or unjust are often ignored by rulers in Christendom who always declare their own wars just, so the word *jihad* is regularly used by rulers and rabble-rousers in Islamdom in senses that are far from religiously correct.

If the traditional ideal of diversity in Muslim-majority lands is this "extreme autonomy for minority communities under Muslim protection" model, what about situations in which Muslims live as relatively powerless minorities in non-Muslim communities? The arch-Orientalist Bernard Lewis has popularized the notion that Muslims view all non-Muslim lands as *dar al-harb* or "the house of war," meaning that there is a permanent state of war between Muslim and non-Muslim lands, and thus no Muslim should be able to exist in a non-Muslim land except as a soldier or spy—including Muslims in today's West.[47] This notion is preposterous, as a cursory glance at history or at today's reality shows. The first emigrant Muslim community went to a Christian kingdom, Abyssinia, and there enjoyed exactly the kind of protection that Islam offers to non-Muslim minority communities. As a general rule, wherever Muslim minority communities are offered the same umbrella of tolerance, autonomy and protection that Islam offers non-Muslim minorities, or even anything short of outright persecution, Muslims have been happy to live as peaceful and productive citizens. This has historically been the case in much of Africa and Asia, and this is still the situation in most of the non-Muslim countries of the world.

Currently Muslim minority communities in the US and Europe face a difficult challenge, as those nations' non-Muslim rulers are supporting wars of aggression against Muslims in Central Asia, the Middle East, and especially Palestine, the second-holiest Muslim land. Many Muslim scholars make a strong case for mandatory *jihad*, or armed struggle, on behalf of the Muslim and Christian ethnic-cleansing victims of Palestine, and for the restoration of the traditional Islamic order of tolerance and diversity, rather than apartheid Jewish racial superiority and ethnic cleansing, in the Holy Land.[48] (There is likewise a strong argument for a

Christian "just war" on behalf of Palestinian ethnic cleansing victims as well, many of them from the Christian minority, but most Christians have been so cowed by the Holocaust narrative that they are afraid to look the facts of Palestine in the face.)

In particular, the greatest of all Islamic religious monuments, the *masjid al-aqsa* which includes but is not limited to the Dome on the Rock, is in extreme peril, and will presumably remain so until the Holy Land is liberated from its invaders and occupiers. Naturally it is to be hoped that the liberation of the Holy Land will come through peaceful political and spiritual persuasion rather than by force of arms; and there is no question that virtually all Palestinians of whatever religion, and virtually all Muslims worldwide, would accept a solution in line with United Nations resolutions mandating right of return with compensation for all ethnic cleansing victims and their descendants, and a return to the original UN borders—or at the very least, the pre-1967 borders—with Jerusalem being either under a pluralistic Islamic mandate, or equally ruled by, and equally open to, all three of the great monotheisms.

The challenge facing Muslim minorities in Europe is augmented by racism and classism, since European Muslim immigrants are mostly working-class and darker-skinned. In the USA, where Muslim immigrants tend toward the top of the socio-economic scale, the challenge is rather different, and stems mainly from what many Muslims view as a sort of terrorist blood libel. By repeatedly linking the words Islam and terrorism, and performing similar repetitions on parallel concept and image linkages, opinion-shapers have, in the view of Muslims, created a hateful caricature of their faith and incited a climate of pervasive anti-Muslim bigotry. From a Muslim perspective, a new crime, "Self-Defense While Muslim" (SDWM) has been created along the lines of Driving While Black (DWB), and used as an excuse for bullying and extra-judicial punishment.

The terrorist blood libel seems aimed at de-legitimizing acts of self-defense that would be accepted as normal and natural if those defending themselves from aggression were not Muslims or linked to Islam in the popular mind. For example, the British Medical Journal studied the killings of 621 children by Israeli soldiers and concluded that "soldiers are routinely authorised to shoot to kill children in situations of minimal or no threat."[49] Chris Hedges, in Harper's magazine, is one of the few American journalists who have reported this hecatomb:

Yesterday at this spot the Israelis shot eight young men, six of whom were under the age of eighteen. One was twelve. This afternoon they kill an eleven-year-old boy, Ali Murad, and seriously wound four more, three of whom are under eighteen. Children have been shot in other conflicts I have covered—death squads gunned them down in El Salvador and Guatemala, mothers with infants were lined up and massacred in Algeria, and Serb snipers put children in their sights and watched them crumple onto the pavement in Sarajevo—but I have never before watched soldiers entice children like mice into a trap and murder them for sport.[50]

Yet Palestinian attempts at self-defense against such ongoing Israeli aggression are labeled "terrorism," while infinitely more brutal acts of Israeli aggression, such as those witnessed by Hedges, are almost completely ignored in the institutional mainstream American discourse.

In the view of most Muslims, this terrorist blood libel has been applied against Muslims through a carefully developed geopolitical "strategy of tension," consisting of equal parts of Goebbels-style media propaganda, the nurturing of obscurantist-extremist groups including al-Qaida/al-CIA-*duh*, and orchestration of false-flag "Islamic terror" attacks, the most notorious of which was the 9/11 Reichstag Fire.[51] This carefully-developed demonization of Islam and Muslims has changed the situation of Muslims in U.S. America from an almost ideal one pre-9/11, in which Muslims freely enjoyed the religious liberty guaranteed them under the US Constitution, to a condition akin to that of Jews in late 1930s Germany. Outside US America, the USA's popularity in the Islamic world has plummeted from its pre-9/11 status as a very popular nation (aside from its support of Israel) to virtually zero.

How can America get out from under its post-9/11 fascist, islamophobic regime, and return to its ideals of tolerance and pluralism? In struggling for their rights, and the rights of other minority communities, might Muslims be able to help America rediscover her roots? I propose an affirmative answer, and offer the model of an Andalusian America as a model of deep pluralism that combines the best aspects of the American and Islamic traditions.

The best roadmap toward an Andalusian America, and the most interesting American meditation on Islamic deep pluralism that I am aware of, is from Maria Rosa Menocal. In *Shards of Love: Exile and the Origins of the Lyric*, Menocal explores symbolic linkages between the fall of

Islamic Spain in 1492 and the lost origins of Provencal lyric poetry in the great exile from Andalusia.[52] In Menocal's vision, the Islamic tradition of the love lyric, with its ambiguous play between human and divine love and its boundless nostalgia for the beloved, shines forth as the esoteric origin of even the most contemporary forms of Western/American love poetry, exemplified by such avatars as Jim Morrison and Eric Clapton, whose *Layla*, inspired by the Islamic love epic of Layla and Majnun, provides the background music for Menocal's extraordinary banquet.

Though *Shards of Love* is an unrepeatable work of genius, Menocal is better known for her follow-up meditation on the lost glories of Islamic Spain. *The Ornament of the World: How Jews, Christians, and Muslims Created a Culture of Tolerance in Medieval Spain* is one of those rare works that give political correctness a good name.[53] *The Ornament of the World*, as its subtitle indicates, celebrates that most facile of modern idols, tolerance, but does so by way of a rich and passionate reading of the history of Islamic Spain, which I will henceforth refer to as Andalusia.

While I do not necessarily endorse every facet of Menocal's version of Andalusian history, I find her vision inspiring, especially as it pertains to today's ideals of tolerance, pluralism and diversity. Menocal correctly points out that Medieval Spain, and even much of the Medieval world in general, was a far more tolerant, diverse and pluralistic place than most of us realize. Indeed, she argues, it was in many ways a more genuinely tolerant, diverse and pluralistic place than are today's Western nation-states.

In Menocal's terms, borrowed from F. Scott Fitzgerald, Andalusia was a "first-rate" place because it, like Fitzgerald's "first-rate intelligence," was blessed with "the ability to hold two opposed ideas in the mind at the same time."[54] Menocal extends Fitzgerald's point by arguing that at its best—and it was at its best in Andalusia—medieval culture "positively thrived on holding at least two, and often many more, contrary ideas at the same time. This was the chapter of Europe's culture when Jews, Christians and Muslims lived side by side and, despite their intractable differences and enduring hostilities, nourished a complex culture of tolerance, and it is this difficult concept that my subtitle attempts to convey."[55]

Menocal's reading evokes what I will term, borrowing from David Griffin, "deep pluralism" rather than mere shallow tolerance.[56] Griffin's term purports to describe how different, irreducible religions may exist side by side, each claiming a unique, unsurpassable and "final" account of the divine message, yet not only remain at peace with each other, but positively contribute to each others' vision. To realize this state of affairs, each religious community needs to have maximal autonomy, imposing its own rules on its neighbors as little as possible. Individuals in religious communities, including local and heterodox ones, would be free to formulate their own codes of conduct and govern themselves, with as little interference as possible from any supra-local body (such as a government that claimed jurisdiction over more than one locality, be that government "religious" or "secular.")

By this measure of things, a "secular" American government using its monopoly of legally sanctioned violence to prevent me from eating peyote is just as oppressive as a "religious" Iranian government preventing you from drinking alcohol. And a "secular" American government that prevents me from taking more than one wife (or prevents my wife from taking on a co-wife, should she be the instigator) is far more oppressive than a "religious" Islamic government that allows each religious community to set its own marriage rules.

In arguing for an Islamic version of "deep pluralism," I am drawing on the traditional notion of protected minority religious communities, or *dhimmis*. In this tradition, which of course varied widely in terms of its application in practice, minority communities were free to set their own rules and govern themselves. While it might at first seem unfair that the Muslims reserved the first position for themselves, and regulated inter-community disputes according to their own code, the notion of local community autonomy could be seen to offer far more genuine freedom than current statist "democratic" models do. To see what can happen to a genuinely autonomous American religious community—one that chooses to regulate its behavior in a way that is meaningfully different from that of the majority community—we need look no further than Waco.

My proposal for Andalusian-style deep pluralism stems from the Islamic notion that religion is not a private affair to be hidden away and brought out on Sundays, but an all-encompassing worldview and code of life. Government *is* faith – or a part of it anyway. If you feel differently about paying your taxes than you would feel about paying off a mob extortionist, that is because there is something inherently sacred about the notion of "government" and "law" that causes you to bow before it and accede to its demands. The sacred quality of law—and critical legal theory has taught us that there is very little to law beyond this sacred aura

and its manipulation by power—is at root a religious phenomenon.[57]
Thus the whole notion of "religious law" is a pleonasm, or tautology, and
"secular law" an oxymoron.

For America to become a genuinely first-rate place, and grow capable
of holding many ideas in mind at the same time, we will need to allow
ideas—and by this I mean the great ideas about the ultimate questions of
life, especially as those ideas are embodied in the time-tested worldviews
and codes known as religions—to freely develop. That means granting
them full autonomy, or as close to it as is practicable. Currently the
imperial USA is bereft of great ideas because it allows no communities
that could sustain them to exist. The closest thing we have to such full-
fledged religious communities—the Native American Church, the Church
of Latter Day Saints, the Quakers, Stephen Gaskin's The Farm in Tennes-
see, and a few other such groups—are so marginalized or neutered that
they cannot grow to their full potential as autonomous worldview-
communities. The Native American church is harassed over its use of
peyote and bombarded by the dominant culture's obsessions with alcohol
and gambling; the Mormons are denied their polytheism and force-
molded into Young Republicans; the Quakers are made to pay taxes to
support the evilest killing machine in human history; Stephen Gaskin's
farm must keep its group marriages and sacral psychedelic use under wraps;
and even the Amish, perhaps the most successful American religious
community in terms of maintaining autonomy and authenticity, survive
only in the furthest margins, often by selling handicrafts to tourists.

What road could bring Andalusia, with its deep plurality of clashing yet
co-existing, mutually-stimulating great ideas, to America? Ironically, the
exotic foreign model of Andalusia could be realized through a return to,
and an extension of, the vision under which the United States of America
was founded, alongside a sloughing off of the more recent toxic
accretions of statism, corporatism, banksterism, militarism, materialism,
and consumerism. (As peak oil puts us in a permanent negative growth
cycle, we will soon be sloughing off these accretions by necessity, if not
by choice.)

The northern parts of the New World, notably the original thirteen
colonies, were originally a sanctuary and haven for religious visionaries,
utopians, dissenters, and assorted riff-raff.[58] These religious communities
were escaping the State and its Church, and seeking local community
autonomy based on radically pluralistic religious codes and worldviews.
Maryland was a haven for Catholics, Massachusetts for Puritans, and

Pennsylvania for Quakers, while "tri-racial-isolate" communities of escaped slaves, indentured servants and Native Americans created syncretic religions out of their respective traditions in backwoods havens. It was out of this ferocious devotion to local autonomy for wildly diverse religious communities, and antagonism toward the State and its Church, that the American revolution was born. This founding national impulse has remained alive in populist and libertarian politics, dropout culture, the life-style movement, utopian religious communities, movements toward ethnic and religious identification and self-determination, and the American anti-imperialist tradition, and it still represents the best hope for America's future in a post-oil age.

This indigenous American tradition of deep religious pluralism and local autonomy can and should be recovered as a blueprint for the kind of country we want to have after fossil-fuel-driven economic growth ends and the "long emergency" is upon us.[59] There are no atheists in foxholes, nor do atheists do well in times of extreme economic hardship. As the material ties that bind us to empire begin to fray, spiritual ties to our neighbors will sustain us.

I invoke Andalusia as a paradigm for this return to our American roots not so much because the American future will look like medieval Islamic Spain—it most certainly will not, at least in any superficial way—but to evoke a kind of nostalgia for our lost origins in a first-rate culture of deep pluralism that has all but disappeared, which remains on the horizon to beckon us toward something we can barely remember, yet which we know to be glorious beyond our present imagination. There is a poetry in the mythology of American utopianism and religious dissent, in our lost heritage of deep pluralism, that can inspire us to see beyond the apocalyptic end of empire that looms before us.

This mythic tradition will provide a much-needed anchor as centralized authority collapses under the weight of energy shortages, economic collapse and environmental crises. The emerging religious attitudes, however deeply pluralistic, will have to go far beyond Romanticist sacralization of a disappearing nature, and inspire a jihad or struggle to preserve the natural world: "The new religious sensibility endows all of nature with a sacred, privileged status. The political implications are acknowledged and lead to new forms of struggle in which modernist centralism and violence are under assault from a variety of postmodern sources. It becomes worth dying for the sake of dolphins, whales, perhaps even on behalf of rivers, mountains, and forests."[60]

Islam urges us to join this jihad against the idolatries of statism, materialism and secular law, and for the preservation of Gaia, the marvelously complex organism that is our home,[61] through socio-political devolution into an intricate web of religiously-based "communities of communities of communities"[62] that can coexist and even enhance each other by holding opposed ideas in mind at the same time. For if in Islam the one unforgivable sin is *shirk*, idolatry, then modern banksterist statism, and the de facto atheism that is its pseudo-religion, are surely one of the worst idolatries that humans have had the misfortune of inventing. Worse, this idolatry wishes to subdue the entire world in its grip, and the greed and egoism that is the driving force behind this worldview is leading to material super-exploitation and a cancerous hypertrophy of technology that is quite literally killing our planet.

Some will question whether Islam, with its history of demanding the lead role in society, its brash self-confidence, its unrelenting orthopraxy, and its all-embracing focus on *tawhid* or oneness, can really coexist with any other religions, much less hold opposed ideas in mind at the same time. Given the prominence of certain overly modernized forms of Islam—the Taliban, for example, is quintessentially modernist in its rigidity and intolerance, not "medieval" as it is sometimes called—this is a fair question. I think the answer is that it is not so much Islam as modernity that is hyperstandardized, rigid and intolerant, as Menocal suggests. Wherever Islam succumbs to modernity, whether by turning into a quasi-Marxian political ideology or by adapting too readily to Western imperial secular fundamentalism, it loses its flexibility and its capacity to foster deep pluralism.

As I understand it, many nations where Islam is invoked as the basis for governance still evince a greater degree of deep pluralism than do their secular Western counterparts. Consider, for example, the two nations of France and Morocco, both of which I admire, and in both of which I have lived extensively. In Morocco, non-Muslims (and Muslims with fake ID) may drink alcohol in bars that are quite visible in all the major cities, whereas in France, the dominant community's definition of which drugs are acceptable and which ones are not is applied to everyone, including the minority Muslim community. The thought of allowing a minority community to autonomously control its own drug preference rules (or marriage, divorce and inheritance rules) is taken for granted in most Islamic lands, but practically unthinkable in Western ones. The same, of course, is true in many other areas of law and custom.

Americans and Muslims—overlapping categories, of course—will both need to adjust the course they are on if we are to realize my vision of a genuinely first-rate place, an Andalusian America. Americans will have to return to their core traditions of tolerance, pluralism, freedom, and anti-imperialism. The traditional American reverence for religion and education, exemplified by daily Bible readings and bookshelves of Shakespeare and the classics in 19th-century middle-class and even frontier households, must be revitalized, and our modern idols of materialism and obscurantism banished. The coming economic decline, cushioned by the retooling of the military industrial complex toward life-sustaining education and infrastructure, could help foster a cultural Renaissance, in part by underlining the futility of purely material pursuits.

American Muslims will also need to undergo a certain attitude adjustment if we are to become Andalusian-Americans. For one thing, we have our own battles to fight with materialism and obscurantism. We Muslim Americans tend to be far too materially comfortable for our own good, and we usually guide our children toward fields like engineering and medicine, not literature and cultural studies. Worse, some of us embrace or tolerate obscurantist trends in our own thought. To me, the epitome of contemporary Muslim obscurantism was the Rushdie affair, in which ignorant loudmouths howling for murder and burning books they hadn't even read became the image of Islam in the world media.[63]

The issue here is not a simplistic defense of freedom of expression. I agree with those among Rushdie's detractors who argue that today's West is characterized by a pervasive tendency to "transgress all bounds," a crucial sin in the Islamic worldview. And I agree that the offending passages in Rushdie's book certainly did that.

But if we are to effectively defend ourselves and our religion against those who transgress all bounds, we need to react to each transgression in proportion to the threat it poses. When Western intelligence operatives blow up the World Trade Center and kill thousands of innocent people, blaming the act on Muslims in order to justify the mass torture and murder of Muslims and the looting of Muslim resources, their transgression of all bounds merits a determined response.[64] When, on the other hand, a literary author produces a parody-within-a-parody that portrays the life of our Prophet in a demented, surreal light—offered as the hallucination of a dying man who has been driven to insanity by the anti-Muslim bigotry he encounters in England—we are faced with an ambivalent "transgression" that should either be ignored or dealt with in a thoughtful, reflective, and relaxed way.

As Muslims, we could learn something from Menocal's observations about the advantages of being able to hold opposing thoughts in the mind. I aspire to this when I read *The Satanic Verses* and simultaneously feel revulsion at the demented parody of prophetic biography, admiration and awe faced with Rushdie's undeniable literary skill, unmitigated appreciation of the "skewering of British racism" reading, amazement tinged with disgust at Rushdie's pharaoh-like attempt to rival God's messenger as a bringer-of-words, and (dare I admit it) a certain envy of Rushdie's genius as a literary *provocateur*. For all of these reasons, I named my dog Rushdie. He is an amazing dog, and I love him very much. But he is, after all, a dog.

Why did so many Muslims fall into Salman Rushdie's trap, and display themselves on the world stage as small-minded fools? In a word: Insecurity. Those who are secure in their faith, like the Andalusians, can co-exist with opposing thoughts. In the classical age of Islam, poets like al-Ma'ari and al-Mutanabbi challenged orthodoxy in rather shocking ways, and Muslims who didn't agree with their theological views celebrated their creative works in spite of, or even because of, their disagreements.

As U.S. America becomes more and more of a mestizo transition zone, and its skin grows browner and its languages multiply, as its religious and racial homogeneity recedes and the melting pot is replaced by a stew in which each ingredient retains its flavor—and as Hispanic immigration brings a powerful Iberian influence to bear—we will be looking more and more like Andalusia, with its mix of Berbers, Arabs, Europeans and Africans, its irreducible heterogeneity, its small-scale local governance and its multiplicity of languages and autonomous communities thinking different thoughts at the same time. Insha'Allah—if God so wills—our Muslims will be studying literature and culture and history and the arts, transcending insularity and insecurity, and helping make the USA the first-rate place that it was always meant to be.

~~~~~

Each one hath a goal toward which he turneth; so vie with one another in good works. – *Quran* 2:148.

There is no compulsion in religion. - *Quran* (2:256)

B. The Official 9/11 Truth Jokebook

Introduction

I recently taught a class on folk narrative at the University of Wisconsin-Madison. The class included a unit on the folk humor evoked by disasters such as the space shuttle explosion of 1986 and, of course, 9/11. For a somewhat dated introduction to 9/11 humor from a folklorist's perspective, see Bill Ellis's "Making a Big Apple Crumble" at http://www.temple.edu/isllc/newfolk/bigapple/bigapple1.html . (Note that every sentence in Ellis's first paragraph, which summarizes the official account of 9/11, now reads like a bad joke.)

Ellis notes that 9/11 shocked would-be jokesters into a "latency period" during which no 9/11 jokes were tolerated. Gradually the shock wore off, and the usual disaster jokes began to spread.

Today, the growing awareness that 9/11 was an inside job has shocked people into over-seriousness, paranoia, or, most commonly, silence and repression. As of this writing (2006) we are still in a 9/11 truth latency period. Just as most people were shocked into confused silence during the first few months, they are now too dumbfounded to deal with the fact that their own government, or high officials thereof, orchestrated the attacks.

One way to cope with horror is through humor. Two notable efforts at desublimation through 9/11 humor are the Deception Dollar at http://www.foneymoney.com and Mondo Terror at http://mujca.com/mondoterror.htm. Also, don't miss the wise words of MUJCA endorser Swami Beyondananda at www.wakeuplaughing.com.

Jokes

George Bush returns to Booker Elementary School to talk to the kids and get a little PR. After his talk he offers question time.

One little boy puts up his hand and George asks him his name.

"Stanley," responds the little boy.

"And what is your question, Stanley?"

"I have three questions. First, why are you President when Al Gore and John Kerry got more votes? Second, why did you just keep reading that book about pet goats? And third, why was Cheney there holding your hand and the Commissioners weren't allowed to take notes?"

Just then, the bell rings for recess. George Bush informs the kiddies that they will continue after recess.

When they resume George says, "OK, where were we? Oh, that's right: Question time. Who has a question?"

Another little boy puts up his hand. George points him out and asks him his name.

"Bobby," he responds.

"And what is your question, Bobby?"

"Actually, I have five questions. Why are you President when Al Gore and John Kerry got more votes? Second, why did you just keep reading that book about pet goats? Third, why was Cheney there holding your hand and the Commissioners weren't allowed to take notes? Fourth, why did the recess bell go off twenty minutes early? And fifth, what the hell happened to Stanley?"

* * *

A man enters a bar and orders a drink. The bar has a robot bartender. The robot serves him a perfectly prepared cocktail, and then asks him, "What's your IQ?" The man replies "150" and the robot proceeds to make conversation about global warming factors, quantum physics and spirituality, evidence against the official version of 9/11, biomimicry, environmental interconnectedness, string theory, nano-technology, and sexual proclivities of Amazon Basin tribes.

The customer is very impressed and thinks, "This is really cool." He decides to test the robot. He walks out of the bar, turns around, and comes back in for another drink. Again, the robot serves him the perfectly prepared drink and asks him, "What's your IQ?" The man responds, "about a 100." Immediately the robot starts talking about football, trucks, NASCAR, baseball, supermodels, favorite fast foods, guns, and women's breasts.

Really impressed, the man leaves the bar and decides to give the robot one more test. He goes out and returns, the robot serves him the drink and asks, "What's your IQ?" The man replies, "Er, 50, I think." And the robot says, real slowly, "So... .ya gonna vote for Bush again?"

* * *

President George W. Bush was scheduled to visit the Methodist church outside Washington, DC as part of his campaign. Bush's campaign manager made a visit to the Bishop, and said to him,

"We've been getting a lot of bad publicity among Methodists because of Bush's position on stem cell research and the like. We'd gladly make a contribution to the church of $100,000 if during your sermon you'd say the President is a saint."

The Bishop thinks it over for a few moments and finally says, "The Church is in desperate need of funds and I will agree to do it."

Bush pompously shows up looking especially smug today and as the sermon progresses the Bishop begins his homily: "George Bush is petty, a self-absorbed hypocrite and a nitwit. He is a liar, a cheat, a bully, and a low-intelligence weasel. He was a drunken cokehead for most of his adult life, and he had Rove scrub his cocaine arrest story by setting up and destroying the journalist who reported it, the late Jim Hatfield. He has lied about his military record and had the gall to dress up in a flight suit landing on a carrier posing before a banner stating 'Mission Accomplished.' Worst of all, he let his cabinet neocons and covert operators murder almost 3,000 Americans on 9/11 so he could invade two countries for oil and money—and he's been lying about it ever since. He is the worst example of a Methodist I've ever personally known. But compared to Dick Cheney, Donald Rumsfeld, Paul Wolfowitz, Richard Perle, Doug Feith, Scooter Libby, and the other neocons, George Bush is a saint."

* * *

A man turned to the woman seated next to him on an airplane and said, "What's that book you're reading?"

"*The New Pearl Harbor* by David Ray Griffin."

"What's it about?"

"It's about how the Bush Administration orchestrated the 9/11 attacks so they could invade the Middle East."

The man's jaw dropped, his face slowly turned red, and he said "That's so ridiculous it's not even worth discussing." Silence.

The woman said, "Okay, then. A horse, a cow, and a deer all eat grass. The same stuff. Yet a deer excretes little pellets while a cow turns out a flat patty, and a horse produces clumps of dried grass. Why do you suppose that is?"

"Jeez," said the man. "I have no idea."

"Well, then," the woman said, "How is it that you think you know what happened on 9/11 when you don't know shit?"

Bush, Dick Cheney and Donald Rumsfeld are flying on Air Force One. The President looks at the Vice President, chuckles and says, "You know, I could throw a $1,000.00 bill out the window right now and make somebody very happy."

The Vice President shrugs and says, "Well, I could throw ten $100.00 bills out the window and make 10 people very happy."

Not to be outdone, the Secretary of Defense says, "Of course, I could throw one-hundred $10.00 bills out the window and make a hundred people very happy."

The pilot rolls his eyes and says to his co-pilot, "Hell, I could throw all three of those 9/11 criminals out the window and make six billion people happy."

* * *

Donald Rumsfeld, Dick Cheney and George W. Bush are court-martialed for 9/11 high crimes and dragged before a firing squad. Donald Rumsfeld is first placed against the wall, and just before the order to shoot him is given, he yells, "Earthquake!" The firing squad falls into a panic and Rumsfeld jumps over the wall and escapes in the confusion.

Dick Cheney is the second one placed against the wall. The squad is reassembled and Dick ponders what his old pal Rummy has done. Before the order to shoot is given, Cheney yells, "Tornado!" Again the squad falls apart and Cheney slips over the wall.

The last person, George W. Bush, is placed against the wall. He is thinking, "I see the pattern here, just scream out a disaster and hop over the wall." As the firing squad is reassembled and the rifles raised in his direction, he grins his famous grin and yells, "Fire!"

* * *

On his trip to Great Britain, George Bush had a meeting with Queen Elizabeth. His smirk looked more like a grimace as he told her:

"I'm in deep doo-doo over 9/11—we're heading for a Constitutional crisis and treason trials. But you folks over here, you have been running a nice stable monarchy for centuries. How does one manage to run a country so smoothly?"

"That's easy," she replied, "You surround yourself with intelligent ministers and advisors."

"But how can I tell whether they are intelligent or not?" he inquired.

"You ask them a riddle," she replied, and with that she pressed a button and said, "Would you please send Tony Blair in."

When Blair arrived, the Queen said, "I have a riddle for you to answer for me. Your parents had a child and it was not your sister and it was not your brother. Who was this child ?"

Blair replied, "That's easy. The child was me."

"Very good," said the Queen, "You may go, now."

So President Bush went back to Washington and called in his chief of staff, Karl Rove. He said to him, "I have a riddle for you, and the answer is very important. Your parents had a child and it was not your sister and it was not your brother. Who was this child ?"

Rove replied, "Yes, it is clearly very important that we determine the answer, as no child must be left behind. Can I deliberate on this for a while?"

"Yes," said Bush, "I'll give you four hours to come up with the answer."

So Rove went and called a meeting of the White House Staff, and asked them the riddle. But after much discussion and many suggestions, none of them had a satisfactory answer. So he was quite upset, not knowing what he would tell the President.

As Rove was walking back to the Oval Office, he saw former Secretary of State Colin Powell approaching him. So he said, "Mr. Secretary, can you answer this riddle for me. Your parents had a child and it was not your sister and it was not your brother. Who was the child?"

"That's easy," said Powell, "The child was me."

"Oh thank you," said Rove, "You may just have saved me my job!"

So Rove went in to the Oval Office and said to President Bush, "I think I know the answer to your riddle. The child was Colin Powell!"

"No, you idiot!" shouted Bush. "The child was Tony Blair!"

(Thanks to Arden Kirkman)

* * *

Back in the 1960s, long before Dick "Chicken Hawk" Cheney became a 9/11 war criminal, he was a draft-dodging dropout at the University of Wisconsin.

One day Cheney was trotting down Mifflin Street and saw a nun standing there. Out of breath he asked, "Please Sister, may I hide under your skirts for a few minutes. I'll explain why later."

The nun agreed.

Just a moment later two draft board enforcers came running along and asked, "Sister, have you seen a draft-dodger running by here?"

The nun replied, "He went that way."

After the MP's disappeared, Cheney crawled out from under her skirt and said, "I can't thank you enough Sister, but you see I don't want to go to Vietnam. I have other priorities."

The nun said, "I think I can fully understand your fear."

Cheney added, "I hope you don't think me rude or impertinent, but you have a great pair of legs!"

The nun replied, "If you had looked a little higher, you would have seen a great pair of balls... .I don't want to go to Vietnam either."

(Thanks to Mia Hamel)

~~~~~

FALSE FLAG FACTS

Able Danger, suspected of being the CIA cell running the 9/11 patsies, destroyed the 2.5 terabytes of data it had collected before 9/11.

Bush and Blair plotted to paint a plane in UN colors, shoot it down and blame it on Saddam Hussein for a false flag pretext for war on Iraq.

It was claimed that the black boxes from the planes in the WTC were vaporized, but witnesses say they were found and confiscated by the FBI.

DOT Secretary Norman Mineta resigned the day after publication of his testimony that Cheney knew a plane was approaching the Pentagon.

An official named Kevin Delaney destroyed the tapes the FAA made of air traffic controllers' statements on what happened on 9/11.

A Dutch demolition expert named Jowenko says WTC 7 was blown up.

Mossad agents kept apartments nearby the alleged hijackers's homes.

Rumsfeld chose 9/10/01 as a convenient date to announce trillions missing from defense budget.

It took 411 days to set up a 9/11 commission, others took only a week.

SF Mayor Willie Brown and others were warned not to fly on 9/11.

Zbigniew Brzezinski wrote that a New Pearl Harbor would be needed to mobilize public support for a military grab to dominate Central Asia.

Dave Frasca, the FBI supervisor who quashed warnings from field agents about the 9/11 plot, was promoted, as were other suspects.

Condi Rice said, "No one imagined that airplanes could have been used against buildings," yet on her visit to Italy with Bush in July 2001, they took extensive measures against exactly this threat.

C. Mondo Terror

Introduction: How Do You Turn Catastrophe Into Art?

"Nowadays the process is automatic. A nuclear plant explodes? We'll have a play on the London stage within a year. A President is assassinated? You can have the book or the film or the filmed book or the booked film. War? Send in the novelists. A series of gruesome murders? Listen for the tramp of the poets. We have to understand it, of course, this catastrophe; to understand it, we have to imagine it, so we need the imaginative arts. But we also need to justify it and forgive it, however minimally. Why did it happen, this mad act of Nature, this crazed human moment? Well, at least it produced art. Perhaps, in the end, that's what catastrophe is for."
—Julian Barnes, *A History of the World in 10 1/2 Chapters*, p.125

"Whenever I hear the word culture, I reach for my revolver."
—Hermann Goering

"'Tis strange—but true; for truth is always strange;
Stranger than fiction!"
—Lord Byron

The directors of the Mondo Cane films of the early 1960s, Gualtiero Jacopetti and Franco Prosperi, were according to Pauline Kael "Perhaps the most devious and irresponsible filmmakers who have ever lived"—at least until the neocons came along. The "Mondo" films purported to be serious documentaries about the deeply strange world we inhabit. And they were. At the same time, they were the crassest form of exploitation. Horrific animal cruelty, hideously masochistic religious rituals, clueless overweight tourists dancing the hula—nothing was too weird or macabre for these guys to put up on the big screen, accompanied by their inimitably cheesy-yet-subtly-sardonic narration.

Mondo Cane is Italian for "it's a dog's life," and their films documented that indeed it was. The black humor of these movies made the word *mondo* synonymous with anything kitchy, horrifically painful, or unutterably bizarre, as long as it was viewed through the prism of existential gallows humor. These films inspired Michael O'Donoghue, the twisted comic genius behind *Saturday Night Live* as well as "Children's Letters to the Gestapo," and were thus indirectly responsible for bringing dark humor to mainstream American audiences. Now, after way too many Bill Murray films, that may not seem like an unmixed blessing.

What does the Mondo sensibility have to do with 9/11? The Mondo filmmakers' pioneering look at animals being tortured and slaughtered, and humans being horrifically abused, often in painful, physically-damaging religious rites, all to show us what a stupid, cruel species we are, is one prism though which to view the events of 9/11. The fact that the heads of government who are supposed to protect us instead appear to have perpetrated such an insanely spectacular act of violence against us, in order to make a two-hour television spectacular aimed at brainwashing us into going along with their idiotic war plans, is the Mondo Cane film to end all Mondo Cane films.

Some people hate me for saying these things. For them, this stuff is just *not funny*. For my part, I agree with Lenny Bruce's Lone Ranger, who, when asked by Tonto how it feels to have all those arrows sticking out of him, says "it only hurts when I laugh." For those who don't get it, let me spell it out for you: It would hurt even more—unbearably so—if I didn't.

~~~~~

FALSE FLAG FACTS

A short list of high-level, well-connected 9/11 suspects:

The Carlyle Group, a Bush-linked investment and defense company, held its annual meeting on the morning of Sept. 11, 2001, with Bush Sr. and James Baker attending. Dubya's brother Marvin Bush and his cousin Wirt Walker III were principals in Stratesec, the company that ran security for the WTC.

Menachem Atzmon, a gangster crony of Israeli Prime Minister Ehud Olmert, controlled the company that ran security for Boston and Newark airports.

Rudy "The Ghoul" Giuliani, then mayor of NYC, said on TV that he knew WTC7 would collapse, and had an office floor there. He illegally had all WTC debris removed in a blitz action before it could be forensically inspected. He was in London during the 7/7/2005 bombings to remind CNN viewers of 9/11.

Larry Silverstein, crony of Israeli ex-PM Netanyahu and owner of building WTC7, took out the lease on the Twin Towers six weeks before 9/11, and said on PBS TV that he gave the OK to "pull" WTC7 on 9/11. Silverstein made an insurance fraud killing of several billion on the WTC hecatomb, enabling him to buy the Sears Tower in Chicago. He acquired the WTC with the help of right-wing Zionist figures Ronald "Estée" Lauder, head of the NY state privatization board, and Lewis Eisenberg, head of the NY-NJ Port Authority, which lost a suit in May 2001 over prohibitive asbestos abatement costs in the WTC. Insurer "Hank" Greenberg and Tycoon Warren Buffett of Omaha may also be linked.

Assistant Attorney General Michael Chertoff oversaw the FBI's investigation of both WTC bombings, in 1993 and 2001, as well as Hurricane Katrina. His cousin Benjamin Chertoff directed the Pop Mech 9/11 truth debunking piece.

"Counter Terror Czar" Richard A. Clarke started the Al Qaeda attack rumor.

9/11 is Already the Worst Movie Ever Made

Five years later, Hollywood is putting out a barrage of 9/11 movies—as if the original cheesy disaster film, somehow marketed to the American people as an actual attack by foreign terrorists, weren't enough.

In *Gravity's Rainbow*, Thomas Pynchon takes us from World War II to the end of the world by way of Hollywood film references. Pynchon's insight—that we're living in a bad movie about the end of the world—seems as applicable to Bush's Reign of Terror as it was to the World War II–Cold War period Pynchon wrote about. So I hope my Broadway play-in-progress, entitled *9/11: The Musical Comedy*, somehow makes the transition to the silver screen as effectively as *Springtime for Hitler* did in Mel Brooks' *The Producers*. (I wonder if Brooks' producers, those experts at turning massive disasters into even more massive successes, were responsible for that even more wildly successful disaster, the "New Pearl Harbor" of 9/11. Come to think of it, wasn't confessed insurance-fraudster and WTC-demolisher Larry Silverstein one of the producers in Brooks' film? Or does life just continue to imitate art, as fiction and history keep repeating themselves first as farce, then as tragedy, then as tragic farce, farcical tragedy, and God knows what next?)

The theme song from *9/11: The Musical Comedy* is called *Usama the Magical Ay-Rab*. It starts out:

> Usama the magical Ay-rab
> Lives in a cave far away
> Eats little Amerikkins for breakfast
> Sure hope you don't get in his way
>
> Usama the magical Ay-rab
> Has a magic dialysis machine
> It works without electricity
> And keeps his bloodstream clean
> (chorus)
>
> So hooray for Usama Bin Laden
> He's long tall handsome strong and brave
> His four bitchin' wives
> All fear for their lives

When he takes turns with them deep in his cave

(barbershop quartet style harmony echoes: "deeeeep innn his caaaaaaave")

And speaking of 9/11 as theater-of-the-absurd...

The blond California al-Qaida kid threatening LA and Melbourne— *Melbourne!!*—with a histrionic finger-across-the-throat gesture and mangled Islam-speak is beyond hilarious. Somebody should hire that kid for a remake of Penelope Spheris's punk rockumentary *The Decline of Western Civilization*. This time it will star a bunch of blond jihadi teens with safety pins through their noses and mohawks sticking up through their turbans screaming "get ready for the wrath of Allah, dude!" over the wail of electric guitars.

But seriously: So much of the "terror threat" footage we've seen is SOOOOO bad. Even their best special-effects effort, the live-on-camera controlled demolition of the Twin Towers, turned out to be almost as cheesy as one of those old sci-fi films where you can see the string dangling from the monster's jaws. The use of explosives was way too obvious, and the whole "19 Muslim hijackers" story turned out to be an absurdly improbable B-movie script at best—hardly worthy of that bestselling work of pulp fiction, novelist Phil Zelikow's grippingly imaginative page-turner *The 9/11 Commission Report* .

And if you haven't seen it yet, be sure to check out Paul Thompson's *The Terror Timeline* on the "arrest footage" of Khalid Shaikh Mohamad or "KLM," the alleged 9/11 mastermind whose "confessions"—whether extracted under torture, or scripted for his job as a CIA asset—were virtually the only source for the "19 hijackers" legend of the Zelikow Report. When they showed the film of KLM's alleged arrest to an audience of journalists, the whole room erupted in laughter at the ineptly-staged "reconstruction" being presented as actual arrest footage. (Thompson has archived mainstream media stories about the journalists' hilarity in the face of the KLM-arrest-film hoax, alongside other mainstream stories suggesting that the KLM arrest never took place.)

Then there's the Disneyland vacation footage used to convict some Arab-American "terrorist" tourists, as seen on the BBC documentary *The Power of Nightmares* . Check out the scene (e.g. on google video) where the camera pans from a roller coaster to Mickey Mouse, passing by one of Disneyland's ubiquitous trash cans. The prosecutor/narrator says "it is believed that the terrorists were scouting trash cans as possible bomb locations." Never mind that the whole video is just typical Disneyland vacation footage given a sinister spin by a paranoid-lunatic narrator, turning this innocent family-vacation video into an unwitting surrealist classic: "Welcome to Terrorland—The Disney Version!"

And how about that stand-in stunt man known as "Fatty Bin Laden"—the actor we are supposed to mistake for the terminal kidney patient living in a cave for several months, who somehow gained 40 or 50 pounds and radically changed his facial features as he "confesses" to 9/11 in ultra-grainy, low-sound-quality footage?

Osama the Gaunt
in December 1998
as presented by
mass-media

Osama the Stout
in November 2001
as presented by
mass-media

But for the ultimate 9/11 cheap thrill film segment, somebody should add a laugh track to Larry Silverstein's confession that he and his colleagues pulled WTC-7 and watched it come down: Larry delivers his confession, canned laughter erupts, and we see WTC-7 undergoing controlled demolition in slow motion as the laughter gets more and more hysterical.

In short, somebody—perhaps a Michael Moore who's grown some guts rather than *a* gut—should collect all the worst "war on terror" footage and make the *Reefer Madness* of the 21st century: A film to keep midnight moviegoers rolling in the aisles for the duration of the 9/11-inaugurated "war that will not end in our lifetimes." Call it *Mondo Terror* . We can pitch it to Hollywood as the BBC's *The Power of Nightmares* redone by the *Mondo Cane* film crew.

The Madman Theory: Or, How I Learned to Stop Worrying and Love 9/11

"Mad?! You call ME *mad?!?!?!*
I who hold the secret of eternal empire?!"

— apologies to The Cramps, "Most Exalted Potentate of Love"

*And you will see and they will see
Which of you is the demented.* –Qur'an 68:5-6

Bringing Stanley Kubrick's name into a discussion of bad movies and worse realities may strike the discerning filmgoer as incongruous. After all, in the whole history of American cinema, there has never been as consistently excellent a director as the late Mr. Kubrick. Sometimes, however, the good can illuminate the bad, just as the bad can illuminate the good. John Waters, avatar of the so-bad-it's-good school of filmmaking, says his bourgeois parents' impeccable good taste helped develop his own considerable understanding of shock and schlock. Conversely, it sometimes takes a Kubrick to remind us that our nation and its cinema is really baaaa-aa-aaad. His masterpiece *Dr. Strangelove: Or, How I Learned to Stop Worrying and Love the Bomb* is a most perceptive commentary on the insanity of American society and its leadership during the Cold War.

Kubrick's film, like the German expressionist masterpiece *The Cabinet of Dr. Caligari* and its hellish brood, is a riff on what might be called the madman theory of power. According to this theory, those who seek and achieve power are quite literally insane. At best, they are control freaks, as Tim Leary and friends euphemistically called them. At worst, they are absolutely psychotic—but, unlike ordinary lunatics, they have the means to impose their own mental breakdowns on whole nations. Power is not, as Henry Kissinger said, the ultimate aphrodisiac, but the ultimate PCP overdose.

Siegfried Kracauer writes that *Caligari*'s theme is "the soul being faced with the seemingly unavoidable alternatives of tyranny or chaos" (*From Caligari to Hitler*, 77). Caligari, the dictator-hypnotist, tyrannically imposes his will on the population, along with plenty of surplus sadism, in order to stave off the nightmare of chaos—a projection of his own mind that is teetering on the brink of collapse. The parallels between Caligari's world and our own fictitious "war on terror" are stark: "Like the Nazi world, that of Caligari overflows with sinister portents, acts of terror and outbursts of panic. The equation of horror and hopelessness comes to a climax in the final episode which pretends to re-establish a normal life... normality realizes itself through a crowd of insane moving in their bizarre surroundings. The normal as a madhouse: frustration could not be pictured more finally. And in this film... is unleashed a strong sadism and an appetite for destruction" (74).

The neocons, like their mentors Strauss/Hitler, seek desperately to impose order and stave off their own inner demons of chaos—which they quaintly project on enemies whom they identify with the "chaotic 1960s." Their minds, like the American empire, are on the brink of collapse; it was not for nothing that Colin Powell has called them "the f* crazies," while others have referred to them as "the crazies in the basement" of the Bush Sr. administration. Terrified by their collapsing minds, and the impending collapses of Israel and the American empire it depends on, the neocon crazies set off the 9/11 firecracker, crawled out of the basement, and imposed their madness on the nation and the world.

The irony is astounding: In an effort to prevent moral-cultural-imperial collapse and re-impose order and sanity, they murdered thousands of Americans in a false-flag terrorist attack aimed at re-establishing the "normalcy" of the two decades after Pearl Harbor, the heyday of the American empire. But this "normalcy" has turned out to be a madhouse; post-9/11 American culture is "a crowd of insane moving in their bizarre surroundings." Beneath the thin veneer of normalcy in the Dawn-of-the-Dead shopping malls, "a strong sadism and an appetite for destruction" has been unleashed, exemplified by the unspeakably horrific US-supervised boxcar massacre in Afghanistan, the re-enactment of Pasolini's *Salo* at Abu Ghraib, and the sprawling CIA sex-torture gulag that metastasized from Guantanamo. Meanwhile, the people of New York continue to go about their daily lives, fully half of them believing that top US officials conspired to commit mass murder and high treason on September 11th, 2001. The cognitive dissonance of unspeakable horror has driven them hopelessly mad, and they wander about like the undead in the last flickering shadows of an empire of doom.

What is the source of madness of such scale and scope? I submit that the madman theory of power is essentially correct—power drives men mad, and absolute power drives them absolutely mad—but that the special neocon madness derives directly from the specter of nuclear destruction. The "crazies from the basement" did not crawl out of just any basement, but from a very special one: The basement where people with very high intellectual IQs and grossly subnormal moral-emotional IQs sit around contemplating the consequences of various varieties of nuclear exchange. Wolfowitz and the other "defense intellectuals" who brought us 9/11 cut their teeth on the so-called science of nuclear strategy—a board-game for certified lunatics if ever there was one. Like Kubrick's *Dr. Strangelove*, Wolfowitz & Co. stared MAD (Mutually Assured Destruction) in the face for too long, and emerged from the experience completely deranged.

Kubrick's *Dr. Strangelove* (aren't you glad we finally got there?) is the definitive statement on the identity of nuclear strategy and madness. Anyone who plays this game will end up, like Dr. Strangelove himself, in a state of paranoid dementia, identifiable by the spastic tic of an involuntary Hitler salute.

Why does nuclear strategy drive men mad? Simply put, the destructive power of nuclear weapons, and the chaos they promise to unleash, are overwhelming and unbearable. They represent absolute chaos—the end of everything we know. Deaths of individuals, and empires, can be borne, because we know that life goes on. The specter of all-out nuclear exchange, however, is different. We cannot be sure that life would go on, in any recognizable form, after such an event. And yet the seemingly inescapable logic of human power relations drives us ineluctably toward that very event. We are caught in a swift current a few hundred feet from Niagara Falls. And the worst part is that *we are the very current that bears us toward our own destruction.*

The mind, overwhelmed by this unbearable image of absolute chaos and helplessness, can respond in one of three ways: Sanity, neurosis, or psychosis. The sane response, of course, is to devote all or most of one's resources to dismantling nuclear weapons and the structure of militarism, nationalism and imperialism from which they emerge. The few sane ones among us are mostly in jail for pouring blood on missiles and attacking warheads with hammers. Most of us, unfortunately, are not that sane; we shrink from the horror and try to go about our daily lives—a classic neurotic response of repression and denial. The third response is psychosis: Embrace the horror, and get a job thinking the unthinkable for the Rand Corporation.

Dr. Strangelove is prince of the psychotics. Modeled on the German Jew Henry Kissinger, the Kubrick-Sellers character sports a German equivalent of Inspector Clouseau's French accent as he cackles his way through a learned disquisition on strategic nuclear options, interspersed with tics, twitches, and involuntary heil-Hitlers. One imagines Paul Wolfowitz in this role pre-9/11, convincing General Buck Turgidson, played by Dick Cheney, that the only way to impose order upon the looming chaos is to build a *pax Americana* on the smoldering ruins of a New Pearl Harbor at the World Trade Center.

The neocon madmen, unlike their precursors of the Kissinger-Strangelove generation, are postmodern lunatics: They are self-conscious about their own insanity. The repulsive Kissinger viewed himself as a suave, debonair gentleman employing clever negotiation and the virtue of moderation to turn the madness of men like Nixon to strategic advantage. Indeed, Kissinger invented the "strategic madman theory" (not to be confused with the madman theory *tout court*) by vaunting Nixon's obvious instability to the North Vietnamese and others, suggesting that if they didn't do what he, Kissinger, wanted them to do, Nixon might just be crazy enough to nuke them. That this was not entirely a ruse is suggested by the historically-documented fact that during Nixon's "final daze" of Watergate-induced inebriation, the keys to America's nuclear arsenal were removed from Nixon's grasp at the instigation of Henry Kissinger.

One-upping the rational calculations of Kissinger's madman theory, the neocons have given us a whole new postmodern strategy of insanity by not just *pretending* to be mad. They really are crazy—and they know it! Richard Pearle revels in the nickname "the Prince of Darkness" as the whole sick neocon crew revels in sex-torture gulags, unprovoked invasions of other nations, a fiscal policy so spendthrift as to be far beyond the bounds of reason, and plans for pre-emptive nuclear strikes. When Colin Powell called them "f*ing crazies" they undoubtedly took it as a compliment.

Perhaps the neocons took their cue from the failure of Kissinger's version of the madman theory. The North Vietnamese had gambled on the probability that the Americans weren't really crazy enough to perpetrate a crime of that magnitude, for no particular geo-strategic reason. The neocons, already half-crazed by the delirious theories of Leo Strauss and hours spent contemplating 1001 flavors of Armageddon, reasoned (if that word may be employed) that the whole problem was that the American leadership during the Vietnam era was *not* crazy. If the top leadership had been truly psychotic, they COULD and WOULD have nuked North Vietnam. After that, NOBODY would have messed with us! A nation with a preponderance of military power and a certifiably insane leadership could easily rule the world!!!!!! Bwa-ha-ha!!!!!!!!!! Intoxicated by their plans, they drafted an unstable dry-drunk and ex-cokehead to play the role of drooling-idiot-in-chief, and set in motion the 9/11 operation, which was designed to drive the American people insane so they would accept insane leadership.

Their mad scheme was quite clever (bwa-ha-ha) in that the 9/11 operation produced massive cognitive dissonance—an irresolvable contradiction between two self-evident, unquestionable truths:

1) Top US officials would never do something so awful; and

2) Overwhelming evidence shows that they *did* do it.

Cognitive dissonance renders people helpless. Even rats in a maze, faced with a blatant contradiction in their perceived reality, simply give up and melt into quivering blobs of furry jelly. The effect is much more powerful in humans. Cognitive dissonance renders people utterly helpless, totally susceptible to manipulation from above. The shocking images of the Twin Towers being blown up jolted us into a state of extreme susceptibility—just as psychic shock is used in cult initiations and other rituals that destroy previously-established identities in order to blast open a space for a new identity. If you want to brainwash someone, first shock them in order to destroy their previous world; then program them, with emotionally-compelling repetition, to accept the new world you are creating for them. That is what was done to us on September 11th, 2001: The shocking images of the exploding Towers were followed by incessant repetitions of pre-concocted propaganda drilling us that this was a new Pearl Harbor, that Arab Muslims had done it, that Palestinians were celebrating the attacks (a lie—the footage had nothing to do with 9/11, but was stock footage of a martyr's funeral conveniently provided to the networks by Israel), and on, and on, and on.

"But surely a plot so complex would have left evidence—surely there would be at least one whistleblower," whine those who are still desperately clinging to their illusions. And they are right. The evidence is overwhelming—so overwhelming it would take volumes to even summarize. David Griffin, in the afterword to the second edition of *The New Pearl Harbor*, offers 40 smoking guns, any one of which, if it is what it appears, is enough to prove that 9/11 was an inside job. If anything, Griffin understated the case here, as he himself has come to admit that the "inside job" thesis is no longer just probable, it is an absolute certainty—an inevitable conclusion from ironclad evidence. And whistleblowers? A whole army of whistleblowers has come forward, from the FBI agents like Robert Wright who told David Schippers about the date and target of the attacks *months* in advance and said they were bullied into silence, to Randy Glass, Sibel Edmunds, Colleen Rowley, Delmart Vreeland, the 6-billion-dollar insurance fraudster and self-confessed demolisher of WTC-7 Larry Silverstein, the Cheney-alibi-shredders Richard Clarke and Norman Mineta, the Wall Street Journal sources who leaked the story of the CIA-ISI $100,000 payoff to Mohammed Atta, the many associates of the non-Muslim non-hijackers in Florida, the top CIA officials who have openly called 9/11 "an intelligence triumph" that was "good, positive, extraordinary," and on and on and on.

Some of the evidence proving 9/11 was an inside job may have been planted, including the cognitive-dissonance-inducing contradictory evidence about the Pentagon strike; much of it presumably emerged accidentally, through the very complexity of the operation. But the point of allowing evidence to emerge at all was precisely to create cognitive dissonance, and imbue Americans with a powerful imprint of learned helplessness. Being forced to accept something as true that you consciously or unconsciously know is not true makes you utterly helpless, passive and manipulable, as Orwell and the behaviorists knew all too well.

Learned helplessness leaves us completely unable to deal with reality, with the actual environment that surrounds us. It is a form of insanity. The neocon madmen know this, and they openly mock those who are still sane enough to try to deal with reality. That's just reality-based politics, they cackle. We're an empire now, we create our own reality, bwa-ha-ha!

But reality has a way of re-imposing itself. Treason trials are coming, and only time will tell whether the insanity defense will save the neocons from the scaffold. Odds are that it won't. When they are hanged by their necks and buried beside Benedict Arnold, their epitaphs will sum up the careers of those who tried to turn the madman theory into a reality:

"Be very careful what you pretend to be, because one day you may wake up and discover that it is what you are." –Kurt Vonnegut, Jr.

"Conspiracy Theorist" Asserts:
Bush and Cheney are Death Lizards from Outer Space!!!

Now it can be told: Bush and Cheney are not human beings at all, but death lizards from outer space.

I realize that this is a bold assertion, and that it will probably elicit a degree of skepticism. Nonetheless I think this is a time for bold assertions. Our planet, after all, is under attack by extraterrestrial death lizards, and they have taken over the White House. So this is no time for cautious, measured statements and appeals to pure sweet reason.

This I know from hard experience. I have been championing the cautious, measured statements and appeals to pure sweet reason of the likes of David Griffin and Nafeez Ahmed for almost two years. Before I get into the alien death lizards angle, I guess I had better explain who Griffin and Ahmed are, for the benefit of those who have spent the past two years on the Planet of the Death Lizards, or on the even more distant and desolate planet of the American corporate media. David Griffin is one of America's most eminent Christian theologians, and he has recently published two books marshalling the abundant evidence that 9/11 was an inside job: *The New Pearl Harbor: Disturbing Questions about the Bush Administration and 9/11*, and *The 9/11 Commission Report: Omissions and Distortions*. Nafeez Ahmed is the brilliant young British scholar whose pathbreaking *The War on Freedom* convinced Gore Vidal that 9/11 was an inside job, and became Griffin's most important source for *The New Pearl Harbor*. Ahmed's new book *The War on Truth* goes on to show, with its formidable scholarly apparatus, that the whole specter of "Islamic Terrorism" is an illusion woven by Western intelligence agencies and their client-state proxies—the same conclusion reached by the recent BBC documentary *The Power of Nightmares* .

Griffin and Ahmed show, in clear, measured, scholarly fashion, that the official "19 hijackers" conspiracy theory of 9/11 is untenable, and that the alternative explanation that best fits the facts is that 9/11 was arranged by elements of the US intelligence apparatus, presumably acting at the behest of the US high command—namely George W. Bush and Richard Cheney. The presumable motive: To double the military budget overnight, increase the power of the executive branch, quash domestic dissent, and launch "the war that will not end in our lifetimes."

After two years of promoting the books of Griffin and Ahmed, I have discovered that there is a limited audience for a rational, factual discussion of 9/11. Even those who accept the fairly obvious conclusion that 9/11 was an inside job often seem to prefer a more excited and imaginative prose style. As for those who do not accept that conclusion —in virtually all cases due to an emotionally-charged refusal to consider the evidence—they are addicted to an even more hysterical prose style driven by the paranoid delusion that a secret army of evil "Muslim extremists" is conspiring to wreak mayhem by randomly blowing things up.

The lesson here is that paranoid hysteria sells, while lucid reality-based analysis does not. Since I have a living to make, and children to feed, I have decided to leave reality-based conspiracy theory behind, and strike out boldly where no theorist has gone before: to the planet of the spacefaring death lizards.

But wait a moment, you ask. Just how do I know that Bush and Cheney are death lizards in disguise?

Because my wife says so, that's why. She has been telling me for years that George W. Bush is obviously an alien. His awkward artificial mannerisms, his peculiar mangling of the English language, his emotional insensitivity that borders on utter cluelessness—these are all signs, my wife says, that this guy does not possess a brain with the normal Chomskyan linguistic deep structure, not to mention the emotional-intelligence deep structure, common to all human beings. Instead, he seems vaguely reptilian—cruel, scaly and manipulative behind those dull, beady little eyes.

For years—I admit it—I did not listen to my wife. Indeed, I scoffed at her whenever she pointed out Bush's nonhuman characteristics. I told her that Bush was just a deeply disturbed, borderline-psychopathic rich kid in the throes of a really bad dry-drunk syndrome made worse by coke withdrawal. "No—he's an alien" was her invariable reply. For years neither one of us could convince the other. Then last year, during Bush's first debate with John Kerry, I watched in horror as the Lizard-in-Chief's left lower lip drooped halfway to the floor, twitching convulsively as the mannikin uttered clumsily alien words beamed through a highly visible remote control unit on its back. After witnessing that bizarre perform-ance I could no longer deny it. Something was terribly the matter with the alleged humanoid in the Oval Office.

Then, while watching Cheney debate Edwards, I noticed that that the "Vice President" displayed some of the same non-human characteristics. Cheney's left lower lip corner, like Bush's, kept drooping downward and twitching spastically as cold, scaly, programmed words were emitted from the Cheney-creature's buccal orifice. Every pore of its body urged icy aggression; if it were capable of anything resembling emotion, it would be sheer contempt. Not the faintest shred of human warmth could be detected in its words, gestures, or bearing.

Suddenly it hit me: These guys were pursuing inhuman policies... because they were inhuman! My wife was right! (Not, she reminded me, for the first time.)

Only inhuman death lizards would spread death and destruction across the planet the way these guys have. Only inhuman death lizards would systematically loot and pillage the meager resources of ordinary Americans for the benefit of the super-rich. Only inhuman death lizards would dare destroy the US Constitution from within. Only inhuman death lizards would slaughter almost 3,000 Americans in a fake terrorist attack designed to trigger religious hatred and mass murder.

After doing some quick research on the intergalactic internet, I discovered that the death lizards have a long and sorry history of wreaking havoc, both on their own planet and on those of other sentient life forms. They are cold, clever, aggressive, and exceedingly manipulative. Though unable to effectively communicate with warm, emotional, empathetic/intuitive mammalian creatures like ourselves, they have learned to manipulate us by mimicking our linguistic-emotional behavior. To this end they have entered into a symbiotic relationship with the venomous slime-toads of Wartron-B, who emit a viscous verbal miasma that paralyzes, hypnotizes, and finally devours the brains of its mammalian victims. ("Karl Rove" is in fact one of these venomous slime-toads.)

So that's what we're up against. It isn't a pretty picture. But the good news is that they can be beaten. The most beautiful love-and-gnosis-driven planets of the Intergalactic Federation have all survived the onslaught of the death lizards and slime-toads. How? By uniting as one planet under the stewardship of the local sentient species. The arrival of the death-lizards and slime-toads, like the coming of the devilish-looking aliens in Arthur C. Clarke's *Childhood's End*, signals that a new era has dawned, and the planet's final exam is at hand. It is time for human beings to unite as one sentient species, the divinely-appointed stewards of planet Earth, and drive these scaly imposters out of the White House and back to the reptile-planet from whence they came.

Physics prof calls 9/11 conspiracist 'fruitcake'— fruitcake talks back!

www.infowars.com/articles/sept11/physics_prof_calls_911_conspiracist_fruitcake.htm

University of Wisconsin Professor M.F. Orwellian's argument that colleague Dr. Kevin Barrett is a "fruitcake," and that only those with physics Ph.D.s are qualified to judge anything involving the laws of physics, was subjected to a calm, thoughtful, scholarly refutation by Dr. Barrett yesterday.

Dr. Barrett began by lucidly laying out the premise and conclusion of his argument: "Professor Orwellian is a wingbat, a dingnut, a moonboot—which is to say, an utter and complete imbecile with the malignant growth on his neck that passes for his head firmly implanted in his hindmost nether-regions. Even Steve Nass, the man with one N too many, whom I have cheerfully described as a moonbutt, does not have a head as empty, as putrid, and as deeply ensconced in his own posterior, as does my esteemed colleague the good Doctor Orwellian." Barrett then politely refused to speculate about what Professor Orwellian's initials might stand for.

Judging that Professor Orwellian's "fruitcake" argument had thus been convincingly refuted, Dr. Barrett moved on to examine the assertions on which that argument was based. Dr. Barrett began with Professor Orwellian's claim that Dr. Barrett is unqualified to teach a Religious Studies course on Islam because he is a Muslim. "The idea that professing a particular religion or religious position makes one unqualified to teach Religious Studies courses will be news to every single member of the American academy besides Dr. Orwellian," Barrett pointed out. "Everybody who teaches religious studies has *some* religious position—be it atheism, agnosticism, or affiliation with a major or minor religious tradition. Likewise, philosophy teachers have their own philosophy. The idea that an atheist existentialist could not teach existentialism, an atheistic philosophy, because he or she happened to be an atheist and existentialist, is too ridiculous to contemplate. And the idea that we should fire almost the whole Jewish Studies department because most of its members are Jewish—or the African-American Studies program because most of its members are African-American—is insane. Obviously the good Professor has taken leave of his senses."

Dr. Barrett next took up Professor Orwellian's implicit claim that nobody without a Ph.D. in physics is competent to judge anything involving the laws of physics. Dr. Barrett—citing Samuel Johnson, who

had refuted Bishop Berkeley's idealist position by kicking a stone—
replied to Professor Orwellian's "physicists-only" argument by intoning
"I refute it thus" and kicking Professor Orwellian sharply in the latter's
gluteus maximus. "According to the law of angular momentum," Dr.
Barrett pontificated, "my foot just described nearly one-quarter of a
complete arc around a fixed reference point in the general location of my
hip joint. And according to the law of conservation of momentum, it
would have tended to continue in that direction unless acted upon by an
outside force—in this case, the soft, flabby hindquarters of Professor
Orwellian. But you don't really need to know that to understand that I
have just kicked him in the ass."

Barrett then proceeded to take issue with Professor Orwellian's
professional qualifications. "Professor Orwellian apparently believes that
the large amounts of molten steel produced by the WTC collapses,
documented in photographs, videos, and eyewitness accounts of 'rivers
of molten steel' in the rubble, were produced by fires whose only fuel
was hydrocarbons—namely, jet fuel, which is kerosene, and office
materials such as paper, wood, plastic, and so on. Yet the melting point
of steel is universally agreed to be in the neighborhood of 2800 degrees
f., while hydrocarbon fires cannot exceed 1800 degrees f. even under
laboratory conditions. Professor Orwellian is one thousand degrees short
of a full melting point. I demand that he resign from his physics post
forthwith, and return to his true calling, which is autoproctology."

The courteous scholarly debate between Dr. Barrett and Professor
Orwellian elicited a decorous ripple of applause from Academic Senate
members.

~~~~~

Physics prof calls 9/11 conspiracist 'fruitcake'

'Since he can't evaluate the evidence presented, he shouldn't have an
opinion'

World Net Daily, September 6, 2006,
http://www.worldnetdaily.com/news/article.asp?ARTICLE_ID=51858

The September issue of Whistleblower magazine takes an objective
look at the "9/11 truth movement" and alternate 9/11 theories, and is
titled "9/11: FIVE YEARS LATER, A TIME FOR TRUTH."

A University of Wisconsin professor who works with 9-11 conspiracist
Kevin Barrett says he's a "fruitcake" who is too biased in favor of Islam
to teach a class on the subject.

Barrett, a Muslim convert, was recently cleared by the college to teach a course this fall titled, "Islam: Religion and Culture." Like many Muslims, he contends the 9-11 attacks were an "inside job" carried out by Bush administration officials and not Islamic terrorists.

Specifically, Barrett argues Bush officials rigged the World Trade Center with incendiary devices to bring it down and start a war against Islam.

"He's a fruitcake," says Marshall F. Onellion, a physics professor at the University of Wisconsin. "He has no education in any engineering or science area pertinent to how, or whether, buildings fall down when hit by airplanes. Since he can't evaluate the evidence presented, he shouldn't have an opinion" that will influence students.

The National Institute of Standards and Technology recently released a report on the WTC collapse that rules out such conspiracy theories about the use of controlled demolitions. It concluded the collapse resulted from structural damage to the buildings caused by the impact from the two Boeing 767 jetliners hijacked by Muslim terrorists.

The unusually large amounts of jet fuel from the planes ignited multi-floor fires reaching temperatures as high as 1,000 degrees, and significantly weakened the floors and columns "to the point where floors sagged and pulled inward on the perimeter columns," the report said. "This led to the inward bowing of the columns and failure of the south face of the WTC 1 and the east face of WTC 2, initiating the collapse of each of the towers."

The independent 9-11 commission also concluded after some 1,200 interviews that Muslim hijackers were to blame.

But Barrett, who heads a group called "Scholars for 9/11 Truth," speculates that pro-Israeli neoconservatives led by Vice President Dick Cheney toppled the Twin Towers with secretly planted explosives or incendiary devices such as thermite rods. It's a popular theory in the Muslim community. The anti-Bush left has also embraced it.

Barrett, who converted to Islam 13 years ago, teaches a course on Islam that critics say whitewashes the 1400-year history of jihad against the West.

His Wisconsin colleague Onellion says Barrett is not qualified to teach the course because his doctorate is in Arabic studies, not Islamic studies. And as a Muslim activist with an ax to grind against the U.S. government, he says he is incapable of teaching the course objectively.

"I simply do not believe that an adult convert to Islam is capable of objectively teaching, or objectively grading, a course on his religion," he told WorldNetDaily. "Never would such a person be objective."

University officials, however, are persuaded that Barrett can teach Islam objectively.

In a July letter to Barrett, Wisconsin provost Patrick Farrell wrote, "I have accepted your assurance that you could control your enthusiasm for your personal viewpoints on the topic of 9-11 and present them in class in an objective and balanced time frame and context."

Onellion, who is co-authoring a book on science and religion called, "Seeking Truth: Living with Doubt," says about half the members of a Wisconsin faculty group for academic freedom sided with the decision to keep Barrett on staff and let him teach the controversial course. The other half disagreed with the decision.

~~~~~

FALSE FLAG PHYSICS

The photograph below is an exhibit in a paper by physics professor Steven Jones of BYU at http://9eleven.info/911JonesPaperhtm7.htm. In color it shows a chunk of red-hot metal dug out of the smoking North Tower rubble – about 8 weeks after 9-11! Molten metal was also reported by *The Structural Engineer*. It appears that thermite, an incendiary agent which burns steel, was used to cut steel columns. Such underground pools of molten metal are unique to the three WTC demolitions of 9/11.

Lavatory-Mirror Terror Plot Exposed!

Bush, Blair Save Civilization from Mirror-Dismantling Muslim Extremists

by Kevin Barrett, http://mujca.com

"One of the most bizarre events in the U.S. occurred on a Continental Airlines flight from Corpus Christi, Texas to Bakersfield, California.

"When staff discovered that the lavatory mirror had been removed, the plane rerouted and landed in El Paso, where passengers were questioned. The questioning yielded no results."

www.zaman.com, 27 August, 2006

A plot to wreak havoc by removing lavatory mirrors from jetliners has been derailed by a joint US-UK task force.

Nineteen Muslims have been arrested in what a source close to the investigation called "a terror plot that would have mirrored the events of 9/11, only on a much larger scale — you know, like those carnival funhouse mirrors that make you look like you weigh 300 pounds." [The source added that the use of such a mirror could explain various anomalies in the "Fatty Bin Laden confession video" of December, 2001, including the impression that the "Bin Laden" in that video is actually a fat guy who looks sort of like him, and that the video shows Fatty Bin Laden writing notes with his right hand, while the FBI's description of Osama Bin Laden indicates he is left-handed. (http://www.whatreallyhappened.com/osamatape.html)]

Had their terror plot come to fruition, the 19 Muslim "suicide mirror-jackers" would have simultaneously removed lavatory mirrors on 19 American cross-country flights, replacing them with Fatty-Bin-Laden-style funhouse mirrors. Passengers subsequently using the restrooms would have been terrorized—with many dying of heart attacks—by the image of themselves looking overweight.

The 19 Muslim mirror-jackers would have then returned to their seats with the mirrors. Having cleverly reserved window seats, they would then use their mirrors to reflect focused sunlight on the little people and cars down on the ground. Michael Cherkoff of the Department of Homeland Security explained: "You know how nasty little kids sometimes use magnifying glasses to focus sunlight on ants and broil them? Well, that's exactly what these Islamo-fascists were going to do to us. Everybody knows that when you're up in the air, the people down on the ground look like ants. That makes them vulnerable to being broiled like ants by Muslims with jetliner lavatory mirrors."

As news of the mirror-attacks spread around the planes, the Muslim extremists would have turned their mirrors on the terrified passengers, forcing them to see themselves as they really are — the most despicably craven, pathetically gullible flock of sheeple imaginable, ultra-cowardly morons who fell for the grotesquely obvious 9/11 hoax and the almost equally-obvious terror-hoaxes that have followed. The shame of seeing themselves as they really are would have killed every single passenger and crew member, and the planes would have plummeted directly to earth, leaving no wreckage and no black boxes, as is customary for jetliners destroyed by "Islamo-fascist suicide hijackers."

In a brief videotaped message from his cave in Afghanistan, Osama Bin Laden offered the following cryptic Qur'an citation:

"So tell the story. Perhaps they will reflect."

Is that why some folks say 9/11 was all done with smoke and mirrors!

* * *

US Terror Paranoia Taking Comic Proportions

By Foreign News Desk

Sunday, August 27, 2006

zaman.com

http://www.zaman.com/2006/08/27/american_b.jpg

The rise in terrorism paranoia that reignited following the "second 9/11 plan" claimed to have been targeted against Britain has reached comic proportions.

Pronunciation of the word "bomb" in American airports can lead to arrest and flight delays. Different versions of this paranoia have created a "comedy-like terror panic," which delayed seven U.S.-bound flights in just one day.

Another plane was forced to land after it was discovered that the mirror in one of the lavatories was not properly secured, and in another event, passengers were made to wait in an airport for hours because of the panic caused by a screaming child that refused to get on a plane.

A false bomb threat forced another plane to land urgently and the discovery of an unclaimed knife in an empty seat caused "terror paranoia" on another flight.

* * *

Continuing to indulge our peculiar brand of toilet humor… in August 2006 we were treated to the liquid bomb terror hoax, in which Muslims were accused of planning to blow up airliners with liquid explosives, which they would carry on board and mix in the laboratory – er, lavoratory. The Homeland's guardians of public safety duly confiscated mountains of water bottles, lipstick and the like from the flying folk of America, whose babies went without their milk bottles, to form a more perfect reign of terror. What a bawl!

I asked a PhD in chemistry about it, and he obliged:

" … TATP is made from hydrogen peroxide solution, acetone and sulfuric acid. The reaction … is best done with concentrated solutions of both peroxide and acetone… the acid must be added, a drop at a time, to the solution, all the while continuously stirring it and keeping it continuously chilled. This step of the process will take several hours, during which the fumes given off will be substantial and quite overpowering, thus a lab-quality air evacuation system is required.

One then must let the resulting solution stand for an extended period at temperatures above the freezing point, but definitely below 10 Celsius (50 Fahrenheit). Above 10 Celsius, the TATP does not form; instead, diperoxide forms, which is so unstable it cannot be worked with. The time required for the reaction to go to completion is at least 24 hours and often several days. … Once the TATP forms, it crystallizes as snowflakes from the solution and must be harvested by filtration and the liquid discarded. The TATP then is dried and carefully stored until needed. It must be stored below 10 Celsius or it converts spontaneously to the unstable diperoxide. etc. etc."

How do they do it? Damn clever, these terrorists! They snowed us again!

D. Readings: Stones the Builder Rejected

For the most part I have not reviewed the best-known books about 9/11—those by Griffin, Ahmed, Tarpley, Meyssan, Chossudovsky, Ruppert, Thompson, Marrs, Zwicker, and so on. These readings are labors of love for books that I'm afraid may be underappreciated. In the case of Rushkoff's *Coercion*, I was concerned that its bearing on 9/11 might, in the absence of my review, have gone unnoticed.

The Broeckers Conspiracy

Mathias Broeckers, *Conspiracies, Conspiracy Theories, and the Secrets of 9/11* (Joshua Tree, CA: Progressive Press, 2006)

Am I a crazy conspiracy theorist or a sane 9/11 truth activist?

That's the question I raised in my introduction. If you started reading this book with a curious and open mind and a willingness to learn, without a firm preconception about my sanity or lack of it, that proves that one of us is unusually sane... namely YOU.

Some people have already made up their mind: Anybody who thinks insiders were behind the assassinations of JFK, MLK, RFK and Malcolm X, or complicit in the Pearl Harbor or 9/11 disasters, is a "crazy conspiracy theorist," and whatever evidence such people offer to support their assertions is not even worth looking at. Most of these folks suffer massive anxiety attacks whenever anyone brings up topics like 9/11 truth. Some of these people are highly intelligent, at least when they are dealing with other subjects. Consider Noam Chomsky, whose neurotic anti-conspiracy hysteria is brilliantly analyzed by Barrie Zwicker.[65] Others are knuckle-dragging boneheads, like my own bête noire, Wisconsin Representative Steve Nass, who has made a career out of attacking his state's world-class university because he is far too stupid to understand anything that goes on there. In the end, Chomsky's superiority complex, and Nass's inferiority complex, find common ground in their shared anti-conspiracy-theory paranoia.

Others have made up their mind in the opposite direction: An evil group of insiders is behind all of these crimes and more... in fact, they're behind just about every evil there is. THEY are behind AIDS. They're behind every major war. They created the Nazis and the Communists. They're suppressing clean, abundant energy technologies. They're behind the UFO cover-up. They shot down Buddy Holly's plane on the day the music died, murdered John Lennon two decades later, and took out Lynard Skynard just to be on the safe side. They've cloned Hitler in a lab somewhere in Paraguay, and those Hitler clones are holding Elvis in cryogenic suspension.

Oddly, the folks who have made up their mind that it's all one big conspiracy can't seem to agree on who the conspirators are. Is it the Illuminati? The bankers? The Jesuits? Skull and Bones? The Chinese? The Council on Foreign Relations? The Trilateral Commission? An "Elders of Zion" style Jewish elite? "Rat-line" Nazis who infiltrated the CIA? Extraterrestrials who consider humans their cattle?

To some of these folks, anybody who doesn't believe in the same villain they believe in... must be part of the conspiracy!

One thing the crazy conspiracy theorists and the equally crazy anti-conspiracy-theorists share is absolute certainty. Chomsky KNOWS 9/11 was not an inside job—and he also KNOWS that even if it was, that would not be important—so he KNOWS that anybody who thinks the question is important is crippling the left—which means they're probably working for the CIA! Chomsky's breathless leaps of paranoid logic aren't very different from thinking Elvis is a Nazi death lizard from outer space.

If you or someone you love is suffering from the Noam's Syndrome, Mathias Broeckers has the diagnosis—and maybe the cure. In *Conspiracies, Conspiracy Theories and the Secrets of 9/11*, Broeckers unpacks 9/11 by way of a great quote from William S. Burroughs: "A paranoiac already knows all the facts." Starting on 9/13/01, Broekkers' columns in Germany's biggest alternative paper, *TAZ*, provided eloquent testimony to the only fact that was 100% certain: the fact that the facts weren't in yet. Broekkers, who had been analyzing the paranoid-conspiracy-theory mentality when 9/11 hit, immediately recognized that the "19 hijackers led by a guy on dialysis in a cave in Afghanistan" official conspiracy theory was just that—a conspiracy theory—until sufficient facts arrived to back it up. As the days, weeks, months, and years went by, he became more and more acutely aware that there were no reliable facts whatsoever in support of the "19 hijackers" legend, and a growing mountain of facts disproving it. Yet most people seemed to accept the legend despite its complete lack of connection with empirical reality.

Broeckers' book is a primer on sanity, if sanity is defined as the ability to think clearly and rigorously without benefit of certainty. Imagining that we already know all the facts, and shutting off our minds to new facts, is a kind of madness; yet because we find it difficult to act confidently and decisively in the absence of certainty, we often prematurely close our minds, clinging ferociously to a preconceived paradigm even in the teeth of overwhelming evidence against it.

This tendency is especially noticeable during the chaos that follows catastrophe, as Broeckers presciently noted on 9/29/01: "In times of crisis, simple solutions are in demand, and nothing works better than a good conspiracy theory, a clear image of the enemy. The vague biographies of the terror pilots are currently a bit disappointing in this respect. The only truly promising lead to the real masterminds would seem to lie on the trail of the stock market speculation before the attacks"(p. 78). Since that trail led straight to the den of the CIA and its Wall Street drug-money launderers, its complexities lost out to the simplistic myth of the 19 villains led by super-villain Osama. In 2004 the *9/11 Commission Report*, in one of its many Marx Brothers moments, claimed that the stock market speculation was all traced to a "single institutional investor" and that we should just forget about it, since this investor had no link to al-Qaida. Given this evidence that a large institutional investor, rather than al-Qaida, was behind the 9/11 attacks, one would think that the *9/11 Commission Report* would have followed up. Instead, it let the matter drop, refusing to even tell us who the investor was. After all, the *9/11 Commission Report* had no interest in finding out who financed 9/11: "To date, the U.S. government has not been able to determine the origin of the money used for the 9/11 attacks. Ultimately the question is of little practical significance."[66]

When chaos threatens to overwhelm the mind, the first simple explanation offered by a parent surrogate or authority figure is likely to be accepted, even fervently embraced. That, as you will recall, is the secret of coercion, the mind-control technique discussed in an earlier chapter. Allowing oneself to be coerced is to give up one's psychic autonomy. When an authority figure coerces us into hating a perceived external enemy, as Hitler convinced Germans to hate Jews, or as the Zio-extremist neoconservatives have coerced Americans into hating Muslims, those who succumb lose not only their autonomy, but their very sanity. They become paranoid conspiracy theorists dedicated to defending the homeland against the dusky Semites, those barbarians who are already inside the gates. Sick comic-book stereotypes about Jews mistreating women (by sexually degrading them) or Muslims mistreating women (by oppressing and veiling them) are driven home by media propaganda, triggering the sexualized blood lust of Dachau or Abu Ghraib.

If that is what madness looks like, Broeckers offers an interesting vision of sanity: Not saintly love or idealistic pacifism, but *rigorous uncertainty*. How can we think rigorously and yet allow for uncertainty? Broeckers suggests that a discipline of "critical conspirology" is necessary if we are to think sanely about such complex and uncertain events as the 9/11 attacks: "In this information age, conspiracies are to critical conspirology as 'dark matter' is to physics, with conspiracy theories resting on indications and theoretical models of the state and workings of the hidden substance."

If that sounds a bit paranoid—could there really be unknowns out there that we have to factor into our worldview?—consider how much more insane it is to *deny the existence of any unknowns*! Anyone who denies that anything he doesn't already know could possibly exist is asserting that he already knows everything that could possibly be known. Such people are the epistemological equivalent of the legion of lunatics who think they are world-bestriding Napoleons. I know a few of them personally, and have noticed that they tend to function quite well in academic institutions, which makes me think that those institutions bear a closer resemblance to the other kind than most of us are willing to admit. One such individual, a former colleague who now teaches history at Stanford, has repeatedly told me that alternative views of 9/11, JFK, and so on are absurd, because all secrets quickly leak out and thus historians know everything important that has ever happened. One of my responses to this kind of argument is, "What about Operation Northwoods, a 9/11-type fake terrorist attack the US military almost pulled off in 1962?[67] They kept it secret for 40 years, and the only reason we know about it is because McNamara violated security procedures and saved a copy of the documents." My friend's rejoinder: "Well, we know about it now, which proves that EVERYTHING leaks out!" But what if McNamara had joined everybody else in shredding the documents? That kind of hypothetical question means nothing to my friend. For him, reality is not reality, it is his own mental representation of reality. And there is no room for uncertainty in the mental map he carries in his head. Nothing could possibly exist if he doesn't already know it—a closed loop of thinking as circular as any conspiracy theory.

Despite his academic position, or maybe because of it, my friend's world view is profoundly primitive. Compared to his plumber or electrician who admits he doesn't know everything, my professor friend is an epistemological simpleton. He is like a mathematician who refuses to use concepts like the number zero or the unknown variable X. "But there's no such thing as nothing! Nothing is not a number! Everything is something! And what's this X? Either it's a particular number, or it isn't! If it is, then I want the number itself! If it isn't, then it doesn't exist!"

Broeckers has a remedy for such know-nothing know-it-alls: *conspirology*, "a sober methodology, an aid to perception of reality, a skeptical science. A conspirological criticism would have taken note of the permanent factor of conspiracy in living systems—that is, to investigate the role of conspiracy in the evolutionary dialectic of competition and cooperation. Such a critical discipline would have been tasked with defining structures and models in the amorphous underworld of the struggle for mutual advantage, and could perhaps develop litmus tests to check the reality of conspiracy theories" (p. 11). And the key to Broeckers' litmus test is to avoid premature closure, to maintain skepticism and uncertainty, despite the psychological pressures of top-down coercion and the follow-the-herd dynamic that governs all social systems. Thus to be sane is to inhabit "the no-man's-land between critical thought and pathological paranoia" (p. 45).

Striding bravely into that no-man's land, Broeckers, like the Zionist Islamophobe and arch-Orientalist Bernard Lewis, reads the 9/11 attacks in light of the myth of the Assassins, the supposedly hashish-crazed heretics who terrorized orthodox Muslims and Crusaders alike during the Middle Ages. The legend, spread by the Crusaders, was that the head Assassin, the Old Man of the Mountain Hassan i Sabbah, brainwashed his followers in the following manner: He would invite a novice into his pleasure garden, and turn him loose with wine, women and hashish until he passed out. When the novice awakened, Hassan explained that the garden was only a faint foretaste of the paradise that awaited him if he died in Hassan's service. If the novice believed that, he was given a job as a suicide warrior or sleeper agent. But if he said, "You're full of shit, Hassan!" the novice would be immediately promoted to the ranks of the elite, whose job was to formulate strategy, use and dispose of the warriors and sleepers, and generally run the show.

Bernard Lewis has long been fascinated by this myth, which he wrote about in *The Assassins: A Radical Sect in Islam.*[68] Why? Is this just another symptom of his obsession with casting Islam in a sinister, radical light? Or is it perhaps because Hassan and his elite are a parable for the neo-conservatism Lewis allies himself with—the bizarre philosophy of mega-Machiavellian Leo Strauss and such cult followers as Perle, Wolfowitz, Libby, and the rest of Bush's 9/11 war cabinet? As Shadia Drury reveals, Leo Strauss was a modern Hassan i Sabbah: "There is a certain irony in the fact that the chief guru of the (Christian-fundamentalist-loving) neoconservatives is a thinker who regarded religion merely as a political tool intended for the masses but not for the superior few. Leo Strauss, the German Jewish émigré who taught at the University of Chicago almost until his death in 1973, did not dissent from Marx's view that religion is the opium of the people; but he believed that the people need their opium. He therefore taught that those in power must invent noble lies and pious frauds to keep the people in the stupor for which they are supremely fit."[69]

Broeckers notes that according to the official theory of 9/11, the Assassins are back: "Without their 900-year-old human-disdaining version of the God conspiracy theory—the teaching that death in the battle against the enemies of God gives direct access to the eternal VIP lounge of paradise—the bin Laden theory of 9/11 would not be possible" (p. 85). Interestingly, the Bin Laden theory derives, in large part, from Assassinologist Lewis, American academia's prime purveyor of Islamophobic myths, who was invited to the White House immediately after 9/11: "Cheney (Snowcroft said) appeared to have been taken with a presentation by Bernard Lewis, an octogenarian Middle East scholar from Princeton University, who had been invited to the White House soon after the Sep. 11, 2001 attacks. According to Scowcroft, Lewis's message was, 'I believe that one of the things you've got to do to Arabs is hit them between the eyes with a big stick. They respect power.'"[70] Broeckers' gay science of conspiracy, as developed by Webster Tarpley, suggests that Lewis's myth of the Assassins could have inspired the psy-ops professionals—and the experts in the creation and maintenance of public myths—who scripted the 9/11 New Pearl Harbor.[71]

If there are indeed any modern day Assassins out there, Broeckers writes, they could be re-educated by inverting the brainwashing program of Hassan I. Sabbah: "So let's send the Taliban our sex bombs; let's pamper them with the gentlest, coziest, most delightful pleasures, sensations, sounds and smells; let's seduce them into using the wonderfully relaxing Afghan hashish. In short, every warrior of God who hands in his shooting iron to Uncle Sam will get a six-week holiday for starters in the paradisiacal 'Club de l'Assassin,' If further re-education should be necessary, it's only a matter of making clear that God is just a conspiracy theory for which there is no collectively accessible evidence. It can only be found individually, and due to the observer principle it is bound to vary so much that it makes no sense to beat each other about over the true God. 'Truth is the invention of a liar'" (p. 85). As it turned out, the Cheney Administration had no interest in re-educating the Taliban; they just wanted to murder Afghans, steal their land, and put in a highly profitable gas pipeline.

Broeckers saw through the nonsensical "19 hijackers" conspiracy theory faster than anyone. But his debunking of the "God conspiracy theory" sounds to me a lot like Hassan I. Sabbah whispering in Leo Strauss's ear: "Nothing is true. Everything is permitted." When I was young and naive I used to believe that. But now I'm older, wiser, and a lot less certain. Neurologists tell us that if the human brain were simple enough to be understandable, our brains would be far too simple to understand it. Likewise with God: The Creator of this almost infinitely complex cosmos must be even more complex, so the chances that a minuscule conscious fragment of that cosmos could fully understand such a Creator would seem rather remote.

Islam may claim to have the last word on God, but that last word is that God is an unknown variable, an X, an abiding *mysterium tremendum*. Islam is about peaceful self-submission to this God, this Reality, that we will never fully understand, about whom we are offered at most glimmering shards of hints, not prefabricated truths. Of the little that we know, most of it involves what God is not: God is not a father—glory be to him, that he could have sons!!—nor a petty tyrant. God is neither male nor female, nor even human-like... though to the few human beings who really achieve peaceful self-submission, God may become a kind of Friend.

I have already suggested that my title *Truth Jihad* is intentionally misleading. The real meaning of *jihad* is not fanatical warfare but struggle, and the truth I struggle for is not a pre-fabricated one. My truth jihad is first of all a struggle against the ready-made "truths" with which others deceive us, and with which we deceive ourselves.

This is not heresy; it is faith. The classical Islamic scholars used to present all of the defensible viewpoints, indicate which if any they found most persuasive and why, and finish with the caveat "But God knows best." That, and not the murderously comforting lies of a Machiavellian elite, is true religion.

The Broeckers conspiracy is a conspiracy to make you smarter. That, in itself, will not lead you to Islam. But it may help free you from any false certainty that the media stereotypes are right, or that Islam is stupid, simplistic, or necessarily wrong. (Likewise, if you are Muslim, it may free you from false certainties that other worldviews are necessarily wrong.)

As for me, I believe that God led me on an apparently pointless trip to New York, to that apparently random encounter with my future wife and our romance in the train tunnel under the World Trade Center just before the first bombing... in order to embroil me in a Pynchonesque plot that has yet to be resolved.

If God is a conspiracy theory, then call me a conspiracy theorist.

* * *

Sander Hicks' *The Big Wedding* (New York: Vox Pop 2005)

Since gonzo legend and 9/11 skeptic Hunter S. Thompson died, journalism hasn't been the same. These days, very few journalists have the guts to tell the truth, or the talent to tell it in searing, crackling prose. Few have the vision to seamlessly weld fearless truth-telling, an awareness of the loathsome absurdities of our current social arrangements, and sharp-edged yet entertaining writing into a work of literary art disguised as journalism.

Sander Hicks is an exception. Hicks is an artist as well as a first-rate journalist. He weaves together the stories of his 9/11 whistleblowers like Mozart weaving identifying music for opera characters. The result is a work of beauty united by a profound, almost Shakespearian insight into human nature in general, and the American mind-control system in particular: The stone that the builders rejected is the foundation upon which our castles of truth and illusion are built.

Hicks shows that his rogue's gallery of 9/11 whistleblowers has been ignored, and the truths they tell suppressed, on the basis of ad hominem attacks unleashed by the cover-up artists and picked up on by an uncritical and naïve media. That shouldn't surprise us; after all, the defenders of the official story have only one argument—the hurling of ad hominem insults against anybody who questions their demonstrably ludicrous narrative. But Hicks shows that the covert operators and cover-up specialists actually set the ad hominem mechanisms in place as part of their secrecy strategy. The spooks go out of their way to choose "flawed" individuals to carry out their operations. They hire contract operators with a skeleton in their closets—and when the skeletons don't already exist, they are manufactured. That way, if the operator should ever attempt to reveal compromising information, he can be easily discredited —and any journalist or media outlet that publicizes the information can be discredited as well. This strategy has for the most part totally silenced the media on such sensitive topics as W's history as a draft-dodger, then an AWOL cocaine arrestee, the CIA's continuing history as the planet's largest cocaine and heroin dealer, and of course the 9/11 covert operation mounted by the Bush crime family and its CIA drug empire partner, according to the instructions of PNAC-linked neocons, the intellectual authors of the 9/11 New Pearl Harbor.

Hicks begins his tale of rejected stones with Jim Hatfield, the unfortunate author of *Fortunate Son: George W. Bush and the Making of an American President*. Hatfield blew the whistle on Bush's 1972 cocaine arrest in his book, before both he and the cocaine arrest story were conveniently suicided and buried. It turns out that the controlled demolitions of both Hatfield and the Bush cocaine bust story were the work of none other than Karl Rove, Bush's slime-exuding Svengali of spin. In August of 1999, mainstream journalists were sniffing around the Bush coke bust story, which would have ended W's presidential aspirations had it been revealed in a credible way. Rove, in a sort of pre-emptive strike, proceeded to leak the story to Hatfield, who, as Rove and Bush's Texas team knew, had a criminal history dating back to his misspent youth—very much like W himself, except that Hatfield went straight, while Bush's crime career was still accelerating toward the acts of mass murder, high treason, human rights violations, and international aggression for which he is now infamous.

Hatfield published his book and was invited onto CBS's 60 Minutes on the false pretenses that his book would be the topic. There he was ambushed and destroyed, as the show focused on his own criminal history, not that of George W. Bush. St. Martin's Press recalled all 100,000 copies of Fortunate Son and burned them. "They're heat! They're furnace fodder!" crowed St. Martin's trade division president Sallie Richardson. Sander Hicks, reading Richardson's quote on page 14 of the New York Times, decided to protest the book-burning by publishing *Fortunate Son* under his own imprint. But although the book was well-researched and well-written, and the coke bust story was authenticated by none other than Rove, Bush's close friend Clay

Johnson, and Bush's minister James Mayfield, the media continued to abuse and/or ignore Jim Hatfield, whose death of a vodka-barbituates overdose in July, 2001 was ruled a suicide. Thanks to Rove's demolition of Hatfield, any mention of the Bush coke bust would be career suicide for mainstream journalists, who would be judged guilty by association, and subjected to the same kind of ad-hominem vituperation that destroyed Hatfield if they showed any interest in the story. By the irrational mechanism of ad-hominem attack and threat, the truth was rendered unspeakable—in much the same way that the truth of 9/11 has been rendered unspeakable by the mindless drumbeat of ad-hominem attacks on "conspiracy theorists."

After apostrophizing Hatfield in his intro, Hicks moves on to the next stone the builders rejected: ex-jewel-thief turned crack FBI informant Randy Glass, "the Jewish Joe Pesci." The smart, smooth-talking Glass was adept at posing as a big-time weapons dealer, and managed to set up various dicey-looking people who were looking for lethal weapons, up to and including WMDs. Among them was a Pakistani with ISI (hence CIA) connections named Rajaa Gulum Abbas. In 1999, Glass was dining with Abbas in Robert DeNiro's Tribeca Grill just north of the World Trade Center, when Abbas pointed out the window at the Twin Towers and said, "Those towers are coming down." During the following year, disturbed by further forewarnings of 9/11, Glass made inquiries among his FBI and ATF colleagues, one of whom directed him to an anti-terror player "in the loop," Francis X. "Frank" Taylor, ex-Air Force intelligence op and then State Department Assistant Secretary for Security who would be promoted to Coordinator of Counterrorism shortly before 9/11.

Glass called up Taylor in summer 2001 and decided to bluff him, saying "Listen, I already know about the World Trade Center." At that time, Glass did not know that the attack would involve airplanes. But his bluff elicited the following remark from Taylor: "Randy, listen, you can not mention any of these things, especially airplanes being used to fly into the World Trade Center." Taylor explained that the planes-into-WTC plot had to remain secret for geostrategic reasons, and added: "Look, Randy, we know you're a straight guy, so we're going to give you some information. You cannot do two things: You cannot go to the media under any circumstances. This is—we're playing in a nuclear minefield now. Secondly, you can't tell the agents that you're working with now because they're out of the loop. They know nothing" (p. 13).

Is Glass telling the truth? Or—as the endlessly-rehashed ad hominem argument against 9/11 truth would have it—is he just a smooth-talking con man, a guy with a criminal record? Hicks offers many reasons to accept the truth of Glass's testimony. For one thing, it is a matter of record that Glass repeatedly contacted the office of Florida Senator Bob Graham in the summer of 2001 in a failed attempt to stop the impending destruction of the Twin Towers. And Glass's former law enforcement colleagues vouch for his veracity. Even the mainstream media, including Dateline NBC, has found him credible—though thus far no mainstream outlet has seen fit to publish or broadcast his description of the conversation with Francis X. Taylor, who was promoted after 9/11 and remains in a high-level anti-terrorism job!

After the Glass material, Hicks takes a two-chapter detour through Daniel Hopsicker's revelations about the unsavory characters connected to Huffman Aviation, the CIA drug import airstrip and pseudo-flight-school in Venice, Florida where the so-called hijackers pretended to train. The chapters suggest that the CIA, in such criminal enterprises as drug dealing and terrorist attacks against its own country, employs such dubious characters as the boozing kitten-disemboweling cokehead Mohammed Atta and the sexual-harassment perp and apparent fraudster Rudi Dekkers as a deliberate strategy—nobody would believe such people if they ever decided to 'fess up, now, would they?

Hicks then moves on to his next stone the builders rejected, Delmart Vreeland, an insider who, like Glass, knew 9/11 was coming and tried to prevent it. Vreeland, whose letter describing the upcoming 9/11 attacks was written and sealed in a Canadian jail in summer 2001, is also the subject of a chapter in Ruppert's *Crossing the Rubicon*. Like Ruppert, Hicks concludes that Vreeland is for real—and that his odd behavior and criminal record are not signs that he did not work for US intelligence, but signs that he did. According to Hicks, Vreeland may be the product of an MK-Ultra style mind control program involving childhood sexual abuse and other techniques designed to produce programmable alternate personalities and a biography that allows the agent to be discredited if necessary.

Whether or not this is the case, it seems well-established that Vreeland was an intelligence agent who attempted to stop the 9/11 attacks and, frustrated by the non-response from US authorities, wrote and sealed a letter describing the upcoming attacks from a Canadian jail cell. The unsealing of that letter by Canadian authorities set off a colorful saga of dramatic courtroom calls and dead cats left on lawyers' porches. Hicks adds to the basic story, already well known by readers of Mike Ruppert, by getting to know Vreeland and discovering that he seems almost as bizarre and dicey as his story. Yet it is people with criminal records like Vreeland and Randy Glass, not the Bushes and Francis X. Taylors of the world, who had the heart to try to stop 9/11. Hicks aptly quotes Ruppert: "None of us are saints, but all of us have moments in which we try to do the right thing, and that's when we need to be supported. This is not over yet" (p. 73).

After meeting attempted-murder conspirator Jim Hatfield, jewel thief turned FBI snitch Randy Glass, and criminal-history-toting apparent pedophile Delmart Vreeland—all of whom made valiant attempts to prevent 9/11, and thus ought to be regarded as flawed but heroic figures—Hicks takes us to meet some truly insalubrious individuals: The members of the Zelikow-directed 9/11 Coverup Commission. Every member was deeply compromised.

Philip Zelikow is a member of Bush's shadow cabinet, an-ex-member of Bush's intelligence advisory board (i.e. a 9/11 suspect himself), a close associate of Condi Rice, and a member of a British-intelligence sponsored think tank, the International Institute for Strategic Studies. **Thomas Kean** is director for the oil giant Amerada Hess, meaning he is thick as thieves with the criminal BCCI/BushBoyz wing of the oil industry. **Lee Hamilton** had chaired the House Iran-Contra Committee and the October Surprise Task Force, choosing to keep Bush the elder out of jail in the teeth of the evidence, at the promptings of fellow Wyoming congressman Dick Cheney, because justice would not be "good for the country." **John Lehman**, a protégé of war criminal Henry Kissinger, covered up a Navy pedophilia scandal in 1982. **Bob Kerrey**, another noted war criminal who personally slaughtered unarmed women and children in Vietnam, is a card-carrying neocon and PNAC associate. In 1989, Kerrey covered up the Bush White House callboys scandal as part of his duties as Governor of Nebraska. **Richard Ben-Veniste**, Hicks points out, "has direct connections to murky underworld figures" and gained notoriety as the lawyer for CIA drug runner Barry Seal, who was machine-gunned to death at a stoplight in Baton Rouge. **Jamie Gorelick** works for the world's biggest drug-smuggling outfit, the CIA, where she is a member of the their National Security Advisory Panel; upon accepting her post with the 9/11 Coverup Commission, she was handed a plum job with the Washington Law Firm Wilmer, Cutler and Pickering, which was defending top Saudi officials against a lawsuit by

9/11 victims' families. **James Thompson** and **Slade Gorton**, like Ben-Veniste and Gorelick, are well-connected creatures of unsavory big law firms. **Fred Fielding** worked for Nixon, Reagan, and Bush, and is suspected of involvement in Watergate and Iran/Contra. After summing up the nefarious careers of this gallery of rogues, Hicks turns to **Timothy Roemer**, "the clean one. Sort of. Well certainly he's the young one." After the sudden departure of the one potentially honest member of the 9/11 Commission, Max Cleland, who huffed that he would not be part of another Warren Commission coverup and resigned to take a plum post offered by the Bush Administration, Roemer did look relatively clean—like a guy who's just spattered with mud while his colleagues are wallowing in pig manure. Hicks summarizes the work of this pathetic, criminally negligent commission: "The 9/11 Commission Report has topped the Warren Report... as the greatest cover-up of all time... God willing, a day is coming when the parties responsible will be tried in a high court" (p. 83).

Hicks actually goes to meet Ben-Veniste, taping a TV interview with him and asking a couple of real questions about 9/11 (a transcript is at sanderhicks.com). Ben Veniste loses it and calls him a whackjob. Once again, we see the ad-hominem attack principle at work: The slimiest, craziest, evilest people in the world perpetrate the greatest outrage in history—and proceed to defame the characters and reputations of anyone who dares to question them. Yet a loose association of brave individuals, collectively known as the 9/11 truth movement, has arisen to ask those hard questions, and brave the "tinfoil hat" jibes of the small cohort of perps and their brainwashed legions of drooling idiots. (If you haven't noticed, I'm employing the ad hominem tactic in reverse. If you want sweet reason, read David Griffin and Nafeez Ahmed.)

In his eighth chapter, Hicks surveys the 9/11 truth landscape and finds it good. His argument that the various "no planes" theories (a misnomer, since most of these theories merely cast doubt on the identity, not the existence, of the planes or plane-like objects that hit the WTC and the Pentagon) are a distraction, and that the 9/11 truth movement is often "dismissed by its most outlandish theory," is developed sensibly and convincingly. Hicks writes: "If there's one theory out there that is obviously false, the masses can be kept in intellectual submission, because the official story will represent safety, validation, and freedom from ridicule... the architects of disinformation take it for granted that people fear ridicule" (p. 107). Personally, I do not find the arguments against Flight 77 hitting the Pentagon "obviously false" nor do I fear ridicule for saying so; after two years of 9/11 activism I have grown a fairly thick skin. I think it is possible that technologies of deception were employed that generated apparently contradictory evidence, making the Pentagon event a sort of Rorschach inkblot designed to create true believers in both the truth and falsity of the official story and set them at odds with each other, generating a smokescreen of confusion.

I say 9/11 skeptics should unite—for unity is everything in this kind of movement—behind an "agreement to disagree" on Flight 77, and to cite the strongest, most intellectually and emotionally compelling evidence first, second, and last: The obvious controlled demolition of WTC Building 7, and the nationally-televised confession that it was "pulled" by insurance-fraudster Larry Silverstein, who made 6 billion dollars on his paltry two month investment in the newly-privatized World Trade Center. The growing national consciousness of the obvious demolition of Building 7 will bear out Hicks' optimistic message: "Once this 9/11 Truth movement works out a few kinks, it's going to be unstoppable" (p. 109).

After his upbeat assessment of the 9/11 Truth movement, Hicks delivers his weakest chapter, titled "Muslim Brotherhood, Team B, PNAC, and the New International Fascist Agenda." The problem is his lumping of the Muslim Brotherhood, a very broad-based group that represents the main democratic opposition to brutal dictatorships in Egypt and other countries, with the actual fascists, namely Team B and PNAC. As readers of Nafeez Ahmed's *The War on Truth* know, Western intelligence services sometimes cherry-pick vulnerable individuals with Islamist leanings for such bogus, false-flag terror groups as Al-Qaida. That does not mean, however, that the Islamist groups and movements are themselves fascist. On the contrary, they often represent a populist, democratic anti-fascist opposition to fascist governments. Fascism is defined as the merging of the corporations, the state, and the military into one all-powerful juggernaut organized on hierarchical lines, and ruling through deception and autocracy. That is an excellent description of the US system post-9/11, and a fairly accurate description of various Western-sponsored regimes in the Islamic world. Islamists usually represent the main domestic opposition to local and foreign fascism, and the vast majority of them work peacefully and gradually toward their goals, which involve a decentralized, religiously-based society.

Islamists oppose the banks and corporations, and generally want the state and the military to have less control over the lives of the people, which they believe should be organized on religious principles according to the dictates of individual believers and families first, and then the informal, non-coercive decisions of religious scholars; and finally, and only as a last resort, through state-sanctioned religious authority. Radical Islamists often want to overthrow or at least weaken the state, the corporations, and the military, which they view as the foreign impositions of Western colonizers, and return to a more decentralized, non-statist, religion-based form of social organization insofar as possible. In short, Islamism is more likely to be anti-fascist than fascist; indeed, it is the chief threat to the corporate-globalist New World Order, which is why the fascists at PNAC and Team B are using manipulated, false-flag terrorist attacks to discredit it. By obscuring that reality, and inadvertently lending support to the disinformation about "islamo-fascism," Hicks makes his only serious blunder. Thus in calling Bush's Homeland Security Chief Michael Chertoff "terror's defender" in a posited alliance of the neocons and the Muslim Brotherhood, Hicks takes it for granted that Chertoff's client, Bin Laden financier Dr. Magdy Elamir, was a real "Islamic terrorist." But as Nafeez Ahmed makes clear in *The War on Truth*, much if not all of Al-Qaeda is a front for Western intelligence agencies. Most of its leadership, including all the alleged key players in 9/11, sport grotesquely un-Islamic lifestyles and spy agency connections revealing them to be intelligence assets, not Islamists. No wonder Chertoff sprang "terrorist" Elamir from jail!

Despite his misconceptions about Islamism—an understandable confusion given the chaos of the times and the layers of deception that surround the subject—Hicks has produced a lively and perceptive work of journalism that doubles as a work of art. A suggestive character study revealing how flaws make us human (in the case of the whistleblowers) or inhuman (in the case of the perps and coverup team), Hicks' book urges us to overcome our fears and pursue the truth. In this his voice joins with the voices of the wisdom teachers of all ages and traditions, including the great Islamic truthtellers, the Sufi saints and pious jurists who spoke truth to power and thereby showed that they did not care about anyone's opinion except God's. If we are to speak 9/11 truth to power, we must overcome our worries about what others think of us, and speak the truth as we see it, whatever the consequences. Fears that our imperfections will be revealed, that speaking an unpopular opinion will unveil us as freaks, must be overcome. Many of today's Muslims, who so often huddle together like sheep for fear that wandering off from the herd means destruction, could take a lesson in real piety from the brave and devoted left-anarchist Catholic, Sander Hicks.

T.H. Meyer's Reality, Truth and Evil: *Facts, Questions, and Perspectives on September 11, 2001* (Temple Lodge 2005)

In *Reality, Truth and Evil*, T.H. Meyer offers a profound philosophical, historical and spiritual meditation on the meaning of the events of 9/11. Meyer's touchstone is the Pearl Harbor attack that catapulted the US into World War II, which he argues was set up by the Roosevelt administration. Meyer's book takes up where David Griffin's "New Pearl Harbor" metaphor leaves off, discussing the abundant evidence that the architects of the 9/11 attacks consciously crafted those attacks to create the kind of war-triggering psychic shock that, on December 7th, 1941, took a public that had been 80% antiwar and turned it into a bloodthirsty patriotic mob bent on racist revenge against that pernicious racial inferior, the "Jap"—a precursor to the demonized Arab/Muslim Other who, according the Bush Administration, may be tortured, sexually abused, murdered, kidnapped, or "disappeared" into secret CIA torture gulags for little reason beyond ethnicity and religion.

Was 9/11 designed using the Pearl Harbor template? In answering with a resounding "yes," Meyer covers the well-known quotes from National Security Advisor Brzezinski and the neocon Project for a New American Century showing that top US foreign policy strategists longed for a "New Pearl Harbor" during the run-up to 9/11. The 9/11 psych-war operation was prepared with the help of Hollywood, which cranked out a barrage of patriotic, militaristic, apocalyptic films to prepare the public for 9/11, including of course the blockbuster *Pearl Harbor*. (It would be interesting to see who got the idea to make that movie at this time, and got Disney to put up the $135 million it cost to make: http://www.hollywood.com/news/detail/id/311906.) Despite the fact that Roosevelt had perniciously slaughtered thousands of Americans on 12/7/41 to lie the nation into war, "All that mattered was that the myth should be effective amongst the populace, who had been reminded of it only a few months before the attacks by a sentimental Hollywood film. But to those in the know (i.e. those who had proper information about the facts [of the Pearl Harbor deception]) this official comparison actually *provided the real key to understanding the attacks of 2001*" (p. 5).

Meyer, like Griffin and others, points out that George W. Bush was reported to have penned an enigmatic diary entry on the evening of 9/11/01: "The Pearl Harbor of the 21st century took place today." Egged on by cues like these, the US corporate media endlessly compared the 9/11 attacks to the Japanese attack on Pearl Harbor. *Time* Magazine, in its special September, 2001 issue, resoundingly called for a response to 9/11 modeled on the US public's response to Pearl Harbor: "What's needed is a unified, unifying, Pearl Harbor sort of purple American fury—a ruthless indignation that doesn't leak away in a week or two."

Meyer goes beyond the above observations, cited earlier by Griffin and others, in calling attention to Donald Rumsfeld's bizarre Pearl-Harbor-propaganda campaign that had begun even before the Bush Administration took office. Rumsfeld spent 2000 and 2001 carrying around extra copies of Roberta Wohlstetter's *Pearl Harbor: Warning and Decision*, praising the book to the skies, and offering free copies to all and sundry. Wohlstetter's book, while it ostensibly supports the official myth that Pearl Harbor was a perfidious surprise attack, includes enough information to the contrary to enlighten the discerning reader to the unspeakable but implicitly acknowledged truth: The Roosevelt Administration provoked the attacks, knew they were coming, and left thousands of sailors in harm's way as an offering to the gods of war. Wohlstetter's book is a perfect illustration of neocon doublespeak: Tell a vivid, simplistic, emotionally-charged lie to the masses ("Perfidious surprise attack! Heroic purple-fury response!") yet include as a subtle subtext the unspeakable truth that only the elite are smart enough to discern and strong enough to handle: "Roosevelt sacrificed thousands of American lives to the greater good of getting the US into the war."

Rumsfeld wasn't the only 9/11 suspect hyping Wohlstetter's doublespeak. 9/11 Commissioner Timothy Roemer cited it at the Commission's very first public hearing: "It [Pearl Harbor—and by implication 9/11] was just a dramatic failure of a remarkably well-informed government to call the next enemy move in a Cold War crisis... Today it might be some of the same words. It wasn't a Cold War crisis and it wasn't the Japanese, but it was al Qaeda." Commission Chair Thomas Kean and his fellow Commissioner, CIA drug runner Barry Seal's lawyer Richard Ben-Veniste "also drew on this deceptive comparison with Pearl Harbor" (p. 7).

Meyer shows that FDR and his brain trust were not surprised or upset after Pearl Harbor, but—like the Bush Administration and the CIA after 9/11—reacted as if they were overjoyed and relieved. The Bush/CIA party commemorating (celebrating?) the 9/11 attacks was apparently a cheerful affair: "At CIA headquarters in Langley, Bush junior celebrated a kind of promotional party just two weeks after the attacks, assuring the assembled CIA officials (including their boss George Tenet): 'September

11th is a sad memory, but it's a memory... And I can't thank you enough on behalf of the American people'" (p. 24). The official White House website story (p. 57) has to be seen to be believed:

September 26ᵗʰ, 2001
President Thanks CIA
Remarks by the President to Employees of the CIA
Langley, Virginia
1:23 PM EDT

THE PRESIDENT: Thank you all very much. Well, George (Tenet), thank you very much, and thanks for inviting me back. (Laughter.) There is no question that I am in the hall of patriots, and I've come to say a couple of things to you. First, thank you for your hard work. You know, George and I have been spending a lot of quality time together. (Laughter.) There's a reason. I've got a lot of confidence in him, and I've got a lot of confidence in the CIA. (Applause.) And so should America.

Meyer is to be congratulated for calling attention to the Bush-CIA celebration of the 9/11 attacks. But that isn't the only evidence that Bush and top CIA officials were overjoyed, not disturbed, by 9/11. Griffin notes Rumsfeld's unseemly crowing and military-moneygrubbing on the evening of 9/11 itself (*The New Pearl Harbor*, 99-100). But it gets worse. The preface of veteran Middle East CIA agent Robert Baer's 2002 book *See No Evil* ends on an astonishing note: "The other day a reporter friend told me that one of the highest-ranking CIA officials had said to him, off the record, that when the dust finally clears, Americans will see that September 11 was a triumph for the intelligence community, not a failure." And in the October 6ᵗʰ, 2005 *New York Times,* an ex-top CIA official claims that the intelligence community's handling of 9/11 was not a failure, but something "good, positive, extraordinary." See: http://mujca.com/orwell.htm

Meyer's argument that 9/11 was modeled after Pearl Harbor is convincing, and his discussion of the historical evidence is concise and compelling. But his real contribution is to sort through the thorny moral and spiritual issues posed by the 9/11-Pearl Harbor comparison. Many American 9/11 truth activists have argued that the false-flag Reichstag Fire is a better metaphor than Pearl Harbor, in part because everyone agrees that Nazism and the Reichstag Fire were heinous—while many argue that even if Roosevelt lied the US into World War II, and sacrificed thousands of Americans at Pearl Harbor to do it, his act was justified by the greater good of defeating Nazism.

Meyer points out that lies, even apparent "political white lies" like
FDR's Pearl Harbor deception, are spiritually pernicious: "...Anyone who
has taken even the first faltering steps in learning the ABC of spiritual
science is aware that every lie is a murder at the level of soul" (p. 49).
FDR, then, was not Hitler's antagonist, but his soulmate, his partner in
unspeakable evil, big lies, and mass murder. The evil of Hitler's
holocaust—which was not opposed by the allies, who chose not to bomb
the railroads leading to the camps—was echoed by the murderous
intentional firebombing of German and Japanese civilians, the use of
nuclear weapons on Hiroshima and Nagasaki, and the endless list of
crimes against humanity of the US National Security State, which was
built upon the smoking ruins of Pearl Harbor. In short, the big lie of
Pearl Harbor only seemed to work; its deadly effects have been poisoning
American life, and the life of the world, ever since the day of infamy.

Meyer calls us back to the eternal wisdom of the perennial philosophy,
echoed in every major religious tradition, that truth is the supreme good,
and lies the supreme evil—though the evil of the lie can never really be
supreme in the sense that truth is supreme, for truth and eternity are
identical, whereas lies are temporal ephemera doomed to dissipate with
the passage of time and rebound against their perpetrators. But a lie that
takes on the aura of truth, and becomes an unquestionable sacred myth,
can have horrifically destructive effects—as have the big lies of Pearl
Harbor and 9/11. Such lies prevent people from thinking clearly—
prevent them from thinking at all, in fact. They produce a harmful
miasma that is as harmful to spiritual and psychic health as radioactive
smog is to physical health. Meyer is a student of the mystic Rudolph
Steiner, whose words spoken on April 4th, 1916 now seem chillingly
prophetic: "Shortly after the year 2000 a kind of indirect prohibition on
thinking will emanate from America, a law which will aim to suppress all
individual thought" (p. 16). The suppression of individual thought in
America, the land of creative individualism, would indeed be a planetary
catastrophe. Such observations show why the 9/11 covert operation was
perhaps the worst crime against humanity ever perpetrated. The gravity
of the crime stems not from the scale of the carnage—less than 3,000
were killed, compared to millions in other holocausts—but from the
scale of the lie, which may, unless quickly exposed, quite literally lead to
the destruction of the world.

Along with his profound meditation on truth and lies, Meyer offers an
interesting Hegelian analysis of the power-machinations behind 9/11. He
argues that Anglo-American policymakers, like the Nazis whom they

helped bring to power, intentionally create conflicts in order to gain power for egotistical ends. The Hegelian dialectic, Meyer argues, is supposed to be about conflict-resolution, not conflict-creation. Spiritual development involves confrontations between opposing forces and finding creative, uplifting ways to reconcile them or otherwise achieve harmony. The Anglo-American power elite, he argues, has taken a "satanic" turn by trying to create or amplify unnecessary conflicts in order to reap a harvest of power. Thus they built up Hitler, the "Communist threat," and now the "Islamic terrorist threat" in order to seize the world's resources and build a despotic global regime under the aegis of the New World Order—an expression first used by Bush the Elder exactly eleven years earlier—on September 11th, 1990!

As a Muslim with an interest in comparative mysticism, I find Meyer's analysis provocative, insightful, and accurate. His emphasis on truth, and abhorrence of lies, parallels the implications of the name al-Haqq, "Truth" or "Reality," which is one of the very highest names of God in Islamic tradition. And his Hegelian road-map to the current spiritual conflict makes sense to those of us who are trying to resolve apparently clashing opposites—such as the Muslim, Jewish and Christian faiths post-9/11—in order to help clear the toxic fog of lies and raise humanity to a higher spiritual state.

~~~~~
### FALSE FLAG FACTS

In his new book, *Verschlußsache Terror (Top Secret Terror),* documentary producer Gerhard Wisnewski analyzes how terrorism works. It's a way intelligence agencies start wars.

The secret service provocateurs have two target groups. The first one they target by an overt terror act; on 9/11, this was the American people and world opinion. The second group – the intended and by far the main victims – are targeted by the furious ensuing reaction, which is always far more immense and destructive than the terror act itself. This is achieved by scapegoating, by faking evidence to frame the second, real targeted group as the terrorists. On 9/11, the real target was the Muslim world.

Secret services employ two types of experts, specialists in propaganda and munitions. The psychological warfare experts decide on the fake scenario, timing, and type of atrocity, the weapons experts carry it out. Only amateurs, naïve hotheads who imitate the icons of terror, attempt to improvise their own bombs and propaganda. Wisnewski agrees with Webster Tarpley that *all* large-scale, spectacular or technically sophisti-cated terrorism – 9/11 was all three – is the work of state agencies.

# Apocalypse of Coercion:
# Why We Listen to What "They" Say About 9/11

First published in *Global Outlook 11* (Spring/Summer 2006)

"Apocalypse of Coercion" is not exactly a book review. Instead, it uses Douglas Rushkoff's landmark book *Coercion* as a touchstone for understanding 9/11 as a psychological warfare operation. Rushkoff, an NYU professor and Esalen Institute teacher, is one of the world's most celebrated media commentators: http://www.rushkoff.com/ I sent him a copy of "Apocalypse of Coercion" and asked if he thought of 9/11 as the kind of coercive psy-op his book analyzed. Rushkoff responded:

"Yeah—terrific stuff. I began thinking about this sort of connection, myself, when I saw the documentary Power of Nightmares. He's got a lot more to say about it than I do; pretty much all my opinions on the matter are just watered down versions of his. Have you seen it? I'm assuming you would have, given your area of interest."

\* \* \*

*"That's just like hypnotizing chickens." —Iggy Pop, "Lust for Life"*

They say suicidal Muslim fanatics did it. They say those radical Muslims hate our freedoms. They say the country is full of sleeper agents who could wake up and kill us at any moment, as soon as their little red-white-and-blue "I hate the USA" wristwatch alarms go off.

They say that Saddam Hussein had something to do with it—he's Muslim, isn't he? They say invading Afghanistan and Iraq was the appropriate response; we had to do *something*, right? They say if you're not with us, you're against us—and if you're against us, you're on the side of the evildoers.

They say those cunning, devious suicide hijackers defeated America's defenses using flying lessons and box cutters. They say it was ordered by a tall, dark, handsome, sinister, hooknosed kidney patient in a cave in Afghanistan—a ringer for the evil vizier Jaffar in the Disney film *Aladdin*, but with a thicker beard to signify "Islamist." They say it was masterminded by a real bad dude named KSM. They say they finally caught KSM, and that the whole story, enshrined in the official *9/11 Commission Report*, is based on what KSM said under interrogation—so it's all right from the horse's mouth.

They say it happened because our defense and intelligence systems didn't see it coming, despite all those urgent warnings from dozens of countries as well as whistleblowers from our own agencies. They say that nobody was really to blame, so nobody had to be prosecuted or fired or even reprimanded. They say that by promoting the very people who made the most outrageously improbable blunders, and giving the screw-up agencies a whole lot more money, we've ensured that they'll do better next time.

They say that anybody who questions what they say is a conspiracy theorist.

"Who, exactly, are 'they,' and why do they say so much? More amazing, why do we listen to them?" —Douglas Rushkoff in *Coercion: Why We Listen to What "They" Say* (NY: Penguin, 1999)

Rushkoff's *Coercion* is a sizzling exposé of mind control, American style. Unlike Chomsky's *Manufacturing Consent*, Rushkoff's book provides a detailed guide to the nuts-and-bolts techniques employed against us every day by advertisers, marketers, public relations specialists, Hollywood filmmakers, salespeople, pyramid-scam artists, and cult leaders —the very same techniques applied for decades, and gradually perfected, by CIA interrogators and psychological warfare experts. These techniques are designed to disable rational thought and manipulate behavior at the unconscious and emotional levels. Anyone curious about why so many otherwise rational people have believed the official story of 9/11 for so long, in the teeth of the overwhelming evidence against it, should start by reading *Coercion*.

The secret of mind-control is simple—so simple that Rushkoff can sum it up in one sentence: "In whatever milieu coercion is practiced, the routine follows the same basic steps: Generate disorientation, induce regression, and then become the target's transferred parent figure" (p. 64). Hard-sell car salesmen, CIA interrogators and psychwar ops, and cult leaders have long used this technique. Under coercion, millions of otherwise rational people can be persuaded to act against their own interests—whether by shelling out big bucks for an overpriced lemon, betraying a comrade and a cause, or allowing a gang of criminals to destroy their nation's Constitution and launch criminal wars of aggression.

How do they do it? Let's start by zooming in on your local automobile dealership. The car salesman carefully leads the mark to be dissatisfied with his current car, and by extension his current life—and as the mark sees his current life through newly dissatisfied eyes, he begins to experience disorientation. The salesman then takes the mark on a test drive and, at the right moment, asks "Is this the type of vehicle you would like to own?" Rushkoff quotes a car-salesman-turned-whistleblower:

> And anyone will tell you this, the vacuum cleaner salesman, the car salesman—the customer has a split-second of insanity. The mind goes blank, the body paralyzes, the eyes get glassy, dilated. And you'd be surprised how many people have an accident at just that moment! Ask any car dealer. We always joke about it (p. 43)

The car salesman's question, like the well-timed words of a good hypnotist, triggers a sudden intensification of the customer's dissociated, suggestible state. Rushkoff explains: "The customer is already in a vehicle, being asked to imagine himself owning the same type of vehicle. It's the same as if I asked you if this is the kind of book you can imagine yourself reading. Your current situation is reframed in fantasy. It creates a momentary confusion, or dissociation, from the activity you're involved in. That's why so many drivers crash" (p. 43).

If the customer answers no, he gets the same treatment in other cars until he answers yes. Then he is brought back to the dealership and infantilized, as the salesman becomes his transferred parent figure:

> He is told where to go, how to walk, where to sit. One training manual instructs the salesman to give the customer coffee whether he wants it or not: "Don't ask him if he wants a cup of coffee—just ask him how he takes it." In this way, the customer is trained to obey, and given his fear and disorientation in the sales environment, he welcomes the commands and their implied invitation for him to regress into the safety of childhood.

Once the customer has been infantilized, he is controlled by various tricks. One of the best-known is the "common enemy" technique. The salesman pretends to be conspiring with the customer against the nasty head of the dealership, or against another salesman who is greedy and dishonest. The "common enemy" technique is also used by the CIA—one interrogator, the "good cop," teams up with the subject against the other interrogator, the "bad cop." Governments, of course, use the same technique: The illegitimate son-of-a-Bush of August, 2001 doubled his approval ratings by infantilizing the American public on 9/11 and rallying them against the "common enemy" of evildoing Muslim extremists.

The CIA, like the automobile industry, has long been refining coercive techniques aimed at eliciting compliance. Whether the Company wants to coerce an interrogation subject into spilling the beans, or a whole nation into supporting a war, the techniques are basically the same as those used by hard-sell car salesmen: Generate dissociation through disorientation, induce regression, and become the target's transferred parent figure.

In an interrogation, the CIA begins by disorienting the subject:

As the minutes, hours, or days go by, the "sights and sounds of an outside world fade away, [and] its significance is replaced by the interrogation room, its two occupants, and the dynamic relationship between them" (*CIA Interrogation Manual*) which is why interrogation rooms are generally devoid of windows and free of all references to the outside world, including time of day and day of the week. The subject becomes completely dependent on the interrogator for all external stimuli and, accordingly, his sense of self (p. 35).

After the subject's sense of self has been broken down, the CIA interrogator chooses from a grab bag of techniques that accomplish the same thing as the car salesman's line "Is this the type of vehicle you would like to own?" These techniques induce a sudden state of radical confusion by disrupting the target's familiar emotional associations. The CIA manual explains: "When this aim is achieved, resistance is seriously impaired. There is an interval—which may be extremely brief—of suspended animation, a kind of psychological shock or paralysis... that explodes the world that is familiar to the subject as well as his image of himself within that world. Experienced interrogators recognize this effect when it appears and know that at this moment the source is far more open to suggestion" (p. 36). At this moment, the interrogator encourages the subject to regress to a childlike state of mind, and becomes the subject's transferred parent figure.

This is a very good description of what was done to the American people on and after September 11th, 2001. The images of the planes crashing into landmark buildings, and those buildings exploding into powder and shards, created a state of extreme confusion, "a kind of psychological shock or paralysis." The bombs that brought down the Twin Towers and WTC-7 literally exploded the world that was familiar to us, and our images of ourselves in that world. We experienced a moment of dissociation, which is why we can still recall where we were and what we were doing when we learned of the attack. As the psychological warfare experts who designed the operation knew very well, this left us radically open to suggestion—to mass hypnosis. Our old world had been annihilated, and we were ready to be hypnotized, and have a new world created for us. We desperately needed a parent figure to tell us how to make sense of the madness.

The government, of course, became that transferred parent figure. The presidency, instituted by George "father of his country" Washington, is a paternal institution. Even an illegitimate son-of-a-Bush could briefly become our idealized national daddy. We believed what "they" told us about 9/11, with little or no effort to discern the actual facts, because we had been coerced and infantilized. When Susan Sontag spoke out against the absurd infantilization of the American people post-9/11, she was subjected to vicious attacks by intelligence-asset pseudo-journalists. Why? Not because what she said wasn't true—it obviously was. The reason Sontag had to be ripped to shreds by the CIA rag *National Review* and its epigones was that she was getting too close to understanding that 9/11 was a psychological warfare operation by US and allied intelligence agencies, not a "terrorist attack" by anti-American foreigners. Sontag understood that the American public had been subjected to induced regression. By calling attention to this fact, she was indirectly calling attention to the psy-op man behind the curtain.

The choice of September 11th as the date of the attacks was obviously made by a psychological warfare expert who wanted to make the American people suffer induced regression and put childlike faith in their government. The number 911 has overwhelming emotional associations in the mind of every American. From early childhood, we are taught that this is the magic number we can call in the event of an emergency. If anything terrible or deeply threatening happens to us, all we have to do is push those three buttons on the nearest telephone, and a benevolent parent figure—the government—will come rushing to help us. With the ongoing breakdown of the family and its authority, and the widespread consciousness of abuse between family members, the number 911 represents the government that has become our real daddy. The planners of 9/11 took advantage of this fact, enshrining their false-flag attack with a number that evokes our desperate, childlike need for the government to be the daddy who comes racing to help us in an emergency. Every time we hear "9/11" we are enveloped in subconscious emotional associations of a benevolent, fatherly government that can be counted on to save us from catastrophe. Unless we have learned how to defend ourselves against coercion, it is these emotional associations, not facts, that condition how we think.

Once our old world had been exploded, our minds regressed to a childlike emotional level, and our faith placed in the transferred parent figure of our government and its paternal figurehead, we were ready to be bombarded by hypnotic words and images. The hypnotic inculcation of thoughts, beliefs, and attitudes is a simple matter. The key is repetition: Repetition, repetition, *repetition*. In the Alice-in-Wonderland world of the so-called war on terror, "what I tell you three times is true."

They tell us over and over that 9/11 was like Pearl Harbor; we accept the paradigm and prepare for a righteous world war. They tell us over and over that Bin Laden did it, and we internalize that belief, without reference to evidence. They tell us over and over that Bin Laden is America's enemy, and we accept the story, even though many of the world's most prestigious journalistic outlets have told us that Bin Laden spent the first two weeks of July, 2001 getting treated at the American Hospital in Dubai and meeting with CIA Station Chief Larry Mitchell. They tell us over and over that the guy in the grainy video confessing to 9/11 is Bin Laden, even though there is very little resemblance between this overweight impostor and the Osama Bin Laden of other photos and videos. They tell us over and over about the 19 suicide hijackers, and we believe them, even when we find out that many of these alleged hijackers are still alive, that these individuals were/are not Muslims at all but intelligence agents, and that the "flight schools" they trained at were actually CIA drug import airstrips. They tell us over and over that (whore-chasing, boozing cokehead) Mohammad Atta put a bizarre parody of an "Islamic terrorist's last will and testament" into a suitcase and checked that suitcase on board his suicide flight—say *what?!*—and that the suitcase was mistakenly put on board a different flight so it could be quickly discovered and offered as "evidence." They tell us that other "suicide hijackers" conveniently left a car full of evidence at the airport. They tell us that a hijacker's passport miraculously floated down from the inferno in the Towers to be discovered as more "evidence." They tell us that the fact that the "hijackers" spent the night of 9/10/2001 in a motel right across the street from the gates of the National Security Agency headquarters is just a weird coincidence. They tell us that a Good Samaritan burglar happened to "steal" the briefcase containing the "evidence" of the "hijackers" concocting their plot in Hamburg, Germany, and felt compelled to deliver the briefcase to the German police. (What they don't tell us is that the German police are rolling on the ground laughing at the absurd pretext, and have publicly stated that the "burglar" was an intelligence agent.) They tell us over and over that the World Trade Center collapsed from diesel-fuel-induced fires, despite the fact that no high rise steel frame skyscraper has *ever* collapsed due to fire, including much worse ones than those on 9/11. They tell us over and over that Hani Hanjour, who could not fly a Cessna training aircraft, somehow executed an amazing stunt maneuver in a hijacked 757 in order to hit the empty, newly-reinforced wing of the Pentagon and cause minimal damage—instead of just diving into the roof and killing thousands.

Even more important than the repetition of such ludicrous propositions, has been the bombardment of the public with words and phrases designed to disable rational thought: *terror, terrorism, the war on terror, hate our freedoms, hate our values, patriot, patriotic, Patriot Act, evildoers, extremists, security, anthrax, homeland, biological weapons, Islamo-fascist, dirty bombs, weapons of mass destruction.* These emotionally-charged terms, drummed incessantly into our brains, reinforce the unconscious emotional predispositions that govern our thoughts. They literally force us to think certain thoughts, and render us literally incapable of even entertaining others. Just as the car salesman's coercive question "How do you take your coffee" literally forces 90% of non-coffee-drinkers to obediently accept a cup of coffee, the psych-war experts' attack of disorientation, regression, and parental transference literally forces 90% of the American public to think patently ludicrous thoughts, adopt those thoughts as a model of reality, and cling to those self-evidently absurd thoughts in the teeth of overwhelming factual evidence.

The question remains, who are "they"? The answer is obvious—just read the Project for a New American Century's manifesto *Rebuilding America's Defenses*, published in September, 2000, which openly calls for a "New Pearl Harbor." The 9/11 "New Pearl Harbor" was brought to us by the neoconservatives, who believe that all human beings except themselves are governed by irrational emotions and incapable of evidence-based reasoning. The neoconservatives are Zionist extremists and cult followers of the demented philosopher-guru Leo Strauss, whose worldview can be summed up in the adage "if you can't beat Hitler, join him." They apparently believed that a massive dose of coercion, in the form of 9/11, could motivate Americans to preserve and expand their imperial domination of the planet in general, and their commitment to a belligerent, expansionist Israel in particular.

Oddly enough, 9/11 was apparently designed with the help of focus groups:

...The trick only needs to work long enough to win (or avoid) a war. Even if "the truth" emerges sometime later, at least the primary objective has already been achieved... when American corporate and governmental interests adopted these techniques for use against the American people, they needed to cloak their assault in a seemingly benign manifestation: the focus group. About ten "average" members of a target population are brought into a room and asked to discuss an issue while a team of researchers, clients, and a camera record their responses from behind a one-way mirror. A researcher stays in the room with the subjects, asking them questions and pushing them in new directions...

Bob Deutsch, an anthropologist [and legendary psy-op focus group guru] who worked for the Department of Defense... led focus groups revealing Americans' irrational beliefs about Japan. "You want to uncover in your audience what I call a "spasm of sentiment," he explained. "It's their illogic—their emotional logic." He told us how in focus groups with average American citizens, he learned that most people still associate the Japanese with Pearl Harbor: "People say, for example, "Japan took our lives in 1941, and they took our livelihoods in 1991." Because Japan disrupted America's self-mythology of being invincible, the nation would never be forgiven in the irrational American sentiment (p. 140).

The authors of 9/11 needed a horrifyingly spectacular, murderous attack on the American "homeland" in order to elicit this "Pearl Harbor effect." They needed to "disrupt America's self-mythology of being invincible" so that Arabs and Muslims "would never be forgiven in the irrational American sentiment." They were not interested in triggering just one quick war in Afghanistan, or a second one in Iraq. They were after "the war that will not end in our lifetimes"—an ongoing war that would remove Americans' Constitutional liberties, massively increase military expenditures, and legitimize attacks against Middle Eastern nations for decades into the future, on behalf of Israeli expansionism and the petrodollar hegemony on which it depends.

9/11, in short, was an apocalypse of coercion. It was a psy-op on a scale of murderousness and mendacity to make the Reichstag Fire look like a kid playing with matches.

Play with fire, however, and you just might get burned. This "apocalypse of coercion" could end up being an apocalypse for its authors, and for coercion itself. The neocons have been revealed and reviled as pathological liars, and only the flimsiest film of reticence is preventing the major media from exposing the 9/11 psy-op and triggering the greatest scandal in world history, and a Constitutional crisis light-years beyond anything in the American experience. As people awaken to 9/11 truth, they grow psychic armor that renders them invincible to coercion in any form. Recoiling from the sheer horror of such murderous coercion, their psychic immune system is strengthened. It is a safe bet that no 9/11 skeptic will ever buy a lemon from a car salesman—or even accept an unwanted cup of coffee. The 9/11 truth-awakened individual will not succumb to the blandishments of advertisers, political pundits, cult leaders, politicians, or Fox News commentators. He or she will smell coercion coming from a mile away, and tell the prospective coercer into which orifice their coercion may be inserted.

The simple truth is, coercion doesn't work any more, and future historians will view 9/11 as its final implosion. In the mid-1990s PR guru Howard Rubenstein saw that the internet had made damage-control coercion obsolete, and began advising clients that they had no choice but to let the ugly truth hang out. Need a coverup? "The lesson is not to do it. Sure, people will come to you and say, 'Let's set up a committee and we'll call it so-and-so, and we'll hire someone to run it,' and my attitude is: What's known is known. Simple. What is known gets published. So it's foolhardy to set up a fig-leaf committee and hope nobody will look under the fig leaf and see what's there" (p. 160). Unfortunately, the Bush Administration didn't take Rubenstein's advice when it set up the 9/11 Commission.

The word "apocalypse" denotes the cataclysmic end of the world, but its original Greek meaning is "unveiling." By unveiling the truth of 9/11, and the mechanisms of coercion it employed, we can avoid the apocalyptic future of endless war that the New Pearl Harbor was designed to trigger. Less obviously, we can expose and discredit the mechanisms of coercion that governments and corporations use to dehumanize us. It is time for coercion-savvy media specialists like Rushkoff and Rubenstein to join the 9/11 truth movement and help us figure out how to communicate 9/11 truth, turn the 9/11 apocalypse of coercion against its perpetrators, and ensure that in our shared human future, communications technologies will be used to empower people, not enslave them.

## E. Op-Eds and Manifestos

## America's Top Bin Laden Expert: Osama's Dead, the Tape is Phony

Published February 14th, 2006, *The Capital Times*, Madison, Wisconsin

As a Ph.D. Islamologist and Arabist I really hate to say this, but I'll say it anyway: *9/11 had nothing to do with Islam.* The war on terror is as phony as the latest "Bin Laden tape." (1)

It's a tough thing to admit, because I know on which side my bread is buttered—and dropping Islam from the 9/11 equation is dropping my slice of bread butter-side-down. The myth that 9/11 had something to do with Muslims has poured millions, if not billions, into Arabic and Islamic studies. I finished my Ph.D. last year, so all I have to do is keep my eyes in my pocket and my nose on the ground, parrot the party line, and I'll be on the fast track to tenure track.

The trouble is, it's all based on a Big Lie. Take the recent "bin Laden" tape—*please!* That voice was no more bin Laden than it was Rodney Dangerfield channeling my late Aunt Corinne from Peoria. I recently helped translate a previously unknown bin Laden tape, a real one from the early 90's, back when he was still alive. I know the guy's flowery religious rhetoric. The recent tape wasn't him.

The top American bin Laden expert agrees. Professor Bruce Lawrence, head of Duke University's Religious Studies department, has just published a book of translations of bin Laden's speeches. He says the recent tape is a fake, and that bin Laden has been dead for years. (2)

Ersatz Bin Laden tapes, "verified" by the CIA, are nothing new. Every "Bin Laden" statement since 2001 has been blatantly bogus. The last we heard from the real Bin Laden came in his post-9/11 statements to Pakistani journalists: *"I stress that I have not carried out this act, which appears to have been carried out by individuals with their own motivation... I have already said that I am not involved in the 11 September attacks in the United States... I had no knowledge of these attacks..."* (3)

Then on December 13th, 2001, as George Bush was whining about the "outrageous conspiracy theories" that were spreading like wildfire, the first and shoddiest of the "Bin Laden speaks from beyond the grave" tapes appeared. The video's sound and picture quality were horrible. It showed a big guy with a black beard, doing a passable imitation of Bin Laden's voice, claiming foreknowledge, if not responsibility, for the 9/11 attacks, and chortling over their success. The trouble was, the big guy clearly was not Bin Laden. He was at least 40 or 50 pounds heavier, and his facial features were obviously different. (4)

The "Fatty Bin Laden" tape was widely ridiculed, and I have yet to meet an informed observer who considers it authentic. (If you haven't figured this out yet, go back and look at the images from the tape, and compare them to other images of Bin Laden.) But the media let the fraud pass without asking the hard questions: Why was the US government waving this blatantly fake "confession" video in our faces?

Perhaps due to the widespread hilarity evoked by "Fatty Bin Laden," the next "Osama from beyond the grave" message had no images—it was an audio tape delivered to al-Jazeera in fall, 2002. The CIA verified it as authentic, and then got a rotten egg in the face when the world's leading voice identification experts at IDIAP in Switzerland reported that "the message was recorded by an impostor." (5)

Every "bin Laden" message since then has been equally phony. They are released at moments when the Bush Regime needs a boost—and the American media goes along with the fraud. Remember the bogus bin Laden tape that made headlines right before the 2004 presidential elections? If you didn't figure out that it was a CIA-produced commercial for George Bush, I have some great bridges to sell you. Walter Cronkite, bless his heart, opined that Karl Rove was behind that tape. (6) But the rest of the media just kept pretending that the Emperor was clothed.

And the fraud continues. Last week's "bin Laden" tape has been ridiculed by America's top bin Laden expert—yet the US media keeps right on holding a transparent fig leaf in front of the Emperor's crotch! Professor Lawrence believes that this phony tape was designed to distract world opinion from the horrific massacre of Pakistani civilians by an errant CIA drone. But it may have another, more sinister purpose: To prepare public opinion for another false-flag 9/11 style attack designed to trigger a US-Israeli nuclear attack on Iran. (7)

As our top Bin Laden expert Professor Lawrence informs us, the real Bin Laden, who insisted that he had nothing to do with 9/11, has been dead for quite some time—probably since 2001. The fake messages have been fabricated by al-CIA-duh to support the Bush regime and its phony "war on terror." It is time for Americans to rise up in revolt against the fake-terror masters who are looting US taxpayers, torching our Constitution, demolishing our economy, and threatening nuclear Armageddon.

References:
(1) "The Making of the Terror Myth." *The Guardian* 10/15/04
http://www.guardian.co.uk/terrorism/story/0,12780,1327904,00.html
(2) ABC News http://abclocal.go.com/wtvd/story? section=local&id=3828678
(3) http://en.wikipedia.org/wiki/Responsibility_for_the_September_11,_2001_attacks
(4) http://911research.wtc7.net/disinfo/deceptions/binladinvideo.html
(5) *The Guardian* 1/30/02:
http://www.guardian.co.uk/alqaida/story/0,12469,851112,00.html
(6) CNN: http://transcripts.cnn.com/TRANSCRIPTS/0410/29/lkl.01.html
quoted in: http://www.whatreallyhappened.com/binladen_cronkite.html
(7) *American Conservative* 8/1/05:
http://www.amconmag.com/2005_08_01/article3.html
discussed in: http://antiwar.com/justin/?articleid=6734

~~~~~
FALSE FLAG FACTS

STATE-SPONSORED FALSE-FLAG
TERROR: THE ROGUE NETWORK

'Covered' by Controlled
CORPORATE MEDIA

PATSIES: FOOLS, FANATICS, FAKES, FALL GUYS, DOUBLES, DUPES, OSWALDS...

MOLES: HANDLERS, DISINFO AGENTS, KEY OPERATIVES INFEST GOVERNMENT, MEDIA

HIT MEN: PROS, Technicians, JACKALS, Mercenary Killers, SAS, *REAL* TERRORISTS.

PRIVATIZED COMMAND CENTER

9/11 Synthetic Terror: Made In USA
PROGRESSIVEPRESS.COM

We saw on p. 169 how two covert teams, weapons and propaganda experts, use terrorism to create war pretexts. In Webster Tarpley's model in *9/11 Synthetic Terror*, they are called hit men and moles, who subvert our media and elected government for the power elite, or oligarchy. It owns the major media too, which retouch any errors made, and trumpet war images. The moles use patsies as actors to create the illusion of an enemy attack, but the actual stunts are done by the hit men. Moles, like the neocons who planned this coup d'état against the Constitution, occupy high-level and other key posts (see p. 130). Under Bush/Reagan, CIA functions were privatized to escape Congressional oversight, giving the permanent, invisible mole government more power.

The patsies are weak-minded or sociopathic individuals who can be manipulated with the blandishments of the CIA stable. Their role is to create a trail of incriminating circumstantial evidence – even if it is absurd, such as luggage left in rental cars. The moles' role is to keep the patsies out of jail until the hit men can carry out the terror deed: no patsies means no scapegoats, no propaganda and no war pretext. Moles may also be handlers or double agents who create terror groups by recruiting and training stooges to make and set off bombs (IRA – see p. 43). The terror pros who carry out spectacular attacks may be mercenaries who like to kill, who believe in the cause, or whose oath of duty and secrecy and fear of reprisals far outweigh any whistleblower tendencies. – JPL

Media Hide Truth: 9/11 was Inside Job

Published May 12, 2006, *The Capital Times*, Madison, Wisconsin

Last Saturday, former Bush administration official Morgan Reynolds drew an enthusiastic capacity crowd to the Wisconsin Historical Society auditorium. It is probably the first time in Historical Society history that a political talk has drawn a full house on a Saturday afternoon at the beginning of final exams.

Reynolds, the former director of the Criminal Justice Center at the National Center for Policy Analysis, and former top economist for George W. Bush's Labor Department, charged the Bush administration with gross malfeasance, and proposed the prosecution of top administration officials.

Normally, if a prestigious UW alumnus and ex-Bush administration official were to come to the Wisconsin Historical Society to spill the beans about a Bush administration scandal, it would make the news. The local TV stations would cover it, and it would merit front page headlines in *The Capital Times* and *Wisconsin State Journal*.

Reynolds' indictment of the administration he has worked for was a stunning, life-changing event for many who witnessed it. As the event's organizer, I have received dozens of e-mails about it from people who were deeply affected.

Despite the prestigious speaker and venue, and the gravity of the charges aired, for most Americans and indeed most Madisonians, the event never happened. Why? Because it was censored, subjected to a total media blackout. Not a word in the *State Journal*. Not a word in *The Capital Times*. Not a word on the local TV news. Not a word on local radio news. And, of course, not a word in the national media.

Why the blackout? Because Reynolds violated the ultimate U.S. media taboo. He charges the Bush administration with orchestrating the 9/11 attacks as a pretext for launching a preplanned "long war" in the Middle East, rolling back our civil liberties, and massively increasing military spending.

When a former Bush administration insider makes such charges, how can the media ignore them? Is Reynolds a lone crank? Hardly. A long list of prominent Americans have spoken out for 9/11 truth: Rev. William Sloane Coffin, Sen. Barbara Boxer, former head of the Star Wars program Col. Robert Bowman, ex-Reagan administration economics guru Paul Craig Roberts, progressive Jewish author-activist Rabbi Michael Lerner, former CIA official Ray McGovern, author-essayist Gore Vidal, and many other respected names from across the political spectrum have gone on the record for 9/11 truth.

Are the media ignoring all these people, and dozens more like them, because there is no evidence to support their charges? Hardly. Overwhelming evidence, from the obvious air defense stand-down, to the nonprotection of the president in Florida, to the blatant controlled demolition of World Trade Center building 7, proves that 9/11 was an inside job. As noted philosopher-theologian and 9/11 revisionist historian David Griffin writes: "It is already possible to know, beyond a reasonable doubt, one very important thing: the destruction of the World Trade Center was an inside job, orchestrated by terrorists within our own government."

A growing list of scientists has lined up behind BYU physicist Steven Jones and MIT engineer Jeff King in support of this position, as evidenced by the growth of Scholars for 9/11 Truth (st911.org) and Scientific Professionals Investigating 9/11 (physics911.net).

As a Watergate-era graduate of the University of Wisconsin School of Journalism, I was taught that exposing government lies and corruption is the supreme duty of the Fourth Estate. I simply cannot fathom the current situation. I do not understand the 9/11 truth blackout. I wish someone would explain it to me.

It is time to break the 9/11 truth blackout. Please put pressure on your local media through letters to the editor, call-ins to talk radio, and phone calls to local and national journalists.

Peter Phillips, director of the media watchdog group Project Censored, will lead a strategy session on breaking the blackout at the international 9/11 truth conference in Chicago: 9/11: Revealing the Truth, Reclaiming Our Future, June 2-4 [2006]. See 911revealingthetruth.org.

The event will feature presentations from dozens of 9/11 truth luminaries, from scientists like Steven Jones to intelligence agency whistle-blowers like David Shayler, and promises to be a historic, watershed event. Be there, or resign yourself to a future of endless war, lost liberty, and a craven media that cannot bring itself to breathe a single word of truth.

The 9/11 Truth Revolution

First published at http://www.serendipity.li/wot/revolution.htm

"It feels like you and I have started the revolution and God bless America."
Charlie Sheen

As 9/11 truth spreads, we are facing a revolution.

A revolution happens when the many at the bottom get together and overthrow the few at the top. At least that's the theory. In practice, it isn't quite that simple. The American Revolution was led by wealthy, well-educated deists, many of them slaveholders. The French Revolution involved the hungry masses, but the instigators were businesspeople, not street people. The Russian Revolution was led by a self-proclaimed vanguard. The anti-imperial revolutions that ended European colonization 50 years ago were led by the colonies' European-educated elites.

Today, thanks to the rapidly-spreading brushfire of 9/11 truth, we are on the cusp of a new kind of revolution—a real one this time, a revolution from below. As conservative columnist Paul Craig Roberts writes, "the real story is what the people are saying about 9/11." (http://aangirfan.blogspot.com/2005/06/paul-craig-roberts-morgan-reynolds.html) What Roberts means is that the powerful few and the institutions they control—the government, the corporations, the armed forces, the major political parties, the foundation-funded pseudo-left, the universities, the mass media, Hollywood—have imposed near-total silence on the issue of what really happened on September 11th, 2001. Worse, most of them have cranked out endless tape-loops of mind-numbing propaganda aimed at reinforcing the official Big Lie. And yet the people are speaking out loud and clear: *9/11 was an inside job—an act of high treason and mass murder by our own leaders.*

In the latest CNN poll, over 80% of respondents agreed with Charlie Sheen that the official story of 9/11 is a cover-up. Earlier polls showed that half the citizens of New York, the city that was so brutally attacked, and Atlanta, the biggest city in the nation's most conservative region, believe their leaders guilty of high treason and conspiracy to mass-murder.

Despite the best efforts of the treasonous billionaires who control all of our major institutions, the popular groundswell for 9/11 truth is unstoppable. The people have refused to be cowed into silence by inane fear-mongering and cowardly name-calling. All across the nation people are rising up and talking truth. "Have you seen *Loose Change* yet?" "That Charlie Sheen is amazing—how could CNN let him say that?" "You've got to read *The New Pearl Harbor*—here's a copy, pass it on." People are burning hundreds of DVDs and passing them to their friends, who are burning hundreds more. If the video-makers were getting full royalties on every copy, they'd be richer than self-confessed WTC demolisher and billionaire insurance-fraudster Larry Silverstein.

The source of this revolution is the courage and intelligence of the people. The neoconservatives, who underestimate the intelligence of other people almost as much as they overestimate their own, apparently thought that their monopoly media could coerce the poor dumb masses into lapping up outrageous lies indefinitely. What they didn't realize was that new communications technologies, in the hands of smart, brave people, can spread the truth with absolutely no help from traditional top-down, one-to-many media systems.

The truth is that people in power are no smarter than the rest of us. They are just greedier. As the French saying goes, *"plus haut qu'il monte, plus que se voit son cul"* – the higher up he climbs, the better you can see his ass.

This is a moral revolution by ordinary decent folks against the greed-heads who will stop at nothing—not even the mass murder of their own countrymen in the service of a genocidal Big Lie—to gain even more wealth and power.

It is a revolution from below at every level, even in government itself. Dozens of honest agents and bureaucrats, stymied by their treasonous superiors, have spoken out. Colleen Rowley and the other Minneapolis FBI agents have made it abundantly clear that Dave Frasca, the mole and former head of the FBI's Radical Fundamentalism Unit, intentionally blocked their most intensive efforts to call attention to the "hijacking plot" before it happened. Yet the traitor and mass-murderer Frasca, who stymied not only the Minneapolis agents, but also the Phoenix FBI agents and others, was promoted after 9/11! The many thousands of honest agents in the FBI, disgusted with their superiors' complicity in high treason and mass murder, are a key part of our revolution from below, and will surely be dealing with the likes of Frasca one way or another.

It is a revolution from below in journalism as well as government. First it was the complete outsiders, the devil-may-care small-time bloggers, the folks at the very bottom of the journalistic food chain. (Note that some of these ultra-outsider bloggers, such as From the Wilderness and Global Research, have been outperforming the "real journalists" on key issues for years.) The outsider bloggers' incessant agitation put 9/11 truth on the radar screen of the more respectable bloggers and the occasional honest academic. When the highly respected David Griffin's *The New Pearl Harbor* came out, compiling and validating the bloggers' research, low-level people at C-Span began urging their company to report "the other side of the 9/11 story." The result was the nationwide broadcast of Griffin's landmark University of Wisconsin talk *9/11 and American Empire* last year. Now it appears that the actual working journalists at CNN have followed their C-Span colleagues away from their billionaire bosses' fantasy land and back toward reality-based journalism, by giving Charlie Sheen a national platform for truth-speaking.

It is a revolution from below in religious communities too. More than a few independent-minded Jews have made major contributions to the 9/11 truth movement, while increasing numbers of evangelical Christians are waking up to 9/11 truth, as the many e-mails we get from them at MUJCA-NET attest. While the self-appointed leaders and Sunday morning money-leeches spew their hatemongering rhetoric at the alleged-WTC-destroying Muslim hordes, whispers are spreading among their flocks: "Wait a minute—look at WTC-7 collapsing, and Silverstein confessing. How the hell did Osama do *that?*" And in the American Muslim community, the silent majority has always known it was an inside job—but the academics, self-appointed leaders and spokespeople, perfect examples of the Qur'an-derided *munafiqeen* (hypocrites) who say whatever makes their lives easier, have managed to obscure that fact with their ongoing nicey-nice drivel that implicitly or explicitly accepts the 9/11 Big Lie. After the 9/11 truth revolution, I hope every one of these "leaders" will resign from their cushy positions and look for real work. Indeed, they might be better advised to crawl into a hole somewhere, for the silent contempt in which they are now held by most of their co-religionists will surely grow less silent.

The 9/11 truth revolution from below will overthrow a good part of the American power structure. Billionaires will have their fortunes confiscated and spend the rest of their lives in prison. Most, perhaps all of the current administration will be tried and, presumably, either hanged or given some kind of truth-for-mercy deal. Its supporters throughout the judicial and legislative branches will be forced to resign. The CIA and other covert-op apparatuses will be broken into a million pieces and scattered to the four winds, finishing the job that JFK was unable to start. The media monopoly that enabled the 9/11 cover-up will be shattered into hundreds of fragments as the mother of all trust-busting eras commences. The uniformed military, and especially the Pentagon, will be purged of neocon moles, as the venerable institution of the firing squad is revived. Every last member of Skull and Bones, starting with the whole Bush crime family, will be hunted down, jailed, and forced to recite his entire sexual history to his cellmates while lying on the floor of the prison shower. And after the troops have pulled out, Rumsfeld, Perle and Feith will be air-dropped into Fallujah as a demonstration of how an undermanned invasion-of-three can be welcomed by adoring crowds strewing flowers at their feet.

Ultimately, though, the 9/11 truth revolution is not about vengeance—it's about hope. The story of the triumph of the 9/11 truth movement, against such apparently insurmountable odds, is a story of ordinary people's heroism, a veritable Frank Capra movie for the information age.

And though this revolution is an American movie, with a cast of thousands of heroes and Charlie Sheen doing an Oscar-worthy job in Best Supporting Role, it's going to be a worldwide hit. You thought they liked Michael Moore's *Fahrenheit 911* at Cannes? Wait till you see the world's reaction to *9/11 Truth: The Reality*. Other nations used to admire certain things about America—like our relative freedom, integrity, and imperviousness to corruption—and this movie will bring it all back, and then some. Better yet, this is the one American film that could really rock the Casbah in the Arab world. Want to lead the region toward freedom and democracy? Try setting an example. Overthrow your own corrupt leaders, and maybe the Arabs will overthrow theirs. And if you're tired of being hated by Muslims, what better way to re-establish friendship than by exploding the 9/11 blood libel and calling off the Big-Lie-triggered war on Islam?

The global ramifications of the 9/11 truth revolution go way beyond ending the ersatz "clash of civilizations" manufactured by the fake-terror-mongers. Our American revolution from below will lead a cascading revolution around the world, as the globalist elites are jailed, trust-busted, and discredited, and corrupt leaders are overthrown like rows of rotten dominoes. In the place of the current top-heavy structure of world finance and governance, this worldwide bottom-up revolution will create a truly democratic, populist order to match the many-to-many

communications revolution of the information age. This is the
"Planetization Revolution" that was foreseen by de Chardin—a sort of
"people's globalization" that will unite the planet freely and
democratically, rather than under murderous globalist tyranny. For
details, see the revolutionary manifesto "Declaration of Union" at:
http://www.planetization.org/declarationofunion.htm .

The checks and balances on abusive power developed in the USA and
elsewhere will be re-instituted and fine-tuned, as the power structure
devolves toward a bottom-up rather than top-down decision-making
model. People will seize control over their own lives, with individuals,
families and local communities—not nation states, banks or corporations
—making the decisions. This model of governance, as proposed by
theologian and 9/11 truth supporter John Cobb, is one of "communities
of communities of communities." It will be realized after the 9/11-truth-
triggered annihilation of the top-heavy institutions and wealth-and-
power-heavy individuals and families that currently run the world.

9/11 truth offers the ordinary person of good will an unprecedented
opportunity to change the world for the better. So what are you waiting
for? Get out there and spread the word. When the time is ripe—and it is
ripening fast—we will have the people, and the soul-power, to take to the
streets.

Two Plus Two Make Four

Two (2) massive, illegal rollbacks of Constitutional civil liberties were
planned during the year *before* 9/11.

1) The Patriot Act was written *before* 9/11, rolled out on schedule after
the attacks, and rammed through Congress after US military anthrax
from Ft. Detrick Biological Warfare Facility was sent to the two
congressmen, Daschle and Leahy, who wanted to block it.

2) June 30 (Bloomberg) —The U.S. National Security Agency asked
AT&T Inc. to help it set up a domestic call monitoring site seven months
before the Sept. 11, 2001 attacks, lawyers claimed June 23 in court papers
filed in New York federal court...

Two (2) illegal wars of aggression were planned during the year *before*
9/11 – wars that could not possibly have been launched without the
"new Pearl Harbor" effect of 9/11 on public opinion.

1) Former Treasury Secretary Paul O'Neill writes that the Iraq war was adopted as official policy, and Iraq's oil fields divvied up, in January, 2001, when George W. Bush ordered an upcoming war of aggression against Iraq: "Show me a way to get it done." The only conceivable way to get such an illegal war of aggression done, of course, would be a 9/11 "new Pearl Harbor" or its equivalent.

2) According to multiply-sourced reports published by the BBC and other sources, the illegal US invasion of Afghanistan was ordered in July, 2001, and its start date set for October, 2001, before the first snows. The Afghanistan invasion, according to these reports, was a response to the Taliban's refusal, formalized in July 2001, to accept the Bush Administration proposal for a gas pipeline project. Thus the invasion had nothing to do with 9/11, which only served as a pretext.

Two (2) pre-planned massive, illegal rollbacks of Constitutional civil liberties

Plus

Two (2) pre-planned illegal wars of aggression

Make

Four (4) good reasons to think 9/11 was an inside job.

"Freedom is the freedom to say that two plus two make four. If that is granted, all else follows." – George Orwell

Two plus two make four!

* * *

Sources:

"The USA PATRIOT Act Was Planned Before 9/11," by Jennifer Van Bergen, http://www.truthout.org/docs_02/05.21B.jvb.usapa.911.htm

"Spy Agency Sought U.S. Call Records Before 9/11, Lawyers Say," www.bloomberg.com/apps/news?pid=20601087&sid=abIV0cO64zJE

"US 'planned attack on Taleban' - The wider objective was to oust the Taleban," by George Arney, BBC. "A former Pakistani diplomat has told the BBC that the US was planning military action against Osama Bin Laden and the Taleban even before last week's attacks." http://news.bbc.co.uk/2/hi/south_asia/1550366.stm

"O'Neill: Bush planned Iraq invasion before 9/11," http://www.cnn.com/2004/ALLPOLITICS/01/10/oneill.bush/

Jessica McBride and Steve Nass, Exposed as MUJCA Agents!

Ambush Interview: A False-Flag Attack

A lot of people thought my letter to the Secret Service was pretty funny. Dylan Avery of *Loose Change* had it posted even before MUJCA did, and it bounced around the blogosphere like the magic bullet pinging around Kennedy's limousine.

If you thought THAT was funny (see page 196), get a load of Jessica McBride's latest diatribe! If I had to invent a perfect fictional character to publicize MUJCA-NET, I could never have come up with anything half so delicious as the walking talking blond-joke known as Jessica McBride, Ann Coulter's evil twin. A rabid-as-she-is-vapid Bush-cultist spewing unintentionally hilarious venom in my general direction, Jessica is giving us publicity we couldn't pay for if Jimmy Walter's rich uncle died and left everything to MUJCA.

Slow-witted as she seems, Jessica is probably one shapely, well-shaven leg up on her intended audience, the dwindling twenty-something percent of the country that approves of Bush's performance. Jessica's ambush interview with me, presumably pre-arranged with Rep. Steve Nass in a harebrained scheme to give me the Ward Churchill treatment and have me fired from my job at the University of Wisconsin-Madison, has completely backfired. I have been getting strong support from ordinary folks on the street, from letter-writers to the local papers, from my colleagues, from the several mainstream media interviewers I've met (and the surprisingly balanced stories I've read)—in fact, from every quarter except one: that ever-shrinking demographic group of Bush supporters known as TFM's, who are apparently the target group of the backfired McBride-Nass hatchet job attempt to shore up Republican support.

Political analyst Max Udargo explains the predicament that drove them to this pathetic, desperate act:

(www.udargo.com/mub/2006/05/bush_losing_core_supporters.html)

Bush Losing Core Supporters

WASHINGTON, May 11 – President Bush appears to be losing support among a key group of voters who had hitherto stood firmly with the president even as his poll numbers among other groups fell dramatically.

A new Gallup poll shows that, for the first time, Bush's approval rating has fallen below 50% among total f*ing morons, and now stands at 44%. This represents a dramatic drop compared to a poll taken just last December, when 62% of TFM's expressed support for the president and his policies.

The current poll, conducted by phone with 1,409 TFM's between May 4 and May 8, reveals that only 44% of those polled believe the president is doing a good job, while 27% believe he is doing a poor job and 29% don't understand the question.

The December poll, conducted by phone with 1,530 TFM's, showed 62% approved of the president, 7% disapproved and 31% didn't understand the question.

Faltering approval ratings for the president among a group once thought to be a reliable source of loyal support gives Republicans one more reason to be nervous about the upcoming mid-term elections. "If we can't depend on the support of TFM's," says Sen. Rick Santorum (R-PA), "then we've got a big problem. They're a key factor in our electoral strategy, and an important part of today's Republican coalition." (for the rest of Udargo's story, see: www.udargo.com/mub/2006/05/bush_losing_core_supporters.html)

* * *

An important part, hell – they're all the Republicans have left, and Jessica McBride and Steve Nass know it. Well, *maybe* they know it... they do give some signs of being TFM's themselves.

Let's take a closer look at some of McBride's barely-passable sophomore j-school prose. Jessica writes:

"We've been at war for several decades with Islamo fascist terrorists who want to destroy our way of life."

Jessica, I have some news for you. First, there is no such word as "Islamo." Second, the main international conflict used to be the Cold War, and semi-morons like you used to brainwash the TFMs into hating the evil Commies, not the evil Muslims. Remember how the CIA recruited Osama, a.k.a. Tim Osman, to fight for us against the Russkies in Afghanistan? Right. I thought you didn't. For you, the whole universe began on 9/11/01. Since then, WE HAVE ALWAYS BEEN AT WAR

WITH THE ISLAMO FASCIST TERRORISTS WHO WANT TO DESTROY OUR WAY OF LIFE, just like in Orwell's 1984, they had ALWAYS been at war with Oceania, not Eurasia, or was it vice-versa. How could all of your pre-9/11 memories have been erased so completely, Jessica? You're not *that* young, Toots. Could it have been through an Apocalypse of Coercion?

Jessica is trying to bring straying Bush voters like Bill Snarpel back into the fold:

Bill Snarpel of Enid, Oklahoma is a total f*ing moron who voted for Bush in both 2000 and 2004. But he says he won't be voting for Bush in 2008. "I don't like it that he was going to sell our ports to the Arabs. If the Arabs own the ports then that means they'll let all the Arabs in and then we'll all be riding camels and wearing towels on our heads. I don't want my children singing the Star Spangled Banner in Muslim."

Bill's fictional comment reads just like a real-life comment on a pro-Jessica blog—it's hard to tell the reality from the satire these days.

Here's another comment that raises the question, just who is the TFM here—Jessica or her intended audience?

"He [Kevin Barrett] refused to say that Osama bin Laden is an evil man, although I asked him this question several times."

Better luck next time, Jessica – maybe you should try water-boarding me while you repeat the question over and over, like the CIA torturers your lovely cult-leader—I mean, president—has unleashed.

But seriously, folks, I could not believe my ears as Jessica kept sputtering in radio baby-talk, "Is Osama a weely, weely evil man? IS HE?? IS HE??!" My incredulous response was, "Jessica, I feel like I'm talking to a three year old." The question remains: is Jessica a mental three-year-old, or is it her intended audience? Either way, Jessica is a perfect illustration of the infantilization of the American mind post-9/11 that Susan Sontag famously deplored:

"The disconnect between last Tuesday's monstrous dose of reality and the self-righteous drivel and outright deceptions being peddled by public figures and TV commentators is startling, depressing. The voices licensed to follow the event seem to have joined together in a campaign to infantilize the public." Susan Sontag, September 2001.

Jessica McBride and Rep. Steve Nass are still living in the America of mental three-year-olds that the 9/11 false-flag attacks were designed to create. But the rest of America is growing up. Since the Nass-McBride ambush attempt, I have yet to hear an unfriendly word from my colleagues, from the media folks who have interviewed me, or from the vast majority of ordinary citizens, who have by and large opposed Nass's call to have me fired from the University of Wisconsin. The online poll is running heavily in my favor, all but one of the call-ins on Ben Merens Wisconsin Public Radio show were supportive, the University administration is standing tall for free speech, my in-box is so clogged with congratulations that I barely have time to do anything else but acknowledge them... and best of all, people are rolling on the floor laughing at Jessica McBride's blathering rant.

The McBride-Nass ambush attempt fell so flat, and played out so perfectly for me and for MUJCA, that conspiracy theorists are already asserting that it was a MUJCA-sponsored set-up. Now, for the first time, it can be revealed that they are right. "Jessica McBride" is in fact the *nom-de-plume* of an America-hating conspiracy theorist named Cruella Bin Snottin, who has infiltrated the Wisconsin Republican party on behalf of MUJCA's devious plan to destroy Western civilization. Cruella, hats off to you—you played your role to the hilt! Never could I have imagined such histrionic perfection in my wildest satirical dreams!

And "Steve Nass," better known as "the man with one N too many," is – buckle your hats and hold on to your seat belts – really the guy with one **S** too many. "Steve Nass" is actually a dumb-ass white-guy persona developed by the Muslim hip-hopper Nas, who decided that hip-hop was dead and decided to disguise himself as a parody of a white TFM to see if he could get himself elected to office. It was all part of a scientific experiment, designed by Nas, to test the hypothesis that "In America, if you're white, you can get away with anything" – a variation on the better-known Charlie Rangel theory that George W. Bush "pretty much debunks the myth of white superiority once and for all."

So there you have it. The conspiracy has been revealed: Nas can quit the Wisconsin Legislature, let his bleached-out skin redarken, and spark a rebirth of hip-hop; Cruella can slink back to her Afghan cave to rejoin Osama's harem; and, assuming the University of Wisconsin Provost's Office continues to do their job sensibly, I can get back to preparing to teach a class on the religion of Islam.

~~~~~

A party of them knowingly conceal the truth. – *Quran*, 2:146.

F. Letters

"Conspiracy theorists" love to spend their time writing crank letters to the editor, to politicians, to their mothers, to anyone who'll listen. So, at least, goes the stereotype. I enjoy having fun with that stereotype, just as I enjoy playing around with "Irish Muslim jihadi" stereotypes.

I began my career writing 9/11 truth versions of *The Lazlo Letters* with a "Kevin Barrett Sells Out!" hoax. It bounced around the internet, and a surprisingly large number of readers took it seriously. Here is the hoax and accompanying letter, followed by other select correspondence.

MUJCA Founder Sells Out!

Kevin Barrett, founding member of the Muslim-Jewish-Christian Alliance for 9/11 Truth, has become the latest 9/11 truth activist to go over to the dark side. Hoping to finally cash in on his Ph.D. in Arabic, Barrett applied for a Secret Clearance US Army Arabic Translator position (see letter below). What led the intrepid idealist to sell his soul? "Mark Rabinowitz convinced me that everybody in the 9/11 truth movement except Mark Rabinowitz and me was a CIA spy—and we weren't too sure about me," Barrett explained. "So I said to myself, 'Hey, if everybody else is getting truckloads of the taxpayers' money to deviate from Rabinowitz's line on 9/11, why shouldn't I'?"

From: kevin@mujca.com
To: mirfan@calnet.com
Sent: Sunday, December 18, 2005 1:19 AM
Subject: Re: Seeking Arabic Language translators
Dear Mr. Irfan,

As an American with a Ph.D. in Arabic and experience as a Lecturer in Arabic at the University of Wisconsin, I am writing to express interest in the Secret Clearance US Army Arabic Translator positions that pay $150,000-$158,000 per year. I would be interested in one of these jobs, on the condition that I be allowed to work with native Arabic speakers on a special translation project designed to win Iraqi hearts and minds over to American-style democracy.

The project I am proposing is the translation into Arabic and widespread dissemination throughout the Arab world, especially Iraq, of the following books (proposed Arabic names in parentheses):

The New Pearl Harbor: Disturbing Questions About the Bush Administration and 9/11 (al-Pearl Harbor al-Jadiid) by David Ray Griffin

The 9/11 Commission Report: Omissions and Distortions (Tadmiir al-kadhaba al-rasmiyya) by David Ray Griffin

The War on Truth (al-Harb dad al-haqq) by Nafeez Ahmed

9/11 and American Empire: Christians, Jews, and Muslims Speak Out (9/11 wal-imbratoriyya al-amrikiyya) edited by Kevin Barrett, John Cobb, and Sandra Lubarsky, featuring essays by Rabbi Michael Lerner, Rosemary Reuther, John Milbank, Marc Ellis, and other leading religious intellectuals: http://mujca.com/newbook.htm

The Arab world has known that 9/11 was an inside job almost from the moment it happened, thanks in part to the statements of Mohammed Heikal, the Arab world's leading political analyst. An al-Jazeera poll (10/2003) showed that 89% of its viewers believe the US government carried out the 9/11 attacks, while only 11% blame al-Qaida. The 89% of the Arab public that knows 9/11 was a hoax is, unfortunately, able to watch CNN and other US media sources, and is thus exposed to the Goebbels-style propaganda that dominates the American corporate media. From this, and from the ongoing torture and massacres in Iraq and the US carte blanche for Sharon's genocide in Palestine, the whole Arab world has concluded, with virtual unanimity, that the US is not a democracy at all, but a brutal dictatorship with a completely controlled media.

The best way to counter that impression, and restore the Arab public's faith in democracy and in the US, would be to sponsor and disseminate the above-listed books. For one thing, if the Army were sponsoring their translation and dissemination, many Arabs might conclude that perhaps 9/11 was not an inside job after all, since anything official US sources say is automatically discredited. And even those who have investigated thoroughly enough to remain firm in their convictions would undoubtedly be impressed by the remarkably free speech enjoyed by Americans, who are free to call attention to the crimes of their leaders even in Army-sponsored publications.

Thank you for your interest in this proposed project, which, though it sounds outlandish, may very well represent America's last, best hope for salvaging any power, influence, and respect, not to mention oil, in the Middle East.

Sincerely,

Dr. Kevin J. Barrett

e-mailed to: http://www.ustreas.gov/usss/contact_usss.shtml

Public Relations Office

United States Secret Service

To Whom It May Concern,

It has come to my attention that Michael Cook, a Muslim-Jewish-Christian Alliance for 9/11 Truth activist in Kentucky, has been visited by four of your agents, and that his lawfully-possessed firearms have been twice confiscated as the result of an e-mail statement Mr. Cook made concerning our twice-unelected, World Trade Center-destroying pseudo-President. Mr. Cook's e-mail statement made no threat, but simply predicted: "Eventually he (Bush) will be shot for treason."

I am writing because I am concerned that Mr. Cook's statement may be incorrect, and I wish to request Secret Service guidelines about how I may correct Mr. Cook's mistake without running afoul of your agents. As I understand it, the usual penalty for treason is hanging, not death by firing squad. In that case, it is likely that Mr. Bush will be hanged, not shot, for treason. By making this prediction, am I running the risk of having my clothesline confiscated? I also think that there is a real possibility that Mr. Bush will be electrocuted for the mass murder of 2,500 Americans in the World Trade Center. By stating this, am I risking a court order shutting off my electricity? I also foresee a small but very real possibility that Mr. Bush will die in the gas chamber. Does raising this possibility mean that my gas could be cut off?

I appreciate the difficulty you guys must be having doing your job right now, with tens of millions of Americans calling for Bush, Cheney, Rumsfeld, Wolfowitz and company to be prosecuted and (presumably) executed for 9/11 high treason. With almost half the country believing the official 9/11 story is a cover-up (Zogby poll, May 2006) it won't be long before an overwhelming majority of Americans joins Mr. Cook in eagerly anticipating Bush's execution—which will put you fellas in a difficult position. Maybe it's time to save the country a lot of heartache, and rat out whoever it was in the SS who kept Bush at that school in Florida long after the second plane hit the building.

Thank you for your attention, and I look forward to not hearing from you—though if my clothesline disappears I'll know who it was.

Sincerely,

Kevin Barrett

e-mailed to rperle@aei.org

June 26th, 2006

Dear Richard Perle,

I understand that you encourage your friends to call you by your nickname "The Prince of Darkness." After reading your Washington Post op-ed railing at Bush and Condi for beating an "ignominious retreat" by "blinking on Iran," I am wondering why. You seem like such a sweet, innocent guy! How could a nice man like yourself, who is only concerned with "the struggle for freedom in Iran" and "support for democracy and human rights in Iran" revel in such a Satanic sobriquet?

My dear "Prince," I am writing to warn you that by dubbing yourself "The Prince of Darkness," you are encouraging your enemies to spread terrible rumors about you. For example, on WORT radio here in Madison, Wisconsin, Ashcroft-gagged FBI whistleblower Sibel Edmonds recently confirmed what she had already indirectly conveyed through an article in Vanity Fair: She says she saw FBI intercepts showing that you and Douglas Feith had arranged the financing for 9/11!

O poor defamed and denigrated Prince, it is my sad duty to inform you that Ms. Edmonds is not the only one who is saying such things. Vile rumor-mongers are claiming that the American Turkish Council (ATC) and American-Azerbaijan Chamber of Commerce (AACC), upon whose boards you and Mr. Feith so innocently sit, are fronts for drug-smuggling, money-laundering, and false-flag terrorism, and prime sponsors of the 9/11 crimes against humanity. These same back-stabbers and chatterers are claiming that Valerie Plame was outed to stop her surveillance of the ATC, which some wags have been calling the American Terrorism Council. These slanderous, conspiracy-crazed moonbats are raising the alarm that ATC and AATC, major players in the nuclear black market, may launch another 9/11-style false-flag terror event to trigger a US attack on Iran. By calling yourself "the Prince of Darkness," you only encourage such speculation.

O purehearted princely master of Machievellian mendacity, these horrific vilifications and disparagements of your royal honor will undoubtedly continue as long as you go around calling yourself "the Prince of Darkness." If you want to avoid the hangman's noose, and continue your idealistic volunteer work for freedom and democracy, I urge you to publicly repudiate your nickname "the Prince of Darkness" and make it clear that henceforth you will be addressed as "the Prince of

Sweetness and Light." That way, when you write editorials urging Americans to risk World War III by turning Iran into an irradiated charnel house, people will believe that you are motivated by a saintly, unsullied love of freedom, democracy, and the Good.

Your humble & unworthy servant,

Kevin Barrett

Coordinator, Muslim-Jewish-Christian Alliance for 9/11 Truth
http://mujca.com

* * *

Lecturer Threatens Governor's Job

(U.W.-Madison lecturer's letter to Governor Doyle warning that the Governor may be fired from his job for his intemperate statements.)

Poll results: Barrett 86%, Doyle 14%

http://www.channel3000.com/news/9457154/detail.html

* * *

A Letter to the Governor

July 5th, 2006

Dear Governor Doyle,

It has come to my attention that you have suggested that I ought to be fired from my job as a University of Wisconsin-Madison lecturer. You apparently believe that I am incapable of performing well as an instructor of Islam 370 because I am convinced that the 9/11 Commission Report is a farcical cover-up, and that overwhelming evidence suggests top US officials were complicit in the attacks of September 11th, 2001.

I understand that you are under political pressure from your right flank, and that you may feel you have no choice but to call for my dismissal. You may be surprised when the 42% of the American people who believe the 9/11 Commission Report is a cover-up – and we may be over 50% in Wisconsin – decide to cast their votes for a candidate with more integrity. I understand that there are Green and Libertarian candidates running for governor, and I predict that the controlled demolition of our corrupt two-party system by the 9/11 truth movement may begin here in Wisconsin this fall, with you and Mr. Green serving as first victims.

Meanwhile, since you believe that those who dissent from the government line on these matters are unable to perform their duties at teachers, I have decided to help you in your crusade to weed out dissenters from the ranks of U.W.-Madison instructors. (Doesn't that plaque on Bascom Hill say we need to do a lot of "sifting and winnowing" of the faculty in search of the politically incorrect?) To that end, I have prepared a questionnaire for immediate distribution to all U.W.-Madison professors, lecturers and TAs.

Sincerely,

Kevin Barrett

PS Attachment for Governor Doyle:

Questionnaire for Instructors at the University of Wisconsin-Madison

Please note that your answers to the following questions will be used to determine your eligibility to teach at the University of Wisconsin-Madison.

1) Do you believe that the Warren Report performed a thorough and unbiased investigation of the murder of JFK, and that its conclusion—that Lee Harvey Oswald acted alone—is correct?

2) Do you believe that allegations of government involvement in the assassinations of Robert Kennedy, Martin Luther King, Jr., Malcolm X, John Lennon, Mel Carnahan, and Paul Wellstone, and the attempted assassination of Ronald Reagan, have been conclusively disproven?

3) Do you believe that Timothy McVeigh acted alone in Oklahoma City, and that the military officers, and others who deny this, and who say his truck bomb could not possibly have done so much damage are crazy?

4) Do you believe that reports on massive CIA drug trafficking by Pulitzer-prize winning journalist Gary Webb—who committed suicide a few years ago with two gunshots to the head—are crazy?

5) Do you refuse to believe that the US government, at its highest levels, is just as corrupt as most other governments?

6) Do you believe that rumors of Western intelligence involvement in the Bali, Madrid, and London bombings are just that—rumors?

7) Do you believe top US officials, including LBJ, did everything they could to expose the truth about the attack on the USS Liberty by Israeli forces, and to gain justice for the victims?

8) Do you believe that FDR did everything in his power to protect the lives of our sailors at Pearl Harbor before the Japanese attack, and that the attack came as a complete surprise to him?

9) Do you believe your government always tells you the truth about gravely important matters?

10) Do you think that questions about the Constitutionality of the Federal Reserve—a private consortium of banks that creates money out of nothing, backed by nothing, at interest, thereby controlling the 80% of the world's currency that is in US dollars—are just a bunch of crazy conspiracy theories?

11) Do you agree that it is the Executive Branch, not the Legislative Branch or the people, that ought to have the power to decide when, where, how, and why the nation goes to war under the US Constitution?

12) Do you agree that the oath to defend the Constitution "against all enemies, foreign AND DOMESTIC" is referring to domestic enemies like Communists and Muslims, not top US officials who violate the Constitution?

13) Do you believe that Spanish forces sunk the Maine in 1898, and that the US invasion, occupation and annexation of Spanish colonies was a justified response to this outrage?

14) Do you believe that the US government did everything it could to protect the lives of the passengers on board the SS Lusitania?

15) Do you believe that the North Vietnamese attacked a US ship in the Gulf of Tonkin in 1964, and that the subsequent US escalation of the war was a justified response to this outrage?

16) Do you think that those who believe in Operation Northwoods—a 1962 plan for war-trigger fake terror attacks involving mass murders of Americans by covert US military forces—are crazy?

17) Do you believe that Iraqi forces in Kuwait threw babies out of their incubators to die, and that the congressional authorization for Gulf War 1 based on the baby-incubator outrage was justified?

18) Do you believe that questions about the "October Surprise," in which George Bush 1 was rumored to have negotiated a deal with the Iranians to keep US hostages locked up until Reagan defeated Carter and took office, have been fully answered, and that the story has been conclusively debunked?

19) Do you believe that the US invaded Iraq in order to prevent Iraq from using WMD's against the US, and that the Iraqi threat was real and imminent?

20) Do you believe that the 9/11 Commission Report fully, truthfully, and adequately answered all of the serious questions that have been raised about the possibility of official complicity in the September 11th attacks?

Please note that "no" answers to any of the above questions indicate absurd beliefs and poor judgment, and may be grounds for immediate dismissal and/or non-renewal of contract.

Signed,

Steve Nass, Reichschancellor

Thoughtcrime Division

University of Wisconsin-Madison

[Upon receipt of the above letter, Governor Doyle immediately called a press conference and announced that I had sent him "some kind of diatribe" that raised further questions about my capacity to function as a university instructor.]

* * *

Gov casts doubts on UW teacher

Says lecturer on hot seat may be unfit for job

By David Callender and Aaron Nathans

(*The Capital Times*, July 8th, 2006: http://www.madison.com/tct/mad/topstories/index.php?ntid=90417)

Gov. Jim Doyle is hinting that a controversial lecturer at the University of Wisconsin-Madison may be unfit to teach.

Doyle told reporters on Friday that based on a letter he received from Islamic studies lecturer Kevin Barrett, the university must look closely at "whether he has the capacity to teach students."

In an interview, Barrett claimed much of the letter he sent to the governor was merely a parody, suggesting that anyone espousing critical or conspiratorial views would be considered unfit to teach at the university.

But based on Doyle's reaction, Barrett said, "I question his ability to govern the state." ...

* * *

Dear Governor Doyle,

Thank you for responding to my recent letter. I am sure most of your constituents get brief form-letter responses from you, so finding my letter the subject of a press conference and a major news story was quite an honor.
(The letter is archived at http://mujca.com/governordoyle.htm; scroll down for my mock-questionnaire for UW teachers.)

I think you're basically a good guy—I used to play pick-up basketball with you at the Nat, and I know you're a ferocious but fair competitor—so I would like to explain that my letter was intended in the spirit of friendly satire, not mean-spirited sarcasm. I studied absurdist literature at an impressionable age, and grew fond of this style of saying serious things in a humorous way.

My headline "Lecturer Threatens Governor's Job" was a humorous "man bites dog" inversion of the story from a few days earlier, when the **governor** had threatened a **lecturer's** job on the basis of political views espoused on a radio program. As conservative professor Donald Downs has written, this kind of threat represents a wholesale rollback of the prevailing norms of academic freedom. The "Lecturer Threatens Governor's Job" headline was also intended to underscore the point that public officials are hired and fired at will by the people, and that it is the ordinary person—the $8,000-a-semester lecturer in this case—who should be hiring and firing the governor, not vice-versa. Effrontery? Unmitigated audacity? Sure. That's the fun of it. As I told Aaron Nathans the other day, there is no Arabic word for chutzpah, but I'm trying to invent one.

As for my questionnaire, that was intended to underscore the point that there is a very important debate in progress that touches on the issues raised in my questions. On one side of the debate are those who promote a mythical view of history designed to inculcate a kind of fundamentalist religious faith in American exceptionalism—the idea that while other governments are corrupt, suffer coups d'etat and inside-job assassinations, have their democratic institutions undermined by plutocrats, use false-flag attacks to trigger wars of aggression, and so on, nothing like this could ever possibly happen here. On the other side are historians, journalists and intellectuals who are critically examining and debating the events listed in my questionnaire, and their implications for our society.

If you want the University of Wisconsin to function as a state church that inculcates fundamentalist religious faith in American exceptionalism, my questionnaire would be a good way to weed out potential heretics. If, on the other hand, you want the University to remain true to its tradition of "fearless sifting and winnowing" and its motto "the truth will set you free," people who raise questions about these issues, and debate them rationally on the basis of evidence, should be sought out and hired, not hunted down and fired.

While I have built up a loyal readership at MUJCA in part on the basis of my satirical writings, some readers have suggested that now that I am reaching a broader audience I should go easy on the satire and speak more straightforwardly, in a manner more in keeping with the conventional tone of academia. Their advice is well taken, and I apologize if my previous letter gave rise to misunderstandings and confusion. In particular, you should know that my speech and writings as a satirist and activist are completely different, in tone, style, and content, from my speech in the classroom.

I would be happy to meet with you, in public or in private, to discuss my teaching record and philosophy and my plans and syllabus for the fall section of Islam 370. I also hope to participate in scholarly debates about the evidence for and against the adequacy of the *9/11 Commission Report*—debates which I believe will sooner or later change your opinion, and received opinion in general, about this gravely important matter.

Thank you for your attention, and I look forward to hearing from you.

Sincerely,

Kevin Barrett

This came to Kevin@mujca.com *from* info@johnkerry.com

Subject: The Difference You Are Making

Dear Kevin,

Over the last 19 months, when you could have walked away, you dusted yourself off, got back on your feet, dug deeper, and you have fought even harder.

[it goes on like this and finishes:]

Thanks so much for all of your help, energy and commitment. I'm proud of what you do, and I hope I live up to your values and convictions in the way I fight by your side.

Sincerely,

John Kerry

Kevin Barrett Replies to John Kerry,

Subject: The Difference You Are NOT Making

Dear John,

You, my "war-hero" friend, are a feckless yellow-bellied WIMP. 19 months ago, when you could have walked away... you did! You let the Bush crime family and their 9/11 perp friends the neocons steal the election you won in a landslide 53%-47%. If you had the slightest shred of guts or integrity, you could have had us all out in the streets taking back the country. Instead, you tucked your tail between your legs and fled like the coward you are. Unless, of course, the two candidates from Skull and Bones had the whole thing fixed in advance. Either way, it appears that masturbating in a coffin in front of your sick Yalie frat buddies doesn't do much for your intestinal fortitude. As far as I'm concerned, you're history. But hey, prove me wrong. Get onboard with 9/11 truth NOW or condemn yourself to historical irrelevance.

Sincerely,

Kevin Barrett

Rupert Murdoch

Bull-Goose Loonie & Fascist Billionaire Extraordinaire

Fox News

Dear Mr. Murdoch,

It has come to my attention that one of your announcers, Bill O'Reilly, has stated on national television that he would like to see me murdered and thrown into Boston Harbor.

Since I already get so many e-mail death threats I can't keep track of them (among the 10% of my 9/11-related e-mails that are negative) this is a pretty inflammatory thing to say. If anything were to happen to me, Fox News would find itself facing the mother of all lawsuits, and my family might very well end up in control of the Murdoch fortune. You may wish to consider urging your friends in the White House to offer me Secret Service protection. Please assign me the guy who said "we're out of here" to Bush when the second plane hit the building at 9:04— not the higher-up who overruled him and kept Bush reading about pet goats while our nation was allegedly under surprise attack. See: http://www.whatreallyhappened.com/9-11secretservice.html . The Secret Service agent who said "we're out of here" before being overruled was honest. That's the guy I want protecting my life.

Also, you might want to tell O'Reilly that HE'S the one who should worry about ending up in Boston Harbor. 9/11 was an act of high treason and mass murder, and media figures complicit in the cover-up will be viewed, a few years hence, the way we now view Dr. Goebbels.

The last time a bunch of empire-builders tried to trample on our rights, we had a little uprising called the American Revolution. It's time for another one. Let's kick it off with another Boston Tea Party—a little red-white-and-blue version of V-for-Vendetta—and throw the whole Fox News crew, along with the traitors in this administration, straight into Boston Harbor.

Sincerely,

Kevin Barrett

* * *

From: Ben Vaughan
Date: December 19, 2006
To: kevin@mujca.com
Subject: To Kevin Barrett: Support after O'Reilly Factor

Dear Mr. Barrett,

Having just watched the O'Reilly Factor on the Fox News Channel, I felt obligated to write to you to voice my support.

While I am rather undecided when it comes to 9/11, I felt it necessary to let you know I thought your spot on The O'Reilly Factor went brilliantly—or as well as any interview can go when the guest has any opinion different to that of Fox/O'Reilly.

I have only recently been introduced to the joys of The O'Reilly Factor. Many of us Brit's watch the show purely as a source of comedy, none of us quite believing that something so utterly right-wing can even be broadcast.

I have watched quite a few O'Reilly shows but rarely do I see a decent guest get to put a decent point across without being cut off by this idiot. Thankfully, you managed it, and for that I thought I would say well done.

Please know that there are a lot of people out there screaming (literally) in support of anyone who argues a valid point against O'Reilly.

Your appearance tonight was a welcomed one.

Thank you, and good luck.

Fondest Regards,

Ben Vaughan

~~~~~

FALSE FLAG FACTS

BBC 2 aired a documentary "The Power of Nightmares: The Rise of the Politics of Fear" – a must-see. In part III, "Shadows in the Cave," which you can see on Google video, producer Adam Curtis goes on the search for Al Qaeda – and concludes that ***Al-Qaeda does not exist!***

So if it is just a bogey that doesn't even exist, how did this non-existent organization execute the huge feats seen on 9/11, demolishing three steel skyscrapers to dust, plus a kamikaze attack on the best-defended building in the USA, the Department of Defense in the Pentagon? Go figure.

23 August, 2006

To the Capital Times

Kudos to American Players Theater and to Kevin Lynch for his perceptive review of *Julius Caesar* (10/21/06). I especially liked the line, "What we bring away from this deeply ambivalent drama is the stuff we'll make of our own times."

Steve Nass probably thinks this Shakespeare guy is some moonbat who should be fired from his job at APT for promoting "conspiracy theories." After all, right-thinking people know that coups d'état never happen, and that political assassinations are always by lone-nut outsiders, not powerful insiders.

Call me crazy, but I still say the assassination of Julius Caesar was an inside job.

Kevin Barrett

* * *

E-mailed to Rep. Steve Nass (rep.nass@legis.state.wi.us) on Tuesday evening, July 11th, and left as a standing debate challenge ever since:

Dear Rep. Nass,

Since you have stated that I have no scholarly basis for my ideas about 9/11, and repeatedly insulted me and my views, I challenge you to a public debate on the topic. You will argue that the *9/11 Commission Report* is a trustworthy account of the events of 9/11, and I will argue that it is not.

The debate format will favor complex argumentation backed by scholarly sources, and allow for sustained cross-examination.

Are you willing to stand behind your ideas and subject them to the light of critical scrutiny? Or are you afraid to go beyond simple name-calling?

Sincerely,

Kevin Barrett

Appendix 1:
Hannity & Colmes Interview – Fox TV 7/10/06

Starts with an excerpt from Barrett speaking on Visibility 9/11 Podcast of 7/1/06:

"... happening, you know, largely through this false flag terrorism. It looks to me like not only 9/11 but also Madrid, 7/7, the Bali hotel bombing and probably most of the so-called Zarqawi style bombings in Iraq are all false flag operations being carried out by a special wing of probably U.S. or Western military intelligence."

Colmes: That was University of Wisconsin Prof. Kevin Barrett, who has recently drawn criticism for plans to teach an Islamic Studies course next fall that will incorporate conspiracy theories that the U.S. government was involved in the events of September 11th. Prof. Barrett joins us now. Professor, can you give us the context within which you teach this?

Barrett: Oh yeah, sure. I'm teaching an introductory course on Islam. And I think it's really important to cover these contemporary political issues. And one of them is, of course, the so-called War on Terror. Now the fact is that the great majority of the world's Muslims believe that 9/11 was an inside job.

Colmes: Okay, that's your opinion, right? You're offering your opinion that 9/11 was an inside job.

Barrett: Well, after studying the evidence pretty intensively for two-and-a-half years, I am convinced that 9/11 was in fact an inside job.

Colmes: And are students required to regurgitate that in some way in order to do well in your class?

Barrett: Of course they're not. That's ridiculous. I'm not interested in making students regurgitate anything. I'm interested in training people how to use critical thinking skills to look at the evidence in any area and come to their own conclusions. And I would hope they'd be able to do that.

Colmes: Is this a required class?

Barrett: No, it's not.

Colmes: So this is basically an elective class. How much of the time is spent focusing on who caused 9/11?

Barrett: Only about one week. We're looking at the War on Terror for one week. And in fact it's not focusing on who caused it. It's looking at the main interpretations of 9/11. And there are really several different ways of looking at 9/11, and one of them, of course, is the standard American story of the War on Terror that changed everything. It set us at war, it rolled back our civil liberties, it doubled our military budget. All those things had been planned before 9/11. Every one of those things had been put into place before 9/11.

Colmes: Okay, do you objectively ... Professor, let me ask you, do you objectively put forth that view as well as the view of how you perceive Muslims viewing us? Are they presented in a fair and balanced manner?

Barrett: Of course. In the classroom I always present things in a fair and balanced manner. Outside the classroom when I'm an activist or a satirist I'll tell it like it is. Inside the classroom I'll present all of the defensible interpretations and let the students use their own critical reasoning skills to come to their own conclusion.

Hannity: All right, Mr. Barrett, Sean Hannity here. Do you really believe that 9/11 was an inside job – not just 9/11 but Madrid and Bali and the Zarqawi operation?

Barrett: Well, you know, actually...

Hannity: I'm asking ... hang on a second ...

Barrett: Yeah, okay, finish up.

Hannity: ... do you believe personally that these are inside jobs – yes or no?

Barrett: It's not quite that simple. I do know – I don't believe, I know that 9/11 was an inside job.

Professor Steven Jones has found residue of thermate on the steel samples from the World Trade Center ...

Hannity: Okay, I don't have a lot of time. Let me ask you this. What evidence do you have that 9/11 ...

Barrett: .... We now know that it was taken down in a controlled demolition.

Hannity: All right. So you believe that the buildings came down in a controlled demolition, right?

Barrett: Well, I don't believe it. I've looked at the evidence and the evidence is overwhelming.

Hannity: Okay, you're right, of course. All right, the evidence is overwhelming to you ...

Barrett: Sure it is.

Hannity: ... because you're a conspiracy nut, but putting all that aside ...

Barrett: No, actually, all of you—I ask your viewers to take a look at this evidence for themselves. They can go to ...

Hannity: That's fine, but ...

Barrett: ST911.org, that's Scholars for 9/11 Truth.

Hannity: All right, you got your free plug in.

Barrett: Take a look. Take a look at the demolitions.

Hannity: Now here's ... here's ... I know you think you're the smartest guy in the world, Professor. But here's the point ...

Barrett: Morgan Reynolds, a former Bush Administration official ...

Hannity: ... the question is, you are ...

Barrett: ... says that the Bush Administration blew the World Trade Center to kingdom come. That's a direct quote from a member of the Bush Administration itself. They blew the World Trade Center to kingdom come.

Hannity: I know, and there were people that said that the Jews were told to leave. We've heard a lot of these sick, bizarre theories.

Barrett: That's not the same thing.

Hannity: I don't believe any of them, but you're allowed to believe what you want. But that's not what's at hand here. The issue is ...

Barrett: Well, it's a question of science.

Hannity: ... whether or not you, with your bizarre theories, are the best, the most competent ...

Barrett: I think you have the bizarre theory. You think it was 19 guys with boxcutters ...

Hannity: ... hang on a second. You're a very angry man.

Barrett: ... led by a guy on dialysis in a cave in Afghanistan? That's ridiculous. I mean, that's the craziest conspiracy theory of all of them.

Hannity: Mm-hmm. Okay. I wish I had the Twilight Zone music. Now, here's my next question.

Barrett: [chuckles] Okay, play it.

Hannity: The issue that's at hand here, you're entitled to have your opinion, and I don't really care what you believe, but if we're talking about a captive group of students in a classroom, the question we've got to...

Barrett: I'm not going to hold them captive.

Hannity: ... hang on a second. Well, they're sitting in a classroom, and you have a position of authority. I'm wondering—the question is whether or not you're the most competent to teach them. And most people think you're a nut. Most people think you're usually not even worth listening to.

Barrett: Well, actually, no, they don't. We just had a poll here in Madison, and we found that 90% of the respondents, a Channel 3000 poll, said that I should be allowed to teach. Only 10% said I shouldn't.

Hannity: Well, that's the question at hand. I agree that that's the question. I don't think what your views are ...

Barrett: And 60% agreed with me about the questions I'm raising about 9/11. 60% of the respondents. You're in the minority.

Hannity: I think you have every right to speak. I don't think this is the proper forum, though, for people that hold extremist views like yourself.

Barrett: No, you guys are extremists. Fox News is the biggest bunch of extremists on the planet.

Hannity: I got it. But reasonable people see you as an extremist, and I don't think you're the most appropriate guy to teach that class. My guess is – my final thought is we can do better than you. That's my point.

Barrett: Well, I don't think you're the most appropriate guy to be on the airwaves spewing your venom throughout this country. I think you guys should be taken off the airwaves because you are the guys who are responsible for high treason, not the New York Times. [The Fox segment before the Barrett interview accused the New York Times of treason for revealing the secret, unconstitutional NSA spy-on-Americans program the Bush administration put in place several months *before* 9/11.]

Hannity: All right, Professor. You want to silence a conservative.

Colmes: We don't want to silence anybody. You teach, and we'll do Hannity & Colmes. Thank you, Professor.

Appendix 2: 9/11 Truth Bibliography and References

Nafeez Ahmed, *The War on Freedom: How and Why America Was Attacked, September 11, 2001* (Joshua Tree, Calif.: Tree of Life Publications, 2002)

——, *The War on Truth: 9/11, Disinformation, and the Anatomy of Terrorism* Northampton, MA: Interlink, 2005).

Kevin Barrett, John Cobb and Sandra Lubarsky, eds. *9/11 and the American Empire: Christians, Jews and Muslims Speak Out* (Northampton: Interlink, 2006)

Global Outlook magazine, issues No. 1-11. Oro, Ontario, Canada (2002-2006). www.globaloutlook.ca

David Ray Griffin, *Christian Faith and the Truth behind 9/11* (Louisville: Westminster John Knox Press, 2006)

——, *The New Pearl Harbor: Disturbing Questions About the Bush Administration and 9/11* (Northampton: Interlink, 2005)

——, *The 9/11 Commission Report: Omissions and Distortions* (Northampton: Interlink Books, 2005)

David Ray Griffin and Peter Dale Scott, eds. *9/11 and the American Empire: Intellectuals Speak Out* (Northampton: Interlink, 2006)

Barbara Honegger, "Seven Hours in September: The Clock that Broke the Lie." In Jim Marrs, *The Terror Conspiracy: Deception, 9/11 and the Loss of Liberty* (The Disinformation Company, 2006)

Daniel Hopsicker, *Welcome to Terrorland: Mohamed Atta and the 9/11 Cover-up in Florida* (Eugene: MacCowPress, 2004)

Eric Hufschmid, *Painful Questions: An Analysis of the September 11th Attack* (Goleta, Calif.: Endpoint Software, 2002)

Peter Lance, *Cover Up: What the Government is Still Hiding about the War on Terror* (New York: Harper-Collins/ReganBooks, 2004)

T.H. Meyer, *Reality, Truth and Evil: Facts, Questions and Perspectives About September 11th, 2001* (London: Temple Lodge, 2005).

Thierry Meyssan, *9/11: The Big Lie* (London: Carnot, 2002)/

——, *Pentagate* (London: Carnot 2002)

Rowland Morgan, *Flight 93: What Really Happened on the Heroic 9/11 'Let's Roll' Flight* (London: Constable & Robinson, 2006)

Rowland Morgan and Ian Henshall, *9/11 Revealed: The Unanswered Questions* (New York: Carroll & Graf, 2005)

Don Paul and Jim Hoffman, *Waking Up from Our Nightmare, the 9/11/01 Crimes in New York City* (San Francisco: I/R, 2004).

Project for the New American Century, *Rebuilding America's Defenses: Strategy, Forces and Resources for a New Century*, September 2000 (www.newamericancentury.org)

Justin Raimondo, *The Terror Enigma: 9/11 and the Israeli Connection* (Lincoln, NE: iuniverse, 2003)

Michael C Ruppert, *Crossing the Rubicon: The Decline of the American Empire at the End of the Age of Oil* (Gabriola Island, BC, Canada: New Society Press, 2004)

Webster Tarpley, *9/11 Synthetic Terror Made in USA* (Joshua Tree, CA: Progressive Press, 2005).

Gore Vidal, *Dreaming War: Blood for Oil and the Cheney-Bush Junta* (NY: Thunder's Mouth, 2002)

Paul Zarembka, ed., *The Hidden History of 9-11-2001* (Amsterdam: Elsevier, March, 2006)

Barrie Zwicker, *Towers of Deception: The Media Cover-up of 9/11* (Gabriola Island, BC, Canada: New Society, 2006)

* * *

The Official Story

The 9/11 Commission Report: Final Report of the National Commission on Terrorist Attacks upon the United States, Authorized Edition (New York: W. W. Norton, 2004) [should be read alongside Griffin's critique]

Der Spiegel Magazine: *Inside 9/11: What Really Happened* (NY: St. Martin's, 2002) It includes useful information as well as disinfo. Sample: "It makes for a great story. A petty thief pilfers files containing critical information about the largest terrorist attack in history and dutifully turns them over to the police. BKA agents do not buy this story for a minute; they suspect that some other secret service was trying to find a way of getting evidence into BKA hands. The question is, whose secret service?" (167)

Steven Strasser, ed. *The 9/11 Investigations: Staff Reports of the 9/11 Commission* (NY: PublicAffairs2004.

Web Resources

mujca.com (note Steven Jones and David Griffin links in upper left corner)

911blogger.com

st911.org

physics911.net

911truth.org

cooperativeresearch.org

911research.wtc7.net

globalresearch.ca

infowars.com

prisonplanet.com

whatreallyhappened.com

Favorite articles:

Steven E. Jones, "Why Indeed Did the WTC Buildings Collapse?" Regularly-updated peer-reviewed scientific paper archived at: http://www.physics.byu.edu/research/energy/htm7.html

David Ray Griffin papers available on the internet archived at: http://mujca.com/newyork.htm

"The Fake bin Laden Video" (http://www.whatreallyhappened.com/osamatape.html).

"Terrorist Stag Parties," *Wall Street Journal*, October 10, 2001 http://www.opinionjournal.com/best/?id=95001298

"Top Ten things You Never Knew about Mohamed Atta," Mad Cow Morning News, June 7, 2004 (www.madcowprod.com/index60.html)

~~~~~

FALSE FLAG FACTS

The real burden of history most Americans don't want to think about: No people has *ever* been mad or bad enough to *want* war with the USA. Like a habitual bully, the US has *covertly* provoked every major foreign war (and hundreds of "interventions"): from the 1846 war on Mexico, 1898 war on Spain, two great wars on Germany, on Korea, Vietnam (Gulf of Tonkin), Cuba (Operation Northwoods), Gulf War I (incubator baby fraud) and II (9/11 and yellowcake), and as we go to press, faked evidence against Iran. Who is really served by this? Not We the People!

Notes

[1] http://www.serendipity.li/wot/571-page-lie.htm

[2] David Griffin, *The 9/11 Commission Report: Omissions and Distortions* (Northampton, MA: Interlink, 2005). A critique of *The 9/11 Commission Report: Final Report of the National Commission on Terrorist Attacks upon the United States*, Authorized Edition (New York: W. W. Norton, 2004).

[3] David Griffin, *The New Pearl Harbor* (Northampton, MA: Interlink, 2004).

[4] Nafeez Ahmed, *The War on Truth* (Northampton, MA: Interlink, 2005).

[5] Webster Tarpley, *9/11 Synthetic Terror: Made in USA* (Joshua Tree, CA: Progressive Press, 2005).

[6] David Bamford, "Hijack 'Suspect' Alive in Morocco," BBC News, Sept. 22, 2001 (http://news.bbc.co.uk/1/hi/world/middle_east/1558669.stm). *Telegraph*, September 23, 2001 (www.portal.telegraph.co.uk/news/main.jhtml?xml= /news/2001/09/23/widen23.xml). In "Subverting Terrorism" Nafeez Ahmed reports that ten of the nineteen hijackers have been reliably reported to have been alive post-9/11: http://reprehensor.gnn.tv/blogs/12624/ Subverting_Terrorism_Nafeez_Ahmed_Part_1_3

[7] For background on the "19 hijackers" see Daniel Hopsicker, *Welcome to Terrorland: Mohamed Atta and the 9/11 Cover-up in Florida* (Eugene: MadCowPress, 2004). For reports of their survival post-9/11, see previous note.

[8] www.cnn.com/SPECIALS/2001/trade.center/victims/AA11.victims.html, www.cnn.com/SPECIALS/2001/trade.center/victims/AA77.victims.html, www.cnn.com/SPECIALS/2001/trade.center/victims/UA93victims.html, www.cnn.com/SPECIALS/2001/trade.center/victims/UA175.victims.html

[9] http://www.whatreallyhappened.com/osamatape.html

[10] Amber Rupinta, *Duke Professor Skeptical of bin Laden Tape* (http://abclocal.go.com/wtvd/story?%20section=local&id=3828678)

[11] Paul Sheridan and Ed Haas, "FBI says, 'No hard evidence connecting Bin Laden to 9/11'" (http://www.theithacajournal.com/apps/pbcs.dll/article?AID=/20060629/OPINION02/606290310/1014)

[12] http://www.cooperativeresearch.org/timeline.jsp?timeline=complete_911_timeline&the_isi:_a_more_detailed_look=mahmoodAhmed

[13] http://www.whatreallyhappened.com/cutter.html

[14] Steven E. Jones "Why Indeed Did the WTC Buildings Collapse?" http://www.physics.byu.edu/research/energy/htm7.html; David Ray Griffin, "The Destruction of the World Trade Center: Why the Official Account Cannot Be True" http://911review.com/articles/griffin/nyc1.html

[15] Griffin, *The 9/11 Commission Report: Omissions and Distortions*.

16 See Griffin, *The New Pearl Harbor: Disturbing Questions About the Bush Administration and 9/11* (Northampton: Interlink, 2004) p.25-48; Thierry Meyssan, *9/11: The Big Lie* (London: Carnot, 2002); Barbara Honegger, "Seven Hours in September: The Clock that Broke the Lie" (http://www.apfn.org/apfn/WTC_target.htm) to be published in Jim Marrs *The 9/11 Terror Conspiracy* (2006); and http://www.pentagonresearch.com/.

17 Rowland Morgan, *Flight 93: What Really Happened On The Heroic 9/11 'Let's Roll' Flight* (London: Constable & Robinson, 2006).

18 "Statement of Secretary of Transportation Norman Y. Mineta before the National Commission on Terrorist Attacks upon the United States, May 23, 2003" (available at www.cooperativeresearch.org/timeline/2003/commissiontestimony052303.htm); Richard Clarke, *Against All Enemies: Inside America's War on Terror* (NY: Free Press, 2004).

19 Dan Eggen, "9/11 Panel Suspected Deception by Pentagon; Allegations Brought to Inspectors General" (*Washington Post* August 2, 2006).

20 "Group of 9/11 Widows Question the Entire 9/11 Commission's Report" (http://www.rawstory.com/news/2006/Group_of_widows_claim_911_Independent_0804.html)

21 Jones, "Why Indeed Did the WTC Buildings Collapse?"

22 Kevin Barrett, "Two Plus Two Make Four" http://mujca.com/masterplan.htm

23 The letters are reprinted later in this book.

24 Literally, ignorance, particularly ignorance of Islam, or paganism. In Arabic history, the pre-Islamic period, marked by decadence and barbarism, but also a flowering of culture, especially poetry.

25 Unlike in Chistianity and Judaism, which have special offices for priests, ministers and rabbis, Muslims allow any competent adult to serve as imam and lead a congregational prayer.

26 Mûlay Muhammad al-Bûzîdî lived in the latter half of the 18th century c.e. He was a disciple of the Shaykh Mûlay al-'Arabî ad-Darqâwî, who granted him the title of autonomous master. Sidi Buzîdî's disciple, Ahmad Ibn 'Ajîba, was a noted author of Sufi works that are increasingly being reissued and translated into French and English.

27 *sâhib ash-shay' yastatî' wa qâdir 'ala kulli shay'*

28 A well-known *hadîth qudsî* makes this doctrinal point clear: "...This morning one of My servants became a believer in Me and one a disbeliever. As for him who said: We have been given rain by virtue of Allah and His mercy, that one is a believer in Me, a disbeliever in the stars; as for him who said: We have been given rain by such-and-such a star, that one is a disbeliever in Me, a believer in the stars." Transmitter Zayd ibn Khâlid al-Juhaniyy. Reported in Bukhârî, Mâlik, and an-Nasâ'i . Ibrahim and Johnson-Davies, 44.

[29] As implied by the doctrine of *fanâ'*, annihilation of the ego in God. A key scriptural source for this idea is the *hadîth qudsî*: "And My servant continues drawing nearer to Me through supererogatory acts until I love him; and when I love him, I become his ear with which he hears, his eye with which he sees, his hand with which he grasps, and his foot with which he walks." William A. Graham, *Divine Word and Prophetic Word in Early Islam, A Reconsideration of the Sources, with Special Reference to the Divine Saying or "Hadîth Qudsî,"* p. 173 no. 49. Quoted and discussed in Ernst, 10.

[30] I used the alien/reptile image in the article "'Conspiracy Theorist' Asserts: Bush and Cheney Are Death Lizards from Outer Space" (see page 140). The article was meant as satire, with the reptile image as a metaphor for the rapacious, coldblooded, unempathetic reptilian quality of the Bush Administration. When I wrote it I had never heard of David Icke, who supposedly claims that the British Royal Family is made up of drug-dealing alien reptiles; although I have not yet read Icke, so I am going on hearsay.

[31] www.whitehouse.gov/news/releases/2002/03/20020313-8.html

[32] Stanley Hilton: "Our case is alleging that Bush and his puppets Rice and Cheney and Mueller and Rumsfeld and so forth, Tenet, were all involved not only in aiding and abetting and allowing 9/11 to happen but in actually ordering it to happen. Bush personally ordered it to happen. We have some very incriminating documents as well as eye-witnesses, that Bush personally ordered this event to happen in order to gain political advantage, to pursue a bogus political agenda on behalf of the neocons and their deluded thinking in the Middle East. I also wanted to point out that, just quickly, I went to school with some of these neocons. At the University of Chicago, in the late 60s with Wolfowitz and Feith and several of the others and so I know these people personally. And we used to talk about this stuff all of the time. And I did my senior thesis on this very subject—how to turn the U.S. into a presidential dictatorship by manufacturing a bogus Pearl Harbor event. So, technically this has been in the planning at least 35 years" (www.rense.com/general57/aale.htm).

[33] See my review of *Neoconned Again* in this volume for a consideration of Luttwak's book.

[34] Michael Ledeen, *Machiavelli on Modern Leadership: Why Machiavelli's Iron Rules are as Timely and Important Today as Five Centuries Ago* (NY: St. Martins, 2000).

[35] The Muslim-Jewish-Christian Alliance for 9/11 Truth has always been open to people from a wide variety of perspectives. Its statement of purpose is as follows:

MUJCA-NET is a group of scholars, religious leaders and activists dedicated to uniting members of the Jewish, Christian and Islamic faiths in pursuit of 9/11 truth. We believe that the process of joining together in search of the truth about 9/11 will bring enormous benefits, regardless of what truths we may discover. While our endorsers and supporters have different views about the probable level of US government complicity in 9/11, all of us agree that a new, honest investigation of the possibility of official complicity is a matter of the most urgent national and global importance. See: http://www.mujca.com

36 As Canadian journalist Barrie Zwicker put it, "It is a war against Islam...It is a war against millions of people who happen to share the same faith." Terry Glavin, "Zwicker loses the 9/11 plot," http://www.straight.com/ content.cfm?id=19718 . Gore Vidal sees a religious factor behind this new crusade: "Mr. Bush is a 'come to Jesus' kind of fellow who believes he is doing God's work." Newsmax article "Gore Vidal Calls Bush, Blair 'Dangerous Jesus Lovers'"(archived at www.informationclearinghouse.info/article2614.htm).

37 See http://mujca.com An early version of Faiz Khan's essay is archived at http://mujca.com/muslims.htm, while a later version is in Barrett, Cobb and Lubarsky, *9/11 and the American Empire: Christians, Jews and Muslims Speak Out* (Northampton: Interlink, 2006).

38 For a link to Feuer's article, and my response to it, see: http://mujca.com/ nytimes.htm

39 Dr. Khan gave a talk based on his essay in *9/11 and the American Empire: Christians, Jews and Muslims Speak Out* (op. cit.)

40 In *Poems of Arab Andalusia,* tr. Cola Franzen, from the Spanish version of Emilio García Gomez (San Francisco: City Lights, 1989).

41 I am playing with the Latin phrase to make a point; as far as I know, no other Muslims have used it in this way, and it is not a part of Islamic discursive tradition.

42 Murata and Chittick have incorporated a lucid look at this cosmology in their introductory textbook *The Vision of Islam* (NY: Paragon House, 1994).

43 I am translating *taqwa* as God-consciousness. It is sometimes translated as God-fearingness, but I think this over-emphaszes the aspect of fear.

44 Marshall Hodgson, *The Venture of Islam: The Middle Period: Conscience and History in a World Civilization v.2: The Expansion of Islam in the Middle Periods.* Chicago: U of Chicago Press, 1974.

45 I will use the term Andalusia as the English translation of *al-andalus,* "the name used for the ever-shifting Muslim polities of Iberia, never quite the whole of the peninsula." Maria Menocal, *The Ornament of the World: How Jews, Christians, and Muslims Created A Culture of Tolerance in Medieval Spain* (Boston-NY-London: Little, Brown, 2002). This meaning should not be confused with the word's more common English sense as a geographical region in what is today southern Spain.

46 Murata and Chittick translate *kafirun* as "truth-concealers." The concept of *kufr* or unbelief is the opposite of *shukr* or gratitude—in this context, gratitude to God for the gift of existence. Hence my translation "ungrateful ones."

47 Bernard Lewis, *The Crisis of Islam: Holy War and Unholy Terror* (NY: Modern Library 2003). Lewis's use of the *dar al-harb* concept is interrogated by Michael Sells at: http://listserv.linguistlist.org/cgi-bin/wa?A2=ind0110&L=arabic-info&P=2993

[48] I offer these controversial comments in the interest of honesty, and because this essay is a personal vision by an author writing as a Muslim. My "Andalusian" vision is of a genuine plurality of voices, in which people with radically different views may feel comfortable expressing their views and co-existing despite their differences. I have close friends who are Jewish and pro-Zionist, and we are happy to "agree to disagree" on the question of Israel-Palestine. I believe that when pro-Zionists and anti-Zionists are willing to get to know each other and even learn to like each other as human beings, despite their differences on one political issue, we will have come a long way toward an Andalusian culture and a viable peace process.

Currently in the USA, established academic, journalistic, publishing and media institutions are enforcing a pro-Zionist line in which the Muslim-majority position on the Israel-Palestine dispute is almost entirely suppressed from public discourse, and a pro-Zionist chorus drowns out all dissent. If al-Jazeera can bring pro-Zionist and Israeli voices into its programming, I do not see why American institutions cannot bring themselves to allow the Muslim-majority position to be heard. I am intentionally resisting suggestions that I tone down my position on Zionist ethnic cleansing, in order to underline my belief that American institutional gatekeepers need to open up to a genuinely diverse array of voices on this question, including those of the Muslim-majority position that I express here.

Regarding the question of whether the term ethnic cleansing is accurate when applied to Zionism: I take the term to mean changing the ethnic demographics of an area by force—i.e. expelling people of a targeted ethnicity, and not letting them return.

Some who resist applying the term "ethnic cleansing" to Israel argue that only if large numbers of Palestinians were forcibly removed from their current residences, circa 2006, would there be an ethnic cleansing. This position is often confused with another misconception—that ethnic cleansing would only happen if it were completely and absolutely successful for all time, i.e. that Palestinians would have a zero chance of reclaiming the land and homes they were ethnically cleansed from. (At which point, crying "ethnic cleansing" would of course be pointless!)

My position, which I take to be the position of the great majority of the world's Muslims, is that Israel's current demographic status, in which Jews and Europeans outnumber Palestinians by perhaps 80% to 20% within Israel proper (meaning either the UN borders or the post-1948 pre-1967 borders) is the product of an ongoing program of ethnic cleansing. The 1948 terror campaign that drove the great majority of Palestinians from their homes, and Israel's ongoing refusal to obey UN resolutions demanding that these refugees be allowed to return, have their property restored, and be paid compensation for their suffering, is an indefensible, illegal, ongoing act of ethnic cleansing. I (and most other Muslims) will regard "Israel" as an illegitimate, temporary entity—a war crime, not a nation—until Right of Return is accomplished. Every time a Palestinian refugee is stopped at the border rather than allowed to return and reclaim her property, another act of ethnic cleansing has transpired. (I think most of us would accept a compromise in which Right of Return is implemented gradually in accordance with the legitimate security concerns of the citizens of Israel-Palestine.)

Non-Muslims can perhaps imagine the emotional as well as logical reasons for this position by thinking how Catholics would feel if Muslim armies invaded Italy, terrorized Christian Europeans into fleeing, and occupied Rome. There would be no peace until the natives were allowed to return, and Rome returned at least to a status in which Christians were the equals of the Muslims who had settled there after the ethnic cleansing. Naturally a great many Catholics would want to drive the Muslims out of Rome and the Italian peninsula altogether, and they would perhaps be justified in so wishing and, in the event of Muslim intransigence, in so doing.

My position is surely not controversial among the vast majority of the world's Muslims. On the early history of modern Zionism and Palestinian nationalism, see Walid Khalidi, ed. *From Haven to Conquest: Readings in Zionism and the Palestine Problem Until 1948* (Washington, DC: Institute for Palestine Studies, 1971). From a Palestinian perspective: Said, Edward, *The Question of Palestine* (NY: Vintage, 1980) and *The Politics of Dispossession: The Struggle for Palestinian Self-Determination 1969-1994* (NY: Random House, 1994). From a Zionist perspective: Benny Morris, *Righteous Victims*. NY: Alfred A. Knopf, 1999). Morris has admitted that the term ethnic cleansing is an accurate description of what happened to the Palestinians in 1948, but he argues that Zionist ethnic cleansing is justified: "There are circumstances in history that justify ethnic cleansing." Ari Shavit, "An Interview with Benny Morris" (*Counterpunch*, January 16, 2004: http://www.counterpunch.org/ shavit01162004.html).

[49] Derek Summerfield. "Palestine: the assault on health and other war crimes." *British Medical Journal* 329: 924 (16 October 1994).

[50] Chris Hedges, "A Gaza Diary" (*Harpers*: October, 2001). http://home.mindspring.com/~fontenelles/hedges/hedges1.htm

[51] The best documented and most comprehensive study to date of Western intelligence orchestration of so-called Islamic terrorism is Nafeez Ahmed, *The War on Truth* (Northampton: Interlink 2005). A thorough study of the inner workings of state-sponsored false-flag terrorism and its relation to 9/11, including the fostering of Islamic fundamentalism and fabrication of "Islamic terrorism" by intelligence agencies, is Webster Tarpley, *9/11 Synthetic Terror: Made in USA* (Joshua Tree, CA, Progressive Press, 2005). The case that 9/11 was orchestrated by US government officials is also developed in three books by David Ray Griffin: *The New Pearl Harbor: Disturbing Questions About the Bush Administration and 9/11* (Northampton: Interlink 2004), *The 9/11 Commission Report: Omissions and Distortions* (Northampton: Interlink 2005), *Christian Faith and*

the Truth Behind 9/11: A Call to Reflection and Action (Westminster: John Knox Press, 2006).

[52] Maria Menocal, *Shards of Love: Exile and the Origins of the Lyric* (Durham and London: Duke UP, 1994).

[53] Menocal, *The Ornament of the World*.

[54] Fitzgerald, qtd. in Menocal 10-11.

[55] Menocal, *The Ornament of the World*, 11.

[56] David Griffin, ed. *Deep Religious Pluralism* (London: Westminster John Knox Press, 2005).

[57] To take just one example, Steven D. Smith writes: "In short, modern constitutional interpretation…is a religious enterprise in the sense that it depends on the (usually tacit) assumption of transcendent authority. More precisely, inasmuch as the transcendent authority on which these theories implicitly rely is illusory, legal interpretation can most accurately be understood as a species of idolatry." "Idolatry in Constitutional Interpretation." In Campos, Paul F., Schlag, Pierre, and Steven D. Smith, *Against the Law*. London and Durham, NC: Duke UP, 1996.

[58] This version of the American story is admirably told in the twenty-five essays collected in *Gone to Croatan: Origins of North American Dropout Culture*. Ed. Ron Sakolsky and Kames Koehnline (NY: Autonomedia, 1993).

[59] James Kunstler, *The Long Emergency* (NY: Grove-Atlantic Inc., 2005).

[60] Richard Falk, "Religion and Politics: Verging on the Postmodern." In David Ray Griffin, ed. *Sacred Interconnections: Postmodern Spirituality, Political Economy, and Art* (Albany: SUNY P, 1990).

[61] Lovelock, James. *The Ages of Gaia: A Biography of Our Living Earth* (NY and London: W.W. Norton, 1988).

[62] John Cobb, "The Evil that Results from Erroneous Beliefs." In Barrett, Cobb and Lubarsky, eds. *9/11 and the American Empire: Christians, Jews and Muslims Speak Out* (Northampton, MA: Interlink, 2006).

[63] I am not, of course, insulting all of Rushdie's detractors – merely some of them.

[64] The case that the World Trade Center was demolished with explosives is presented in Steven Jones, "Why Indeed Did the WTC Buildings Collapse?" http://www.physics.byu.edu/research/energy/htm7.html

[65] Barrie Zwicker, "Chapter 5: The Shame of Noam Chomsky and the Gatekeepers of the Left." In *Towers of Deception: The Media Coverup of 9/11* (Gabriola Island, BC: New Society, 2006) pp.179-224.

[66] www.9-11commission.gov/report/911Report_Ch5.htm

[67] Discussed in James Bamford's *Body of Secrets*, the Operation Northwoods documents have been widely posted on the internet and may be easily found through a Google search.

[68] Bernard Lewis, *The Assassins: A Radical Sect in Islam* (NY: Basic Books, 1968).

[69] Shadia B. Drury, "Leo Strauss and the Grand Inquisitor," from *Free Inquiry* magazine, Volume 24, Number 4 (http://www.secularhumanism.org/index.php?section=library&page=drury_24_4).

[70] "Frustrated Scowcroft Assails Neo-Cons, Cheney." Published October 25, 2005 by Inter Press Service (www.commondreams.org/headlines05/1025-05.htm).

[71] Webster Tarpley, "Bernard Lewis: Bin Laden's Flack" in *9/11 Synthetic Terror: Made in USA* (Joshua Tree, CA: Progressive Press, 2005) pp 146-147.

~~~~~

Also from Kevin Barrett:
9/11 & American Empire: Christians, Jews, and Muslims Speak Out

Inspired by David Ray Griffin's internationally acclaimed book *The New Pearl Harbor: Disturbing Questions about the Bush Administration and 9/11*, this anthology presents a variety of perspectives on 9/11 and empire from authors who identify with one of the major Abrahamic traditions. Co-edited by a major Christian theologian (John Cobb), a Jewish scholar (Sandra Lubarsky), and a Muslim scholar (Kevin Barrett), the book features essays by 9/11 revisionists and activists alongside those of noted writers and scholars, including several of the leading religious intellectuals of our time. The writers offer reflections on 9/11 and empire informed by the moral principles of their religious traditions as well as by the obligation to engage in thoughtful dialogue with those of other traditions. While the question of the Bush administration's and US military and intelligence leaders' possible complicity in 9/11 – and the moral implications of facing that possibility – is at the forefront of the book's agenda, it also addresses the way 9/11 has been used to expand the US empire's "global domination project" – raising profound moral questions that confront all of us, whatever our views on 9/11 complicity and whatever our faith, worldview, or national / ethnic identification.

Contributors include Nafeez Mosaddeq Ahmed, Kevin Barrett, Faiz Khan, Enver Masud, Yasmin Ahmed, Tamar Frankiel, Roger Gottlieb, Marc Ellis, Sandra Lubarsky, Rabbi Michael Lerner, John Cobb, David Ray Griffin, Carter Heyward, Catherine Keller, and Rosemary Radford Ruether.

Released by Olive Branch Press, Oct. 15, 2006, 336 pages, $20.

~~~~~

Listen or call in to Kevin Barrett's radio talk shows!
For schedule information and call-in numbers, visit
http://mujca.com/airwaves.htm

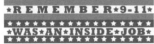